Carol Ann Tomlinson

Kay Brimijoin | Lane Narvaez

The Differentiated
School

Making Revolutionary Changes in Teaching and Learning

 Association for Supervision and Curriculum Development
Alexandria, Virginia USA

Association for Supervision and Curriculum Development
1703 N. Beauregard St. • Alexandria, VA 22311-1714 USA
Phone: 800-933-2723 or 703-578-9600 • Fax: 703-575-5400
Web site: www.ascd.org • E-mail: member@ascd.org
Author guidelines: www.ascd.org/write

Gene R. Carter, *Executive Director;* Nancy Modrak, *Publisher;* Julie Houtz, *Director of Book Editing & Production;* Leah Lakins, *Project Manager;* Greer Beeken, *Senior Graphic Designer;* Valerie Younkin, *Desktop Publishing Specialist;* CarmenYuhas, *Production Specialist;* Mike Kaylan, *Production Manager*

PAPERBACK ISBN: 978-1-4166-0678-9   ASCD product #105005   s6/08

Also available as an e-book through ebrary, netLibrary, and many online booksellers (see Books in Print for the ISBNs).

Quantity discounts for the paperback edition only: 10–49 copies, 10%; 50+ copies, 15%; for 1,000 or more copies, call 800-933-2723, ext. 5634, or 703-575-5634. For desk copies: member@ascd.org.

Library of Congress Cataloging-in-Publication Data
Tomlinson, Carol A.
  The differentiated school : making revolutionary changes in teaching and learning / Carol Tomlinson, Kay Brimijoin, and Lane Narvaez.
      p. cm.
  Includes bibliographical references and index.
  ISBN 978-1-4166-0678-9 (pbk. : alk. paper) 1. Individualized instruction—United States. 2. Individualized instruction—United States—Case studies. 3. School improvement programs—United States. 4. School improvement programs—United States—Case studies. I. Brimijoin, Kay, 1945–II. Narvaez, Lane, 1951–III. Title.

  LB1031.T652 2008
  371.39'4—dc22

                                                                              2008006362

18 17 16 15 14 13 12 11 10 09 08   1 2 3 4 5 6 7 8 9 10 11 12

With appreciation to

the faculties, administration, students, and parents

of Conway Elementary School in Ladue School District,

St. Louis, Missouri, and Colchester High School

in Colchester, Vermont, for teaching us

what teaching can be and for modeling

professionalism at every turn.

You make us proud to call ourselves teachers.

The Differentiated

School

Making Revolutionary Changes in Teaching and Learning

Appendixes

Acknowledgments

When we began to discuss the idea of this book, our intent was to tell the story of Conway Elementary School's remarkable change journey to illustrate the way in which a faculty can transform itself to teach with the needs of each individual student in mind. Along the way, we learned about—and ultimately also studied—Colchester High School, which was similarly engaged in a transformation for more academically responsive teaching.

We entered the lengthy and demanding process of authoring a book with our eyes open and with a pretty good sense of how that process intrudes on an author's life. By contrast, Joyce Stone, Bill Rich, and Brad Blanchette at Colchester High were conscripted into the writing process. They first gave us access to the school, faculty, and students. Then they answered thorny questions and picky ones. They sat for interviews. Then they pulled together documents at our request. Then they generated copy for us. That cycle repeated numerous times over many months through school years, holidays, and vacations until the book became the story of two schools that are unlike in many ways—and alike in all the really important ways. The book has a wider reach because of the addition of the Colchester story. That story would not have come to life without them.

And so, we offer enduring gratitude and respect to Joyce Stone, Bill Rich, and Brad Blanchette, who invested sacrificially in helping us with this work while they continued to exemplify the best in educational leadership with their colleagues and for their students.

Introduction

Education, like all other professions, has a literature of best practice—a collective wisdom born of research and experience—that points the way to success. It's not a formula, of course. There is no recipe that guarantees infallibility. Humans are varied, messy in their wants and needs. Young humans are certainly no less so. There is no error-proof way to teach them.

Nonetheless, we know a great deal about teaching and learning. Research and practice have clarified, and continue to clarify, pedagogical principles and procedures that merit careful attention and application. In short, we generally know what more effective classrooms look like in comparison to less effective ones. We also recognize that it is devilishly difficult to move from the latter to the former.

The metaphor of adopting a healthy lifestyle works as a proxy for adopting a best-practice classroom. Most of us know intellectually that good health is fundamental to a robust life. Most of us also know principles and practices that enhance health. Certainly some grey areas and unanswered questions remain, but some habits we know we should cultivate: sleep enough, eat more fruits and vegetables, exercise, stay out of direct sun, eliminate smoking, and so on. We have plenty of research and experiential evidence to commend those practices—and most of us mean to incorporate them into our lives. Evidence and intentions notwithstanding, however, it's perversely difficult for most of us to live healthy.

Junk food tastes good. It requires more thought to cook for health. It's tough to add 30 minutes of exercise to a schedule that's already on overload. A tan is nice—and, in fact, makes us look fit. Besides, we've lived with our foibles to this point, and we're still in pretty good shape. There are other folks who are a lot less fit than we are. Maybe when summer comes and there are fewer pressures, we'll be more attentive to a healthy regimen.

Many of us never get much further than worthy intentions to adopt practices that stand a high likelihood of improving our health. Even if the intentions are vivid in our thinking, it is a considerable journey from *meaning* to do better to *doing* better.

Sure, most of us make forays into a healthier life. We buy a health club membership—and go for a while. We go on a diet—until we are overcome by the desire for a hamburger and a shake. We use sunscreen—until it feels sticky or until we run out.

Few of us convert from comfortable and familiar habits to practices that seem as though they will forever define someone else but not us. The point is that change is aversive when it calls on us to reinvent ourselves—to shed the cocoon of the customary—even when we really know we would benefit significantly.

So what's the solution? Should health-related practitioners quit championing the cause of a healthy lifestyle? Should they simply give up on research and exhortations?

To do so would, we think, be unethical. The practitioners have information we need to know. They also have evidence that when folks follow their advice, the outcomes are worth the effort. So they have no option but to continue learning; to make their advice clearer, more palatable, or more compelling; and to provide better support for the change they commend.

So it is with educational leaders—whether those leaders are teachers, principals, researchers, curriculum coordinators, staff developers, or specialists. By assignment or conviction, they have information about what constitutes "healthier" educational practice. They too have little choice but to continue learning; make their advice clearer, more palatable, or more compelling; and provide better support for the change they commend.

The goal of this book is to help educational leaders more effectively support changes regarding effective classrooms for academically diverse student populations—in other words, for differentiated instruction. Most of us are keenly aware of the range of learning needs represented in our students. Most of us know we miss the mark with too many students in our classrooms. (If we miss the mark with even one student, that's too many.) Yet most of us persist with one-size-fits-all teaching.

It's so hard to change the familiar classroom patterns. Anyhow, mostly we're good teachers. There are lots of classrooms less effective than ours. And the pressures are so great—standardized tests, too little time, too many students, parental expectations. It might make intellectual sense to pay attention to varied learning needs in the midst of all that, but in reality, that kind of teaching belongs to someone else. It's just not for me. Or at least not now . . . Maybe when things let up a little . . .

How does a leader promote change when the prevailing winds all seem to blow against it? Again, there is no formula, but there is a body of knowledge about school and classroom change. We know things that are more likely to work in favor of change and things that are more likely to impede change. A leader armed with that body of best-practice knowledge is in a better position than an equally well-intentioned leader who repeats the familiar, comfortable—and often ineffective—patterns viewed as leadership.

To support leaders who, in turn, want to support development of more classrooms that work better for more students, this book will take a three-pronged approach. It will clarify the goals and attributes of best-practice differentiation. It will highlight important principles of best-practice approaches to change. It will provide illustrations from schools and leaders who understand both differentiation and school change—and who have been effective in moving from comfortable and familiar ways of teaching to ways of teaching that support the academic health of a far wider sphere of learners.

To that end, Carol Tomlinson has drawn heavily on the work and reflective writing of Lane Narvaez, principal of Conway Elementary School, and Kay Brimijoin, faculty member at Sweet Briar College in Virginia and staff developer at Conway for more than six years, as well as on observations at the school and conversations with many of its staff. She has also drawn generously from the work and reflective writing of Joyce Stone, principal of Colchester High School; Bill Rich and Brad Blanchette, Colchester faculty members; observations and interviews at Colchester; and research data gathered by Cindy Strickland and Kristina Doubet, University of Virginia doctoral students at the time they spent two years researching the Colchester site.

The book is not about formulas or recipes. We and our key collaborators have a combined educational experience of nearly 150 years. If we ever had the illusion that there is a single right answer to successful teaching, we've long since abandoned it. What we do believe, however, is that the research-based body of educational knowledge matters, that we can learn from the experiences of others, and that it is possible to change schools and classrooms for the better if we do so from a solid understanding of why the change matters and how change happens.

For us, and for the other educators whose experiences we'll share in this book, the change journey has been both evolutionary and revolutionary, both frustrating and exhilarating, both depleting and renewing. In the end, it has been reconstructing in highly positive ways. We are not through learning, but we believe that what we have learned to this point is worth sharing. We hope you will think so as well.

1

Setting the Stage for Change Toward Differentiation

Students in today's schools are becoming more academically diverse. There are more students identified for more exceptionalities in special education, more students for whom English is not their first language, and more students struggling to read. There is a need to ensure challenge for advanced learners when accountability pressures focus on basic competencies, and a growing economic gap exists between segments of the student population.

It seems unrealistic to think that all those students will thrive in classrooms that disregard their learning differences. In fact, a look at indicators such as grades, student discipline, attendance, college acceptance, dropout rates, and standardized test scores confirms that school is not working well for too many students.

Differentiated instruction seems promising as a response to the variety of learning needs students bring to school every day. It makes sense to encourage teachers to be mindful of and responsive to their students' diverse learning needs. But what would the school leaders be asking teachers to do by encouraging them to differentiate instruction? What does differentiation look like? And would benefits to students and teachers be worth the tension and effort such a change would require? Are there avoidable errors that leaders should keep in mind?

What does it mean to lead for schoolwide change for differentiation?

Fostering Enduring, Deep Change

We often hear fellow educators say, "We're doing differentiation in our school this year. Could you come help us?" Not surprisingly then, we also hear, "Our teachers know about differentiation, but nobody seems to do much with it in their classrooms." We also visit classrooms where "differentiation is happening," go to conference sessions, and even read books that revisit the truth that a little knowledge is a dangerous thing.

On the one hand, it's positive that educators are having a conversation about how to teach with an eye to individual learner needs. As we'll discuss later, there is more than ample evidence of a need for that conversation. Further, it speaks well of us as educators that we see and acknowledge the varying needs of our students. On the other hand, shallow approaches to differentiating instruction for academically diverse learners will serve neither the students nor the profession well.

Mandates for classroom change and drive-through approaches to staff development likely will do more harm than good. They may result in some modifications for some people over some period of time, but they are seldom catalysts for broad, widespread, and enduring change. In addition, surface approaches to deep issues trivialize problems and convince teachers that shortly the wind will shift and the gnats that are pestering them will go away until a new breeze blows through.

In this book, we hope to provide a more substantial way to think about substantial change on behalf of a substantial need in our schools. It is our intent to (a) clarify the tenets of "defensible differentiation," (b) specify key principles and practices of leadership for meaningful change in classrooms and schools, and (c) illustrate how it looks when educators commit to making durable changes in teaching—in this case, to implement differentiated instruction in classrooms throughout a school.

To set the stage for the rest of the book, this chapter will first highlight some key elements of defensible differentiation. Next, it will take a look at the complexity of educational change. Finally, it will introduce two schools that made differentiated classrooms a schoolwide reality and whose change journey will provide practical and concrete illustrations through the rest of the book.

Defensible Differentiation: What It Is and Is Not

There is a great deal already written about what we call "differentiated instruction." This section of the chapter will not try to repeat or even summarize that writing. What it will do is address some misconceptions by outlining what differentiation is and is not, and it will highlight essential elements of defensible differentiation. The point is to remind educational leaders (a term we use to include teachers and administrators who are wise and informed pace setters for their colleagues) that solutions to educational problems do not lie in names or in labels but in quality practice. Calling something "differentiation" provides no guarantee of its efficacy for students. Leaders must continually be attuned to fidelity of practice and continually ask themselves and others, "How does what's happening here make sense for learners?"

Differentiation that's likely to make a positive difference for students will have some attributes and—more to the point—will not have others. Figure 1.1 suggests some misconceptions about differentiation that, turned into practice, can dilute or damage student outcomes. It also points to some indicators of defensible differentiation.

Key elements of effective differentiation are important for leaders to understand. They are the mileposts that change efforts should be moving toward—nonnegotiables of the model. Each of the nonnegotiables is aimed at one shared goal—greater academic success for the broadest possible student population. The nonnegotiables are respecting individuals, owning student success, building community, providing high-quality curriculum, assessing to inform instruction, implementing flexible classroom routines, creating varied avenues to learning, and sharing responsibility for teaching and learning.

Respecting Individuals

With genuine respect comes a desire to know a person more fully, understand him or her more deeply, and connect with that person. Respecting individuals looks, sounds, or feels like the following:

- Listening
- Asking for input
- Making time for the person
- Using positive humor
- Accentuating the positive
- Accepting the person "as is," while helping him or her grow
- Learning and demonstrating an appreciation for each person's culture and background
- Providing the best (respectful tasks—everyone's work is equally important and equally engaging)
- Expecting the best—always "teaching up"—pushing the student beyond where he or she believes achievement is possible
- Holding the person to a high standard
- Ensuring a positive environment for growth

Figure 1.1

What Differentiated Instruction Is and Is Not

What Differentiation Is Not	What Differentiation Is	Explanation
Just for students with labels	For every student	Every student has particular interests and learning preferences as well as a readiness level that varies over time and context. Each learner needs appropriate support.
Something extra in the curriculum	At the core of effective planning	Differentiation is not something you do when the real lesson is finished. It's integral to ensuring that each student has access to success with key content goals.
An approach that mollycoddles students—makes them dependent	Teaching up; supporting students in achieving at a level higher than they thought possible	Effective differentiation always enables a student to do more than would be possible without it, not less.
Incompatible with standards	A vehicle for ensuring student success with standards	A goal of differentiation is ensuring that each student succeeds with whatever is important for him or her to know, understand, and do.
Use of certain instructional strategies	Use of flexible approaches to space, time, materials, groupings, and instruction	Flexibility is a hallmark of differentiation, but no single instructional strategy is required to differentiate effectively.
Tracking in the regular classroom	The antithesis of tracking	Effective differentiation requires use of flexible grouping patterns so that students consistently work in a variety of groups based on readiness, interest, learning preference, random assignment, teacher choice, and student choice.
Assigning students to cross-class groups based on assessment data	Within a classroom	When students are removed from their classrooms and placed with students deemed similar in other classrooms, a kind of tracking is taking place. Real flexibility is lost.
All or mostly based on a particular approach to multiple intelligences	Systematic attention to readiness, interest, and learning profile	Learning profile is one-third of the domain of differentiation and consists of learning style, intelligence preference (there are two strong models addressing intelligence preference), gender-related preferences, and culture-related preferences. A single approach to intelligence preferences in the classroom is a narrow segment of the big picture of differentiation.

Figure 1.1—(*continued*)
What Differentiated Instruction Is and Is Not

What Differentiation Is Not	What Differentiation Is	Explanation
All or mostly based on learning style preferences	Systematic attention to readiness, interest, and learning profile	See note above. Attention to learning style is helpful for some students some of the time and helps teachers learn to be more flexible, but it leaves other needs unaddressed.
Synonymous with student choice	A balance of teacher choice and student choice	There are times when it's important for teachers to assign particular work to students because it will move them forward in key ways. At other times, it makes good sense for students to call the shots and learn about making wise choices.
Individualization	Focused on individuals, small groups, and the class as a whole	Although it is an aim of differentiation to focus on individuals, it is not a goal to make individual lesson plans for each student.
More problems, books, or questions for some students and fewer for others	Varied avenues to the same essential understandings	Struggling students don't often benefit by doing less of what they don't understand, and it's not helpful for advanced learners to do more of what they already know. Differentiation asks students to work with essential understandings at varied degrees of complexity and with varied support systems. Information-based tasks and skills-based tasks should be congruent with students' current needs.
Something a teacher does because it's the thing to do	Something a teacher does in response to particular needs of particular human beings	Differentiation should be responsive instruction, not mechanical instruction.
Something that happens all day every day	Something that happens when there is a need for it	At times, whole-class instruction is important and effective. Teachers need to build community as well as attend to individual needs.
Something a teacher does on the spot when it becomes evident that a lesson isn't working for some students (reactive or improvisational)	Something a teacher plans prior to a lesson based on assessment evidence of student needs (proactive)	The most powerful differentiation is based on pre-assessment and ongoing assessment of student progress toward key goals. The teacher uses the assessment information to make proactive plans to address student needs. Some improvisation is still needed, but it is not a dominant means of differentiation.

Owning Student Success

When a teacher owns the success of a student, that teacher operates with a "whatever it takes to make this work" approach. When a teacher owns the success of a student, that student cannot fall through the cracks. Owning student success looks, sounds, or feels like the following:

- Making sure students know what's required for success
- Viewing success as the only acceptable outcome
- Persistently studying student progress
- Adapting instruction to provide support for personal next steps
- Ensuring student access to information, materials, supplies, and support
- Being unwilling to overlook gaps in knowledge
- Being unwilling to let a student wait for others to catch up
- Teaching the student how to make wise decisions and choices that support success
- Giving useful feedback
- Ensuring student action on the feedback
- Finding another way to teach and learn
- Being a persistent, positive presence in the student's life

Building Community

A teacher who focuses on community building understands that teams don't just happen. They are built. Community building looks, sounds, or feels like the following:

- Modeling democracy in the classroom
- Speaking of students with respect
- Teaching students to be respectful of one another
- Pointing out legitimate student strengths
- Making sure everyone has an essential role to play
- Helping students experience and understand the power of positive interdependence
- Establishing positive shared experiences (building positive group memories)
- Making students aware of common goals with varied routes to achieving them
- Helping students learn how to help one another in productive ways

Providing High-Quality Curriculum

Teachers who understand the centrality of high-quality curriculum in differentiation know that students can become powerful learners only if what they are asked to learn is powerful. Providing high-quality curriculum looks, sounds, or feels like the following:

- Teaching for understanding (emphasizing the concepts, principles, and essential understandings of a discipline)
- Teaching for transfer (making sure students use what they learn in authentic contexts)
- Insisting on and supporting consistent growth in high-level thought
- Guiding high-quality discussions to explore important ideas
- Ensuring that students examine varied perspectives and the relative merits of those perspectives
- Helping students connect the important ideas of content with their own lives and experiences
- Vigorously supporting students in developing the skills and attitudes necessary to do quality work
- Starting with what the most able students need and supporting all students in success with that level of curriculum

Assessing to Inform Instruction

The teacher who emphasizes assessment to inform instruction understands that only by staying close to student progress can he or she guide student success. Assessment to inform instruction looks, sounds, or feels like the following:

- Systematically observing students at work
- Using pre-assessments to understand students' starting points—including status of precursor skills
- Using ongoing assessments to trace student progress and identify trouble spots
- Asking students to share interests
- Listening and looking for student interests
- Asking students about learning preferences
- Observing students working in different contexts and modes
- Asking students what's working for them and what's not
- Acting on student suggestions

• Using assessment information to plan for reteaching, teaching in a different mode, extending understanding, developing tasks, modifying time expectations, and so on

Implementing Flexible Classroom Routines

A teacher who strives for flexible classroom routines understands the power of using classroom elements to benefit learners and learning. Flexible classroom routines look, sound, or feel like the following:

• Allowing more time for students who need it
• Enabling students to move ahead who are ready to do so
• Using varied seating arrangements to support the work of individuals and small groups
• Systematically planning and using flexible grouping of students based on readiness, interest, learning preference, random assignment, student choice, and teacher choice
• Ensuring text and supplementary materials at appropriate reading levels
• Using varied support systems to ensure access to information
• Teacher instruction for the whole class, small groups, and individuals

Creating Varied Avenues to Learning

Teachers who provide varied avenues to learning understand that most students can learn most important things if they can do it in a way that works for them. Ensuring varied avenues to learning looks, sounds, or feels like the following:

• Teacher presentations in varied modes
• Student exploration and expression of content in varied modes
• Student suggestions for ways to learn
• Options for a variety of working conditions
• Tasks at different levels of difficulty and appropriate support to move to the next level of difficulty
• Whole-to-part and part-to-whole reminders
• Offering miniworkshops or clinics on key skills
• Interest-based options for how to apply essential knowledge, understanding, and skill
• Small-group instruction to target student interests and needs

• Periodic use of varied homework assignments to consolidate or extend learning
• Creative, practical, and analytical explorations of essential content

Sharing Responsibility for Teaching and Learning

Teachers who share responsibility for teaching and learning understand that students have valuable perspectives on teaching and learning, that a team approach to making the classroom work is more efficient than the teacher having to manage everything, and that students learn to take charge of their own academic success by being taught how to do so. Sharing responsibility for teaching and learning looks, sounds, or feels like the following:

• Ensuring student voice in establishing classroom guidelines
• Ensuring that students take responsibility for implementation of classroom guidelines
• Carefully defining and teaching classroom routines to ensure student success
• Consistent debriefing about classroom routines to help students compare how things worked with how they were supposed to work
• Guiding students in establishing classroom rules
• Helping students understand the teacher's work, goals, feelings about progress toward goals, and need for assistance
• Assigning "teacher roles" to students (passing out materials, providing help while the teacher works with small groups, designing interest centers, establishing due dates for projects, etc.)
• Teaching students to play those roles effectively
• Asking for student input on how the class is working for them and what could make it work better
• Teaching for student independence

This brief capsule of differentiation is not meant to be exhaustive. Readers should feel free to add elements, descriptors, misconceptions, and so on. The intent of this section of the chapter is simply to serve as a reminder that the kind of differentiation that is likely to make a difference in the lives and achievement of students is both fundamental to good teaching and very complex. As the book proceeds, it's important to have a sense of the scope and degree of change that defensible differentiation requires. Only in science fiction do individuals arrive at distant destinations in an instant. Nonetheless, it's critical to have a clear sense of the destination, the distance to it, and the reason for going there in the first place.

To understand those things is to begin to develop a sense of why real change in schools is so challenging.

The Challenge of School Change: Why It's Hard to Go from Point A to Point B

The literature on school change is rich, varied, and multifaceted. Again, there is no formula or recipe for change, yet persistent themes arise in the literature. Two of those themes appear contradictory. The first is that in schools "real change is real hard" (Urbanski, 1993, p. 123). The second is that change is quite possible and not beyond the reach of ordinary educators in ordinary schools (Fullan, 2001b).

In fact, these two themes are not as oppositional as they may seem. A fair translation of the literature on school change is that we know a lot about what supports change and a lot about what discourages it. If we just did what we know to do, we'd generally find improved outcomes for students and their teachers. The challenge—as always—comes in living out the details.

For this book, we have drawn on the expertise of researchers who have devoted their careers to understanding the process of school change. Our intent is not to represent all that these experts have to say. Our intent is to capsule and spotlight key insights from that literature as it relates to change for more academically responsive classrooms.

Through the rest of the book, we'll be looking at principles and practices from the current best understanding of school change. These principles and practices offer no guarantees of success, yet they support educational leaders' efforts to be catalysts for schools and classrooms that can better help each student construct a promising future.

To establish a context for what follows in the book, Figure 1.2 provides some themes from the literature of school change that suggest why our efforts at change too often fall short.

This book focuses on how to support classroom changes that result in teaching that is more responsive to—more effective with—academically diverse student populations. The movement toward defensibly differentiated classrooms is a particularly complex kind of change. It affects virtually every facet of how teachers think about and carry out their

Figure 1.2

Factors That Contribute to the Failure of Change Efforts

Factors That Contribute to Failure to Change Classroom Practice	Brief Explanation of the Problem
Underestimating the complexity of the change	We are unaware of or unprepared to deal with implications of the change in classroom practice. We tend to deal with the change on a superficial level, tend to neglect fidelity to the change, and are often unprepared to deal with the fear, tension, loss, and conflict that inevitably accompany change. We often overlook what teachers perceive to be competing mandates.
Mandating change vs. providing a vision	It's profoundly difficult to change major life routines even when we have a good reason to do so. A mandate seldom seems like a good reason to the people receiving the mandate.
Insufficient leadership	Leaders for change are necessarily keepers of a vision, well informed about the vision, communicators, cheerleaders, taskmasters, diplomats, and ministers. Leading is a very different thing from telling.
Insufficient support and resources	The more the change effort affects actual classroom routines, the more support it requires. That implies long-term and reliable presence of information, coaching, feedback, collaboration, guided reflection, materials, and reassurance—to name a few elements.
Failure to deal with the multifaceted nature of change	It's easy to assume that we can merely ask people to change a practice. In fact, making change requires alteration in beliefs, attitudes, practices, use of materials, and the culture of the school itself. To neglect any of these is to undermine the possibility of change.
Lack of persistence	Significant change is evolutionary. It does not happen as a result of a few professional development sessions or because a school "does" the initiative "this year." It is likely that evoking significant change takes many years and then must be nurtured indefinitely.
Inattention to teachers' personal circumstances	Teachers have high-stress jobs as well as personal lives—and varied levels of professional expertise, varied approaches to their work, and varied ways of learning. Those factors must be accounted for to support change.
Lack of shared clarity about a plan for change	No blueprint for change will endure exactly as it was conceived. Nonetheless, it is critical to have a plan and to ensure that stakeholders understand the plan, what is expected of them in the plan, and what support will be available to them throughout the process.
Weak linkage to student effects and outcomes	It's easy, but unfortunate, to discuss a change initiative without ensuring that it remains focused on the students who will experience it. If a change initiative positively affects students, teachers will find a ready motivator to continue. If it does not, leaders need to reexamine the implementation or reconsider their direction. It's not about the initiative. It's about what it can accomplish.
Missteps with scope and pacing	We often ask teachers to do too much all at once. We move too fast and overwhelm people, or we move too slowly and lose momentum. The scope and pacing of change are critical to its outcome.

work. It is therefore demanding for teachers and demanding for those who provide leadership and support for that journey. As noted earlier, we believe such leadership includes administrators, classroom teachers, specialists, media specialists, counselors, and other key personnel with the potential to improve classroom instruction.

We examine change for differentiation at the school level rather than at the individual teacher or district level. We have made that decision for two reasons. First, it is always the case that some individual teachers and small groups of teachers seek out ways to alter their classroom practices as a matter of professional growth. Those teachers are gifts to the schools in which they work and the students with whom they work. The value of their efforts should never be underestimated and should always be affirmed and supported. Nonetheless, it is unlikely that the degree of change needed in schools will result from one-teacher-at-a-time, self-initiated efforts. Second, although district-level change is certainly necessary for educational equity and excellence, it is far more difficult to achieve than school-level change. In any case, district-level change must ultimately happen on a school-by-school basis.

A major goal of this book is to clarify what we know about school change as it relates to change for defensible differentiation. It has made a world of difference for us to see the principles of change move from the pages of books and into faculty meetings, classrooms, professional development sessions, coaching sessions, collaborative teaming, and hallway conversations. Therefore, we have elected to illustrate the principles that guide effective school change as we have seen them play out in two schools that have accomplished buildingwide change toward defensibly differentiated classrooms for the purpose of improved school experiences and achievement outcomes for more students. In the final section of this chapter, we'll introduce the two schools that have helped us see change in action and that we believe will help readers of the book in similar ways.

Two Schools That Made Defensible Differentiation a Schoolwide Reality

Because, as the experts tell us, school change is both difficult and possible, it is important to examine settings in which people have come together to examine beliefs, change how they think about what they do, and ultimately change classroom practice to the benefit of students. In this book, we'll share experiences from two such schools. The illustrations they provide help make concrete the more abstract principles of defensible differentiation and school change. Our goal is not to tell the story of either school in a linear way, but rather to select instances that illustrate key facets of the change process as each school developed classrooms designed to better serve each student.

A couple of caveats are useful here. First, these are not perfect schools. There is no such thing. The educators in the schools would be the first to say there are—and always will be—facets of their work they would like to change. What sets them apart, in fact, is not perfection but dogged determination to improve. Second, their work with differentiation is not finished. In both instances, the educators in the schools would be the first to say there is still hard work to do. Third, their change journeys have not been neat, tidy, or without conflict. The educators in both schools would be the first to say there have been periods when the journey seemed overwhelming.

That said, the educators in these two schools have done more things right and fewer things wrong along the course to change than is often the case in schools. For that reason, they have much to teach us about how deep classroom change can become a reality—and more specifically, how deep classroom change in regard to academically responsive or differentiated instruction can unfold. Figure 1.3 provides some basic demographic information about Conway Elementary School and Colchester High School.

Conway Elementary School

At the time when the Conway Elementary School staff began its formal work with differentiated instruction in 2000, Lane Narvaez had been the principal at Conway for five years. Prior to that, she had been a high school assistant principal for five years and a teacher at all levels. Ladue School District, in which Conway Elementary is located, is a high-achieving district with approximately 92 percent of graduates attending college. The district has one of the oldest merit pay programs in the country. These factors converge to create high parent expectations and a stable, well-paid teaching force with high standards and a strong work ethic.

On the one hand, it would be easy to look at Conway and conclude that working conditions were ideal and change would be easy to accomplish. In fact, Conway was a good place to work. It was characterized, however, by two factors that often work against change. One is a highly

Figure 1.3
Demographic Information on the Two Exemplar Schools

School	Conway Elementary School	Colchester High School
Location	St. Louis, Missouri	Colchester, Vermont
School District	Ladue School District	Colchester School District
Principal	Lane Narvaez	Joyce Stone
Grade Levels	K–5	9–12
Enrollment	Approx. 330	Approx. 855
Number of Faculty Members	29 (including music, physical education, specialists, and media)	65
Demographics	Suburban, 81%; Caucasian, 12% African American, 7% Asian, Hispanic, and East Asian; 5% on free or reduced-price meals; 25% identified for special education services; serves students from predominantly middle- to upper-middle-class homes	Rural and suburban; 97% Caucasian, 3% African American, Sudanese, Congolese, Bosnian, other; 19% on free or reduced-price meals; 16% identified for special education services; serves students from million-dollar homes and the two largest trailer parks in Vermont

aspirational, highly involved group of parents who can effectively derail change if they feel it will negatively affect the status quo. A second characteristic that makes change very difficult is that Conway was already widely known to be a "very good school." Given the aversive nature of change, when a teacher or a school has the reputation of being excellent, it is natural to eschew suggestions about making significant changes in practice. Why would a faculty undertake the rigorous and risky journey to an uncertain destination when their current place in the world is celebrated? If it's difficult to achieve commitment to school change among faculties in general, it is far more difficult to achieve buy-in for change in schools whose names are synonymous with quality. There is much to learn from the Conway faculty about making a very good school great.

Colchester High School

At the time when Colchester High School began its formal work with differentiated instruction in 2000, Joyce Stone had been principal at Colchester for one year. Prior to that, she had been a high school teacher for 24 years, an assistant principal and special education coordinator in a rural district for seven years, and the assistant principal at Colchester for two years. At that point, Colchester High was a school in trouble both academically and affectively. Student discipline was poor, there were intractable divisions between academic "haves" and "have-nots," test scores were low, the dropout rate was high, and the community was growing increasingly uneasy with the school.

Unlike Conway, the Colchester faculty did not have a record of unimpeachable quality to shield them from a need to change. Nonetheless, it is profoundly difficult to bring about schoolwide change in a high school when that change requires pervasive alteration of teachers' perceptions about students, scheduling of classes, and classroom instruction. The faculty of Colchester has undergone an individual and group metamorphosis in all those areas. There is much to learn from them about rethinking fundamental aspects of schooling—even at the secondary level.

Outcomes of Change

Undertaking substantive change in a school is not—or ought not to be—for the sake of change. It should be designed with specific positive teacher, student, and schoolwide benefits in mind. It is toward those intended outcomes that the initiative should progress and against which the success of the initiative should be assessed both formatively and summatively. Over time, it is likely that some of the initial goals will change. Some may not be fully realized, and there may be unanticipated benefits as well.

Specific outcomes targeted by the Conway and Colchester faculties for their work with differentiated instruction will be discussed in Chapter 2. Here, we want to highlight positive outcomes of the change initiatives in the two schools during their first few years.

Sergiovanni (1999) reminds us that if we judge the success of a school solely on test scores, we set our sights too narrowly. Excellent performance would include good test scores but should also extend to student, parent, and teacher satisfaction, increased student engagement with learning, enhanced professional efficacy of teachers, and so on.

Both the Conway and Colchester faculties are appropriately proud of standardized test scores that show broad growth across the student population. They are also proud of other indicators of success. The suggestions of success noted for both schools in the following sections are just that—suggestions of success. These are not data derived from an experimental study but rather garnered in the course of living out several academic years in particular schools.

Indications of Change at Conway

At Conway, two achievement tests have served as benchmarks for academic improvement—the TerraNova and the Missouri Assessment Program (MAP). The TerraNova is a nationally normed test administered annually to 5th grade students with test scores reported in terms of a Normal Curve Equivalent (NCE) with a mean of 50 and a range from zero to 99. Because Conway students are generally high performing, the school uses an NCE of 65 as its indicator of comparison. Figure 1.4 shows pre- and postdifferentiation scores for Conway 5th graders. Although the table shows an increase in scores during the years of differentiated instruction, other factors played a role during the six years under study. First, enrollment decreased, causing smaller class sizes. Second, Conway's Voluntary Transfer Program ended, resulting in fewer students transferring to Conway from city schools. In order to determine the effect these variables had on test results, the general linear model was used to implement analysis of variance (ANOVA) and a regression. Results showed that differentiated instruction was associated with a significant difference in test scores. That is, student test scores were higher during the years that differentiation was in place.

The MAP is a state-administered criterion-referenced test that includes multiple-choice items, constructed-response items, and performance items. Scores are reported in five steps, with Step 4 (Proficient) and Step 5 (Advanced) indicating students are above grade level and have met state standards. MAP test results likewise show a dramatic and positive shift during the first three years of the differentiation initiative in comparison to the three years prior to the beginning of the initiative (see Figures 1.5 and 1.6).

A simple average of the percent of students who met the state standards during the three predifferentiation years in comparison with the first three years of the differentiation initiative shows communication arts pass rates moving from 61 percent to 69 percent, science from 71 percent to 76 percent, math from 64 percent to 79 percent, and social studies from 59 percent to 83 percent. The state scores were not only lower during the six years, but they also remained relatively static. Figure 1.6 also shows that the percentage of students scoring in the top level (Step 5) increased during the years of differentiation. It is also important to note that the number of students receiving Step 1 and Step 2 MAP scores (lowest levels) at Conway decreased during the first three years of the differentiation initiative.

Figure 1.4

Conway Elementary Predifferentiation and Postdifferentiation Student Scores for Grade 5

Scoring Category	Predifferentiation			Postdifferentiation		
	1998	1999	2000	2001	2002	2003
Percent of Students with Reading Scores ≤ 65	34%	41%	38%	19%	18%	24%
Percent of Students with Language Scores ≤ 65	40%	56%	52%	31%	39%	34%
Percent of Students with Math Scores ≤ 65	43%	58%	52%	31%	35%	34%
Percent of Students with Reading Scores > 65	66%	59%	62%	81%	82%	76%
Percent of Students with Language Scores > 65	60%	44%	48%	69%	61%	65%
Percent of Students with Math Scores > 65	57%	42%	48%	69%	65%	66%

Note: Scores based on TerraNova Normal Curve Equivalent of 65. The school uses 65 as a point of comparison because of the large number of students who score above 50, which is the typical point of comparison in schools.

Test scores from the 2004 and 2005 school years show this test pattern continuing. Using either the TerraNova or the MAP as the test measurement, Conway students demonstrated dramatic improvement in performance during the years of the differentiation initiative.

During the first three years of the differentiation initiative, Conway ranked as one of the state's top 10 scoring schools in reading, math, and social studies. In 2003, it was named a Gold Star School of Excellence by the Missouri Department of Elementary and Secondary Education and, in 2007, a No Child Left Behind Blue Ribbon School by the U.S. Department of Education in recognition of the school's high test scores, professional development initiatives, programming, and parent involvement.

Student, parent, and teacher response to differentiation was also largely positive. Those perspectives will be discussed in later chapters.

Figure 1.5

Percent of Students with Advanced and Proficient Achievement on the Missouri Assessment Program

Scoring Category	Grade and Subject	Predifferentiation			Postdifferentiation		
		1998	1999	2000	2001	2002	2003
Levels 4 and 5 Conway	4th grade math	56%	64%	71%	83%	77%	79%
Levels 4 and 5 State	4th grade math	32%	35%	37%	37%	38%	38%
Levels 4 and 5 Conway	3rd grade science	71%	63%	80%	71%	73%	84%
Levels 4 and 5 State	3rd grade science	39%	35%	45%	45%	48%	48%

Figure 1.6

Percent of Students with Advanced Achievement on the Missouri Assessment Program

Scoring Category	Grade and Subject	Predifferentiation			Postdifferentiation		
		1998	1999	2000	2001	2002	2003
Level 5 Conway	4th grade math	17%	16%	15%	24%	34%	24%
Level 5 State	4th grade math	5%	6%	8%	8%	8%	7%
Level 5 Conway	3rd grade science	15%	7%	23%	27%	27%	41%
Level 5 State	3rd grade science	6%	4%	10%	10%	9%	10%

Indications of Change at Colchester

Unlike Conway Elementary School, student achievement scores at Colchester were generally mediocre to weak when the differentiation initiative began. Results on the New Standards Reference Examinations (NSRE) indicated substantial growth during the first six years of the differentiation initiative at Colchester, as shown in Figure 1.7.

In addition to noteworthy increases in standardized test scores, the Colchester data suggest other equally important, and likely interrelated, outcomes during the first five to six years of the differentiation initiative. During this time, significant demographic factors, such as eligibility for free or reduced-price meals, did not change substantially. However,

- College attendance increased from 68 percent in 1999 to 74 percent in 2006.
- The number of Advanced Placement sections increased from six in 1999 to 13 in 2006. (The number of students achieving honors status on the NSRE between 1999 and 2006 rose in every subject tested—often dramatically (for example, from 17 percent to 29 percent of students achieving honors status in writing conventions, from 19 percent to 46 percent in math skills, from 15 percent to 25 percent in math concepts, and from 8 percent to 15 percent in math problem solving).
- Disciplinary interventions dropped by 42 percent between 2000 and 2006.
- Expulsions declined from seven in 2001 to one in 2006.
- The dropout rate decreased from 6.9 percent in 1999 to 1.03 percent over five years.
- Qualitative measures documented significant improvement in school climate for teachers.

Looking Ahead

On the surface, Conway Elementary School and Colchester High School appear to have little in common. Located in two different regions of the country, one serves younger students and one serves older students. One began the change journey as a school of excellence; one began as a school in trouble. One school's student population is relatively affluent; the other school's student population represents the haves and have-nots. As will become evident in later chapters, one school's principal

Figure 1.7
Percent of Students Passing the New Standards Reference Examination at Colchester

Assessment Area	Before Differentiation 1999	After Differentiation 2006
Reading Understanding	53%	61%
Reading Analysis/Interpretation	51%	66%
Writing Effectiveness	58%	75%
Writing Conventions	82%	84%
Math Skills	44%	72%
Math Concepts	33%	56%
Math Problem Solving	25%	52%

envisioned differentiation as a way to ensure challenge for the school's most able students; the other school's principal envisioned it as a means to ensure equity for the school's struggling students.

In the end, however, the two schools also share important attributes: courageous leaders with a clear vision and the will and skill to act on the vision, faculties willing to engage in sustained reflection, and a blueprint for change sufficient to the challenge of change. In the chapters ahead, we'll examine how the schools reconceived instruction to focus more effectively on individual learner needs, how they created guidelines for navigating this type of change process, and how the change played out in these two schools.

2

Leadership for Change
Toward Differentiation

Principals in many schools are keenly aware of the need to develop classrooms that make room for a broad spectrum of students—not just classrooms that physically include all kinds of students, but classrooms in which teachers proactively plan for student differences and teach flexibly with student needs as a central consideration. To greatly expand the number of such classrooms, however, would require major change for many, if not most, teachers.

It's one thing to realize a need and quite another to lead a faculty to see that need as well. How would the leader of a school create a shared vision? What attributes of leadership would enable the principal to develop the trust of faculty members that the proposed change is more promising than threatening? When should the principal *invite,* and when is a *push* necessary? At what pace should change occur? How well would the principal have to understand the process of school change? Differentiation? And would the philosophy of differentiation have any bearing on the way the principal plans for and guides change?

Understanding and Expecting Resistance to Change

Change in life is inevitable. We see it in the cycle of birth, growth, and death. We watch it in the natural and man-made landscapes that are the scenery of our lives. We want better medicines, fabrics, technologies, and homes than our ancestors had, and these things demand change. Nonetheless, change in our own lives is, more often than not, discomforting at best and gut wrenching at worst. Robert Evans (1996) reminds us that human beings are pattern-seeking creatures who fight to preserve the fabric that gives predictability and stability to our lives. Thus change is a paradox. We must have it to grow, and we resist it energetically.

Change is inevitable in teaching, as in other human endeavors. The individual teacher must progress beyond typical first-year fumbling in order to be viable, let alone to become a professional. The field as a whole has a body of evolving professional knowledge. To do our jobs as effectively as possible, educators need to evolve in response to that knowledge just as physicians or engineers change in response to new insights in their fields.

Logic notwithstanding, however, teachers typically do not embrace change. The reasons for the disinclination to change are many. Certainly one of the reasons it is difficult to sell change to teachers is that the classroom itself is a living organism that changes on a minute-by-minute basis. Students come and go. They grow. Moods ebb and flow. Relationships mutate. Mental lightbulbs go on and off at inopportune moments. Textbook adoptions and new technologies insert themselves. It is as though a teacher practices his or her profession in a house of mirrors. Thus the teacher clings to what can be controlled as an antidote to what is beyond control. Teachers develop habitual practices as defense mechanisms, and in so doing, they become more confident in their capacity to have some dominion in an unpredictable setting. To ask teachers to change is to ask them to return to the swampy ground of the initial months in the classroom—to invite teachers to embrace "the humiliation of becoming a raw novice at a new trade after having been a master craftsman at an old one" (Kaufman, 1971, p. 13).

Educational leaders who seek change, then, may find themselves peddling goods for which there is little market. Although leaders understand that their role includes improving classroom practice and that improvement requires change, it can be difficult to know how to proceed. Good teachers tend to be independent, passionate, and questioning (Hoerr, 2005).

Two approaches to evoking substantial change clearly do not work. First, mandate-driven change is unlikely to succeed and, at best, would have a life span that mirrors the tenure of the person who mandated it. Second, "change lite" will not work. Substantial change does not occur as a result of a few staff development sessions or a few faculty discussions. "Our school is doing differentiation this year" is an anemic approach to change.

Change toward more effectively differentiated classrooms is second-order change. First-order change is incremental, can occur in small steps, and does not require a dramatic departure from the way things are. It allows teachers to retain current beliefs about teaching and to generally retain current classroom routines and practices. Second-order change necessitates a dramatic departure from the status quo. It asks teachers to alter beliefs and practices—often dramatically. School leaders tend to approach all change as though it were first-order change and thus could be implemented in an almost casual way—slowly and a little at a time. It is likely that underestimating the complexity of major change leads to the downfall of many change initiatives (Marzano, Waters, & McNulty, 2005).

Although second-order change is predictive of greater complexity and more problems than first-order change, it is also generally predictive of greater gain because more is being attempted (Fullan, 2001b). This book targets leaders who want to bring about second-order change for differentiation.

We know a good bit about the nature of leaders who guide second-order change. It is clear that they understand the why, what, who, and how of change. This chapter will first examine the characteristics of leaders and leadership for second-order change, then examine the implications for second-order change toward differentiation, and finally provide illustrations from two schools.

The Nature of Leadership for Second-Order Change

Because this book examines change at the building level, the pivotal leader for change is the principal. Said differently, significant school-level change is unlikely to occur without effective principal leadership for that change (Fullan, 2001b). Nonetheless, robust principal leaders cultivate leadership in others and share leadership with others (Duke, 2004). At later points in the book, we will examine an array of leadership roles in the change process. This chapter focuses on the role of the principal as "head leader" and how the principal's leadership is guided by his or her knowledge of the why, who, what, and how of leadership for significant change.

The Why of Leadership

It may well be that one of the most important aspects of leadership for significant change is one of the least attended to. Effective leaders for second-order change operate and motivate from a vision for the change. Such leaders do not *suggest* what teachers might do. They do not *demand* change and retreat to the sidelines. Instead, potent leaders for meaningful change are propelled by values, a vision, and passion (Duke, 2004; Evans, 1996; Fullan, 1991; Lambert, 2005; Reeves, 2006; Saphier, King, & D'Auria, 2006; Sergiovanni, 1999). These leaders ask themselves and ultimately their colleagues key questions (Schlechty, 1997; Sergiovanni, 1999):

- What is school about?
- What do we believe in?
- Why do we do what we do the way we do it?
- How are we unique?
- What do we want to become?
- What role might each of us play in becoming something better?

Despite the complexity and demands of change, teachers will reach beyond comfort to invest in a vision that dignifies their students, their work, and themselves. A suggestion or a mandate to jump on a bandwagon does not inspire the same kind of intrinsic motivation. A vision establishes a need for change. It also casts teachers as "moral change agents" (Fullan, 2001b) whose work makes a difference in the short- and long-term lives of students by creating a new, more rigorous kind of classroom (Sarason, 1996). Such a vision enables teachers to seek virtue in teaching—that is, to seek to teach in an exemplary way, to pursue valued social ends, to embody a caring ethic in classroom practice, and to apply state-of-the-art knowledge in their work to address the needs of students as human beings (Sergiovanni, 1999).

A vision is not a speech or presentation that takes place at the outset of a change initiative. It is the oxygen that permeates and enlivens the process at every stage of the journey. Sergiovanni (1999) reminds us that viable schools require technical or managerial leadership, human resources leadership, and pedagogical leadership. Schools that move beyond competence to second-order change for excellence also require symbolic leadership and cultural leadership. It is these last two kinds of leadership that provide a vision, nurture it, and lead others to embrace and enact it. The leader's passion for the vision becomes a source of authority. The daily actions of the leader attest to the pervasiveness, stability, and centrality of the vision. There simply is no leadership if there is nothing to follow. Vision enlists followers.

The Who of Leadership

Leaders for second-order change understand that the change is dependent on the will and skill of others. They do not see teachers as factory workers (Sarason, 1996). Rather they are respectful of the people whom they ask to invest in the demanding work of change. They are mindful and respectful of the complexity of teachers' personal lives (Evans, 1996) and professional lives (Kennedy, 2005), and they understand the anxiety-producing nature of change.

A key role of leaders for significant school change is relationship building (Fullan, 2001a, 2001b; Reeves, 2006). Effective leaders persist in getting to know teachers, understanding their particular strengths and needs, and listening to their ideas and concerns. They connect with those whom they lead. Such leaders know that "the single factor common to every successful change initiative is that relationships improve. If relationships improve, things get better" (Fullan, 2001a, p. 5).

Therefore, leaders for complex change invest heavily in developing productive relationships and a climate of respect and caring among faculty members (Saphier, King, & D'Auria, 2006). They help all members of the school community communicate more effectively, tolerate ambiguity, and appreciate the varied perspectives represented in the group. They build community even as the group grapples with difficult issues. They help the group make meaning and enlist diverse human beings for a common cause with common beliefs, shared ideas, shared principles, and shared responsibility (Saphier, King, & D'Auria, 2006; Sarason, 1996; Sergiovanni, 1999). As is the case with vision, positive relationships motivate and support change. Thus, the leader serves as minister to both the message and the flock (Sergiovanni, 1999). These leaders demonstrate that they are trustworthy for the journey ahead (Duke, 2004; Fullan, 2001a).

Further, such leaders understand the importance of expanded views of leadership. An emergent concept called "distributed leadership" (Spillane, 2006; Spillane, Halverson, & Diamond, 2001) emphasizes that followers are not passive but rather can significantly affect leadership practices. Leadership exists in many places and forms in organizations; it does not reside merely in assigned leaders. Therefore, leaders must be attuned to interactions between leaders and followers and must be sensitive to understanding how particular situations affect change. The interaction among leaders, followers, and the situation informs successful leadership.

The What of Leadership

Leaders for second-order change understand the nature of the change process and engage in strategic thought about it (Fullan, 2001a, 2001b; Lambert, 2005). They understand the following aspects of change:

- To move too quickly is intimidating to many people, but to move too slowly results in missed opportunity (Fullan, 2001b; Saphier, King, & D'Auria, 2006).
- Change requires both pressure and support from leaders (Fullan, 2001b). An organization that changes must change beliefs as well as practices. An organization that changes practices without changing beliefs will quickly revert to the old practices (Evans, 1996; Fullan, 2001a; Schlechty, 1997).
- Change necessarily causes ambiguity, tension, and self-examination (Duke, 2004; Evans, 1996; Fullan, 2001a, 2001b; Saphier, King, & D'Auria, 2006), and an absence of mistakes likely indicates an absence of growth (Fullan, 2001a; Hoerr, 2005; Saphier, King, & D'Auria, 2006).

With these realities in mind, effective leaders for significant change expect an uneven road. They know that disagreements and dips are as much a part of change and growth as are consensus and peaks. They accept that learning is an individual and a group process and that both aspects of learning can be planned for and yet defy planning. They are, in short, able to interpret and guide the journey.

In addition to understanding and attending to the change process, leaders for significant change understand the initiative they are commending to their colleagues. They use their strong working knowledge of teaching and learning to gain a clear sense of how the initiative works and how it will help the widest possible range of students succeed (Lambert, 2005; Marzano, Waters, & McNulty, 2005; Sergiovanni, 1999). In other words, the change initiative is inextricably linked with the vision for change. The leader understands precisely how the change will contribute to a stronger culture and a stronger practice for the school. However, the leader does not necessarily have, or pretend to have, absolute knowledge of all aspects of the commended change. Rather, the leader should have sufficient knowledge to be sure that the change—effectively implemented—will ultimately benefit teachers and students in ways that make the effort worthwhile. It is also critical that the leader understand the initiative accurately and deeply enough to recognize and guide fidelity to the change model as teachers' implementation efforts mature.

The How of Leadership

Closely related to understanding the change process is understanding how to successfully traverse the change process—messy and unpredictable as it will inevitably be. Leaders for significant change stay focused (Duke, 2004). They understand that neither they nor their colleagues can attend effectively to multiple initiatives simultaneously. Therefore, they ensure that what matters most for the change stays in the foreground (Reeves, 2006; Sergiovanni, 1999). They do not contribute to so-called "Christmas tree" schools in which new initiatives collect like ornaments on branches (Fullan, 2001b).

Importantly, leaders who bring about meaningful change stay the course (Duke, 2004; Taylor et al., 2006). They understand that real change takes a long time, and they plan accordingly with specific short- and long-term goals (Kanold, 2006). Even though they know that plans will inevitably change, the plans communicate the message that the focus of the change is here to stay. When the change process becomes difficult, they display the energy, hope, and enthusiasm necessary to proceed (Fullan, 2001a). When times are good and progress is noteworthy, they act as celebrants (Fullan, 2001a; Saphier, King, & D'Auria, 2006). In every instance, they preserve and renew the core values and shared mission of the group (Kanold, 2006; Sergiovanni, 1999). These leaders are highly visible and involved in classrooms. They pay attention and practice "high touch leadership" (Fullan, 2001a; Reeves, 2006, p. 59). Further, they monitor progress, and they are willing to be held accountable for the process in which they engage others (Marzano, Waters, & McNulty, 2005). Principals who lead for second-order change do not necessarily encounter fewer problems than other principals do, they simply look at the difficulties differently and deal with them in different ways (Fullan, 1993).

Because leaders for second-order change are keenly aware of the complexity of the change process and requirements for its success, they also provide intensive, intelligent, and sustained support for those asked to implement the change. In Chapter 3, we examine in detail the kinds of support necessary for meaningful school change.

The research-based work of Robert Marzano and his colleagues (2005) serves as an appropriate summary of the responsibilities of leaders who are successful in bringing about second-order change. These responsibilities are above and beyond those necessary for the daily management of a school, are listed in order of importance, and include the following:

- Being knowledgeable about how the initiative will affect curriculum, instruction, and assessment and being able to provide appropriate guidance in those areas.
- Being the driving force behind the initiative and fostering trust that outcomes will be important and positive if the group works hard and implements the initiative appropriately.
- Being knowledgeable about the research and theory behind the initiative and guiding the group in developing an understanding of that knowledge base.
- Challenging the status quo and moving forward on the innovation despite the difficulty and uncertainty of the journey.
- Consistently monitoring the effects of the innovation and the change process.
- Being both directive and flexible about the change as the evolving situation warrants.
- Operating in a manner consistent with one's ideals and beliefs relative to the innovation.

Building principals who undertake second-order change do so as an act of courage and professional integrity. They are not content to manage a school operation—even one that is deemed very good. Rather, they accept that leaders are entrusted with significantly improving conditions for those in their care; that doing so requires conviction, knowledge, and risk; and that the dangers of not undertaking change are greater than those of change itself (Fullan, 2001b). These leaders are not superheroes whose work is beyond the scope of ordinary human beings. What they do can be done by others who have moral purpose, a sense of direction, a willingness to engage with others to solve problems that defy simple answers, and the foresight to support an evolution of belief and practice (Fullan, 2001a).

Differentiated Instruction and Implications for Second-Order Change

Seeking to develop classrooms that attend to the learning needs of the broadest possible range of learners is undeniably seeking second-order change. Such change challenges how teachers think about the students they teach, the role of the teacher, the nature of instruction, uses of assessment, and implementation of classroom routines. Such change cannot be addressed by the application of a single strategy. There are no streamlined solutions, no once-and-forever answers; yesterday's answers aren't enough (Marzano, Waters, & McNulty, 2005).

Change toward differentiation is unequivocally deep change and absolutely requires leadership for second-order change. Two elements of such leadership are important to discuss here. One of those relates to the vision for differentiation; the second relates to the leader as a model for differentiation. Examining these two elements sets the stage for looking at two leaders for change toward differentiation and for much of what follows in the book.

A Vision for Differentiation

As will become evident in the final section of the chapter, leaders who envision a particular change will envision it somewhat differently. There is no unitary vision for what we call "differentiated instruction." Nonetheless, there are important components of a philosophy of differentiation that merit a brief exploration here. These components are both visionary and practical in their scope and are a worthy engine for energizing change in a particular school—and in schools in general. Among the underpinnings of differentiation are the following beliefs:

• Human beings differ as learners as a result of factors such as prior experiences, culture, interests, approaches to learning, adult support, maturity, and heredity.
• Such differences are normal and should be dealt with as normal in classroom settings.
• When students are separated out because of learning differences, all students receive important, and often negative, messages about the worth of individuals.

• Ignoring student differences in classrooms leads to frustration, boredom, and possible alienation from school learning.

• Virtually all students benefit from very high-quality curriculum that promotes understanding, complex thought, and application of key knowledge, ideas, and skills. Reserving curriculum of that sort for select students is indefensible.

• Differentiation for all students should stem from very high-quality curriculum with appropriate support for a full range of students in achieving and extending meaningful, complex, authentic goals.

• Attending proactively and effectively to student differences in readiness within more heterogeneous settings supports student growth.

• Attending proactively and effectively to student differences in interest within more heterogeneous classrooms supports student motivation.

• Attending proactively and effectively to student differences in preferences about how to learn within more heterogeneous classrooms supports learning efficiency.

• Persistent, ongoing assessment that is used to follow student progress toward and beyond clearly articulated and important learning goals and subsequently to allow teachers to adjust instruction to support the growth of varied learners toward and beyond those goals is key to effective teaching and learning.

• Effective teaching and learning are rooted in a teacher's acceptance of responsibility for each student's success and grounded in relationships of acceptance and trust between the teacher and each student.

• Defensible differentiation equates to teacher flexibility in using classroom elements to maximize the growth of individual students in the context of a community of learners.

The notion of a homogeneous classroom is, of course, a myth. One educator noted that the only time he believed in a homogeneous class was when he was in a room by himself. After a pause, he added, "and even then, I'm not convinced." No two students consistently learn at the same pace, with the same support, and in the same modes. Clearly, some spans of heterogeneity are greater than others. Regardless of the degree of learner variance, differentiation should be a reality in any classroom. However, the core vision for differentiation embraces greater, rather than less, heterogeneity. Differentiation is a means for enabling broad swaths of students in our increasingly diverse world to learn effectively together. It is an alternative to the two prevailing modes of dealing with learner differences—either sorting and separating students in order to deal with their differences or placing them in the same classroom and ignoring the differences.

John Stroup, a University of Virginia graduate student, potently synthesized the vision of differentiation when he explained:

> Few would argue that opportunity in life is strongly connected with educational opportunity. However, we have often misconstrued the notion of equal access to education to mean that all students should receive precisely the same pacing, resources, and instruction. The result is a one-size-fits-all education system. Differentiated instruction recognizes that students are not the same and that access to equal education necessarily means that, given a certain goal, each student should be provided resources, instruction, and support to help them meet that objective. . . .
>
> Differentiated instruction pushes teachers to reevaluate the purpose of teaching and learning. Teachers have an obligation to increase the participation of all students in healthy and productive ways. But what is an "obligation"? Edward Farley wrote in his book *Deep Symbols* that "obligation is being responsible to the other, and that means that when we are seized by obligation, we are seized by the needs, aims, vulnerabilities, sufferings, and even autonomy—in short, the total condition—of the other." Obligation is a state of being that includes the needs of another in the formulation of an individual's own desires. That is, obligation no longer is something I am doing for you, but becomes something I am doing with you for both of us. . . .
>
> Differentiated instruction asks teachers to become ethnographers of their students. . . .Of course the teacher can never fully know the desires, needs, and wants of all students. It is an impossible task. However, the imaginative teacher can escape his or her own socially bound meanings and become a better interpreter of students. That teacher can explore the possibility that some teaching techniques and ways of learning may be limiting to some students. . . In differentiated instruction, students participate in the formation of their own identity, and thus they transform the environment in which they live and learn. Likewise, the more knowledge an individual acquires about him or herself, the more power and agency that individual has to engage in that particular community. When all students participate in the collective learning of a classroom, the environment is changed positively. Thus the quality of learning of the individual also changes positively—even for those who may already be learning to their fullest capacity. . . .
>
> Differentiated instruction is a way of taking into account the needs and wants of others without either relinquishing our own needs and wants or dominating and controlling the other person. In that way, differentiated instruction is more than just a method of teaching. It is a way of being human. (J. Stroup, personal communication, 2006)

The goal of differentiation, to borrow from Schlechty (1997), is to invent a system of education that provides an elite education for virtually every student—a system in which each student is regarded as an individual of worth, provided with the best curriculum and instruction available, and supported in maximizing his or her potential.

The Leader as a Role Model for Differentiation

The philosophy of differentiation is predicated on respect for individuals and their potential and is aimed at providing necessary support for individuals to become the best they can be. Although that perspective is easy to agree with, it is far more difficult to enact. Effective differentiation requires progression from lip service to service. It is harder than it might seem for teachers genuinely to accept the value of the people whom they lead, accept responsibility for their academic welfare (which inevitably also includes some issues of personal welfare), seek to know each individual at some meaningful level, establish trust with each individual, adapt professional practices and procedures to address varied needs of varied individuals, and do so in a demanding and complex environment. It is difficult to understand how it looks when a teacher aspires simultaneously to help every student reach the same articulated understandings and to acknowledge and attend to important student differences.

Obviously then, teachers need to see differentiation in action in classrooms. They also need to live it as a faculty. At least three key needs are addressed if the principal is a consistent model of differentiation. First, the message is clear that the principal believes that the philosophy makes a positive difference in the lives of all learners—educators included—and is therefore willing to invest effort in enacting the model just as he or she asks teachers to enact it. Second, teachers have an enduring and personal way of understanding differentiation when they experience it and see their colleagues experience it. Third, differentiation respects and dignifies people—and people who are treated with dignity and respect are more likely to interact with others in their environment in the same way, thus enhancing the possibility of community at the school and classroom levels.

The principal who models differentiation for a faculty becomes, in this way, a teacher of learners. Just as in an effectively differentiated classroom, the principal communicates the following fundamental messages to their faculty:

- We have very important work to do.
- I want us all to see why the work matters.

- All of us will work toward essential goals.
- As we grow individually in our professional knowledge, understanding, and skill, we need to become increasingly effective as a team.
- We share many things in common as people and as learners.
- We care about our work, the people we love, and the places we live and work.
- The similarities we share are a kind of glue that helps bind us in a common mission.
- We also have important differences that affect us personally and professionally.
- We represent different experiences, talents, perspectives, cultures, genders, idiosyncrasies, and so on.
- Because of our differences, we will work toward our goals in different ways, on varied timetables, with different support systems.
- We will not always agree on ways to reach our core goals, but we will learn how to reach them better by sharing our varied perspectives.
- It is my job as a leader to help provide you necessary encouragement and support to achieve essential goals.
- Our progress toward essential goals is not negotiable, but how we do so is negotiable.
- I will keep the essential goals in front of us.
- I need your partnership and feedback to ensure that we all grow.
- You need one another's partnership to ensure that we all grow.
- I will consistently monitor our progress toward our key goals, will share data about the progress with you, and will use what I learn to support our journey individually and as a group.
- I will also be asking you to share your perspectives on our work and how we can accomplish it more effectively. I want to hear and learn from your varied perspectives.

It is imperative that a leader for second-order change toward responsive teaching model that philosophy. An effective leader for second-order change helps others make meaning of that change (Duke, 2004; Sergiovanni, 1999). There is no better way to make meaning of a new way of thinking and acting than through positive personal experience with it. Yet even while the leader commends and represents a common vision to the faculty, he or she must consistently remember and act on the truth that a faculty is a collection of diverse individuals. It is no less true at the building level than at the classroom level that "by treating all people as if they were the same, we respect no one's unique contributions. Whenever we homogenize people, we all lose" (Hoerr, 2005, p. 158). The leader for second-order change toward differentiation cannot give less than he or she asks others to give.

Two Leaders for Second-Order Change

Conway and Colchester were strikingly different schools as they each began work with differentiated instruction. Their principals had different characteristics as well. Despite clear distinctions, however, both principals undertook the focus on differentiation because they identified a need for it in their schools. Both principals understood the model well. Both had a strong conviction that the model—appropriately implemented—would address the needs they identified. Both undertook change toward defensible differentiation as a second-order change, ensuring focus on the initiative and long-term persistence in pursuing it. Both were—and remain—attentive to the personal and professional needs of faculty throughout the change process. Thus, despite dramatic differences in virtually all key school characteristics, the principals of the two schools adhered in common to the traits of leaders for second-order change. That is, both leaders had significant knowledge and understanding of research behind the model and how the initiative would impact curriculum, instruction, and assessment. Both leaders were the driving force behind the initiative and engendered trust that outcomes would be important and positive if the faculties worked hard to implement the initiative. Both leaders challenged the status quo in their schools and accepted the rigor and unpredictability of the change process. Both were directive as well as flexible in guiding the work of the faculty related to differentiation. Both consistently monitored the results of the change initiative on teachers and students, and both modeled differentiation in their interactions with teachers (Marzano, Waters, & McNulty, 2005).

Leadership and Vision at Conway Elementary

Principal Lane Narvaez, who previously had administrative experience at the elementary, middle, and high school levels, spent her first year in Conway observing in classrooms and listening to teachers, students, and parents. She realized there were important inconsistencies in approaches to teaching reading as well as a need for scheduling changes to facilitate collaboration among grade-level teams, a need for improved communication with parents about academics, and a need to align curriculum objectives with new state standards.

As teacher teams began working with Narvaez to address these initial concerns, conversations often turned to a need for "differentiating instruction." The teacher-generated interest reflected an additional concern the principal had developed during her first years of leadership. She had not discussed this concern with the faculty because she knew that introducing change in this arena would lead to teacher overload. Persistent classroom observation across all grades had led the principal to conclude that although sound supports existed for struggling learners at Conway, advanced students were underchallenged much of the time. Narvaez felt that the issue would be most effectively addressed by providing appropriate challenge for these students in their regular classrooms. She also knew that such changes would necessitate major adjustments in teacher beliefs and classroom practices. Working with teachers on the initially identified (generally first-order) changes would allow her to get to know her staff better and to establish trust with them—important prerequisites for the impending second-order change.

In their early meetings, teachers raised concerns that pullout programs for students identified as gifted, those having special education exceptionalities, and those requiring additional support in reading or math addressed students' needs for only a small portion of the school week. Further, the teachers were concerned about the state mandate that all students master the same knowledge and skills, despite their obvious differences as learners. As they continued to work on the first-order changes, teachers noted that their understandings of pre-assessment were limited, that faculty members had different conceptions of differentiation, that few teachers systematically and effectively addressed student readiness and interest in their classrooms, and that many teachers were not equipped to do so.

Narvaez wanted a common dialogue among faculty members on the topic of differentiation so that collegiality—already a Conway positive—would continue to grow. This goal called for a shared, schoolwide learning experience on differentiation. To conceive what this might look like, the principal felt that she needed a deeper understanding of the model, and so she attended an intensive multiple-day workshop on differentiated instruction. This experience enabled her to refine her vision for differentiation, develop a vocabulary that the staff would need in common, and begin to think specifically about how she would introduce the vision to faculty.

In Narvaez's mind, the vision had three prongs. One element of the vision involved ensuring that a very good school continued to get better rather than being content with its current status. Conway, she felt, could not be as good as it might be (and perhaps not as good as community members thought it was) if it did not aspire to continual improvement. A second element in her vision had to do with her observation that bright students were seldom stretched in their classrooms. Narvaez felt strongly that the school had a responsibility to be a good steward of the time and trust of advanced learners—as it was of the time and trust of others. Of equal if not greater importance to Narvaez was the third aspect of her vision. She felt quite strongly that by ensuring challenge for high-end students, the quality of curriculum and instruction for all students would improve. The sort of curricular and instructional adjustments necessary for advanced challenge would open up possibilities for a higher quality of learning and more personalized instruction for all Conway students. She was also convinced that a powerful result of such an initiative would be a staff that worked at an even higher level of professional efficacy and confidence—a fourth element in her vision for second-order change. Narvaez understood that the scope of change necessary to make differentiation a reality in classrooms across the school would require a sustained, multiyear commitment on her part, as well as that of the Conway teachers.

When the initial first-order changes had been addressed, the principal met with her staff to share her vision for change toward defensible differentiation and to link the vision with the teachers' own insights that had emerged over the previous couple of years. She began the session not by talking about differentiation but by examining stages of teacher development (Burke, Christensen, & Fessler, 1984).

Narvaez described for the group eight stages of teacher growth: preservice preparation, induction, competency building, enthusiasm and growth, career frustration, stability with stagnation, career wind down, and career exit. She focused on the competency-building stage, during which teachers see their work as challenging and thus are receptive to new ideas and eagerly seek out opportunities to improve their knowledge base; and the enthusiasm and growth stage, during which teachers are enthusiastic about going to school and about their interactions with students, are eager about doing their work, experience high levels of job satisfaction, and search for new ways to enrich their teaching. "Who would *not* want to work at these levels of professionalism?" she speculated.

As Narvaez discussed research on and descriptions of these two peak stages of practice, she and the teachers agreed that working as a team at these two levels was a worthwhile professional objective. She then introduced them to her vision for differentiation, and she invited them to join her in a book study on differentiation so that they could begin an informed dialogue about ways that differentiation could benefit students and staff. This step marked the beginning of targeted staff development for differentiation at Conway.

Leadership and Vision at Colchester High

When Joyce Stone became principal of Colchester High School in 1999, she found a school in trouble. There were strong and contentious divisions among economic groups of students in the school that mirrored a long standing class divide in the community, and many students often felt uncomfortable, if not unsafe, in school. Parents became more concerned about school tensions following events at Columbine High School. The sense of unease escalated after the tragic deaths of two Colchester students. Following seven bomb threats, the school board insisted on metal detectors for the school and a permanent lockdown approach. Furthermore, the district had eliminated the guidance director position in the mid-1980s; teachers were working under an imposed contract; school budgets were routinely voted down by community members; and the state educational authority had identified the school as being in need of technical assistance in reading and math, based on standardized test scores in those areas. In the face of those and other pressures, the principal of Colchester High School resigned. Stone—a veteran high school administrator and former special education coordinator—took on the leadership role.

The local school board gave Stone three mandates: create a safe and secure school environment, ensure teacher accountability, and bring about improved student outcomes academically and affectively. Stone, in turn, asked the board for backing in three areas: commitment to support genuine success for all learners in the school, restoration of eliminated leadership positions, and support for the principal in taking the steps necessary to meet their mandates. Both Stone and the board agreed on those conditions.

If there was not already ample evidence of need for change at Colchester, a visit by the New England Association for School Certification early in Stone's tenure resulted in 78 broad recommendations for change. Stone began immediately working with her staff to create a school environment that was not only safe but nurturing for all students and to ensure academic focus in all classes.

An early step toward school improvement came when Stone wrote a proposal for five teacher leaders to form a school leadership team that would provide guidance to the principal on the work ahead and also provide a strong link to the rest of the faculty. The Leadership Team would later be invaluable in movement toward differentiation.

As Stone began classroom observations, it was immediately clear to her that many of the school tensions between students from different economic backgrounds were fed by the long time system of tracking at Colchester. Students from more affluent homes consistently enrolled in college-prep or Advanced Placement classes. Students from low-economic backgrounds consistently enrolled in general-level classes. The result was an "us and them" mentality that spilled over into the hall, cafeteria, and auditorium. Student tensions were so high and student-to-student behavior was so negative that Stone did not hold school assemblies for two years. She felt that the students could not learn to be proud of themselves in settings where negative behaviors dominated.

Beyond Stone's immediate concern about the negative impact of tracking on the school's environment, she was profoundly disturbed by what she perceived to be a perpetuation of academic inequity in what was already an environment of economic inequity. Simply put, affluent students at Colchester were receiving a quality education that positioned them for positive and productive futures. Students from low-economic backgrounds were taking courses likely to ensure that they would continue on their current economic paths. For this principal, what she observed was morally indefensible. In addition, she believed strongly there was no way to improve either the school environment or student performance as long as the academic inequity persisted.

As Stone talked with her faculty about a new direction for the school, she encouraged them to give meaning to the district mission, which stated in part, "All students will develop the academic proficiency, social skill, and character to be fulfilled, responsible, and involved citizens." It was evident that the words had little practical meaning at Colchester High. Faculty members and the principal agreed that to invest them with significance would require that all students have challenging educational experiences, that the school work far more closely with families, and that the community become the school's partner in forging success. From the beginning, Stone was direct with the faculty. Her vision was clear. All

Colchester students deserved the best education the school could offer. If some students were better prepared for that quality of learning, it would be necessary for teachers to support other students in learning to learn at a much higher level than in the past, even as they ensured high ceilings of opportunity for traditional high achievers. Actualizing the new Colchester vision of equity and excellence in an atmosphere of respect, responsibility, and pride would ultimately require detracking of classes, teaching the new classes at a very high level, and preparing teachers for differentiating instruction to support the success of the widest possible spectrum of students at that level, she told the faculty. "Differentiated instruction," she said on many occasions, "is a civil right."

In addition to the school's Leadership Team, in time Stone would implement best-practice faculty meetings, summer curriculum work, Saturday seminars, a teacher liaison position, grade-level facilitators, faculty forums, voluntary committees, task forces, learning circles, and collaborative work groups to bring about change. Together, teachers and the principal changed the tone of the school by implementing teacher advisory sessions, peer mentoring, conflict resolution, personal learning plans, celebration assemblies, and a restructured student government. Likewise, the teachers and principal changed the academic profile of the school by escalating the quality of curriculum and ensuring wide access to success via differentiated instruction.

Like Narvaez at Conway, Stone was very self-aware in her leadership role. "I had to be sure I understood the complexities of change, to do the research so I asked the right questions, to internalize a vision for the school and make sure our actions were consistent with that vision, and to find the best people to do the job," said Stone. She noted also that she worked very hard to model the values and beliefs embodied in the vision, to communicate in ways that were passionate and thoughtful, to be both directive and collaborative, and to identify and provide the resources, incentives, and supports necessary for the vision's success. Because of the urgent need for change at Colchester, Stone said, "I had to listen, plan, and act simultaneously."

Lessons About Leadership and Vision for Change

As different as Conway and Colchester were—and as different as their principals were—both leaders understood themselves as people and as leaders and had clarity of values. Narvaez and Stone shared the following characteristics:

• Each was sensitive to the context and culture of her school setting.
• Each had a strong belief in equity and quality.
• Each saw movement toward differentiation as a nonnegotiable part
of attaining her school's goals.
• Each thought strategically about the evolution of school improvement.
• Each made herself vulnerable to the faculty by risking change and
trusting faculty members.
• Each had a strong knowledge of teaching and learning—including
differentiated instruction.
• Each was realistic about the complexity of the change process and
sought feedback from the faculty about what was and was not working for them.
• Each was able to develop capacity in their colleagues and the organization (Duke, 2004; Lambert, 2005).

Each principal also derived her vision for differentiation from the
heart (what she believed), head (sound knowledge of pedagogy), and
hand (the actions she took and asked others to take [Sergiovanni,
1999]). Narvaez and Stone both earned trust and inspired commitment (Duke,
2004)—that is, each was able to identify a purpose that drew followers
and then provided "the conditions and support that allow people to function in ways that are consistent with agreed-upon values" (Sergiovanni,
1999, p. 29).

The next two chapters will examine the support system developed
by the two principals to enable teachers—individually and collectively—
to make second-order changes for differentiation in their classroom
practices.

3

The Nature of Professional Development for Change Toward Differentiation

Clearly, the leader of a school that changes and grows in positive ways generates an environment and learning opportunities that support change. But what is it exactly that distinguishes such an environment and such learning opportunities? What is the focus of conversations between the principal and faculty members? What are the messages that the leader will persistently communicate?

How does the principal deal with viewpoints that differ or even clash with his or her perspectives? Does the leader focus on feedback or evaluation? How much help will teachers need for required changes? How often? Where will the help come from? How soon should classroom implementation be an expected outgrowth of professional development support?

Pockets of responsive teaching already exist in the school. How does a principal build networks that lead to shared conversation, problem solving, collaboration, and ultimately shared practice in a school? How does a principal simultaneously maintain and share leadership for change toward schoolwide differentiation?

Supporting and Sustaining Persistent Efforts for Change

Although a vital role of the building principal in bringing about second-order change is focusing and sustaining attention on a vision for change, it is the teachers who will have to do the hard work of change. In the Meredith Willson musical *The Music Man*, the leader of a proposed marching band knows little about music but is a persuasive salesman. He convinces the townspeople—including the prospective musicians—to use the "think system" to become musicians. If they just keep thinking the score in their heads, he tells them, they'll play like pros when the instruments arrive. In the movie, the plan works like a charm. In education, the chance that teachers will suddenly "play new music" because the principal has a good sales pitch is vastly unlikely. To move from vision to implementation absolutely requires intelligent, sustained, focused, and flexible professional development. This chapter will examine the *nature* of such professional development. Chapter 4 will examine the *content* of such professional development.

Leaders for second-order change are not grandiose visionaries. Rather, they are more likely to work from "the blueprints of the architect than the uncertain and cloudy visions of the dreamer" (Reeves, 2006, p. 35). These leaders plan specifically and systematically to support teachers in developing the necessary knowledge, understanding, and skill to enact the desired changes in their classrooms. As is the case with learning designs for students in the classroom, leaders ensure clarity of essential learning outcomes, specify evidence that can serve as demonstration of proficiency with the outcomes, design a step-by-step plan to support the learners in achieving the outcomes, and build in flexibility necessary to attend proactively to learner variance evidenced through formal and informal assessment of learner growth—all the while ensuring a learning environment that supports active engagement of each learner (Tomlinson & McTighe, 2006).

Fullan (2001b) suggests that where deep change is concerned, success is 25 percent having the right idea or vision and 75 percent implementing the right processes. Professional development is foundational to the process of change. The degree of support for professional growth must match the degree of change asked of those who will have to do the changing. To provide lesser support is to doom the potential for pervasive change (Marzano, Waters, & McNulty, 2005).

Effective support will continually help participants answer five key questions that Schlechty (1997) has identified as arising from initial and ongoing conversations about a vision:

- Why is the change needed?
- What will it mean for us and for our students when the change comes about?
- Is what we're being asked to do possible?

• Can we see it in practice?
• How will we develop the skills necessary to enact the change?

Further, effective support for genuine professional growth will necessarily be sustained. A great deal of time is required for a faculty to move from "anemic" understanding to effective understanding of the change (Reeves, 2006). Coming together around a vision is big. Staying together around its implementation is success (Taylor et al., 2006). Effective support for professional growth provides tools and a map for the journey ahead.

Professional development for second-order change has at least three key and interdependent attributes. It ensures an environment safe for growth and change, it develops a professional community of learners, and it establishes and maintains clarity of focus.

Ensuring an Environment Safe for Change

Professional development that ignites deep change is about more than providing technical requirements for teachers. It must also model the new and enduring values and provide conditions conducive to the values commended by the change initiative so that, in time, the faculty comes to embody those values (Sergiovanni, 1999). Support systems for substantial professional growth seek to develop a group of educators who function from a sense of commitment rather than commandment (Schlechty, 1997). To enable people to risk the uncertain and enter the unknown, professional development must create and sustain an environment that is safe for learning and change. To that end, professional development support for second-order change will do the following:

• Establish and foster a caring, personal climate in which it is clear that people matter (Evans, 1996; Saphier et al., 2006).
• Show respect for diverse and divergent viewpoints and model equanimity when faced with disagreement (Duke, 2004; Fullan, 2001b; Saphier et al., 2006).
• Make it easy to ask for and receive help (Saphier et al., 2006).
• Model curiosity and constant learning that encourage teachers to create knowledge as they practice (Joyce & Showers, 2002; Saphier et al., 2006; Sergiovanni, 1999).
• Provide varied learning, coaching, and other support options for teachers based on their particular fears, needs, and points of development to ensure that they grow in confidence and efficiency with

the change (Evans, 1996; Glickman, 2002; Joyce & Showers, 2002; Schlechty, 1997; Sparks & Hirsh, 1997; Taylor et al., 2006).

• Ensure that the process of growth and the feedback received on the process are nonevaluative (Joyce & Showers, 2002).

Developing a Professional Community of Learners

It is difficult in schools for teachers to find time for sustained reflection about their practice and to keep the routine work of the day from swallowing up visions of a new way of doing school (Evans, 1996; Fullan, 2001b; Joyce & Showers, 2002; Kennedy, 2005). Nonetheless, schools are, by their nature, communities of learning and operate on the assumption that teachers and students can improve themselves through the process of learning (Glickman, 2002; Hoerr, 2005; Joyce & Showers, 2002; Sergiovanni, 1999). Actualizing the learning potential of the faculty as a whole develops a culture of collegiality through which administrators and teachers learn together and learn from one another (Glickman, 2002; Hoerr, 2005; Joyce & Showers, 2002), with the principal being the "head learner" (Sergiovanni, 1999, p. 59). Professional development "is the essence of teaching and learning to teach better" (Fullan, 1995, p. 257) and as such must be seen as central to everything that happens in a school, not as an add-on.

Over time, collegiality becomes a professional virtue, and the attention of those involved moves from concern about one's own practice to concern about practice in general (Sergiovanni, 1999; Sparks & Hirsh, 1997). Professional learning communities also play other key roles in moving a faculty from vision to implementation. They help keep everyone together and focused on the initiative, ensure a forum for modeling as well as exploring the initiative, provide the support and pressure needed to bring about second-order change via peer accountability, and strengthen working relationships as well as teacher leadership at the grade, department, team, and school levels (Danielson, 2006; Fullan, 2001a; Joyce & Showers, 2002; Saphier et al., 2006; Schmoker, 2006; Taylor et al., 2006). Effective professional learning communities focus on the following:

• Dealing with hard questions and discussing the undiscussable in an atmosphere of respect and safety (Duke, 2004; Saphier et al., 2006; Sarason, 1996).

• Fostering nondefensive examination of one's own practice (Fullan, 2001a; Sarason, 1996).

• Developing common professional knowledge related to the initiative and to high-quality teaching and learning in general (Fullan, 2001b; Joyce & Showers, 2002).

• Developing a shared and deep meaning of the initiative in the context of high-quality teaching and learning (Fullan, 2001b; Joyce & Showers, 2002).

• Establishing and nurturing a practice-based action inquiry throughout the faculty (Fullan, 2001b; Joyce & Showers, 2002; Kanold, 2006).

• Ensuring that teachers' tacit or private knowledge becomes explicit or shared knowledge (Glickman, 2002; Joyce & Showers, 2002; Marzano et al., 2005; Schmoker, 2006).

Establishing and Maintaining Clarity of Focus

Support for second-order change necessarily establishes and maintains focus on what matters most for those involved in the change. School life is replete with potential distractions, side trips, and escape hatches. Making time for the hard work of change is one challenge for leaders. Ensuring focused use of that time over the long term is equally critical. Professional development for deep change keeps participants focused on the following:

• Student welfare and achievement as the motivation for the change (Darling-Hammond & Sykes, 1999; Glickman, 2002; Joyce & Showers, 2002; Kanold, 2006; Reeves, 2006; Saphier et al., 2006; Sarason, 1996; Schmoker, 2006).

• Teacher capacity in the knowledge, skills, and dispositions necessary for pedagogical expertise in general and for the change in particular (Darling-Hammond & Sykes, 1999; Fullan, 2001a; Joyce & Showers, 2002; Saphier et al., 2006).

• Fidelity to the core intent, principles, and practices of the model being implemented (Evans, 1996; Fullan, 2001b; Kennedy, 2005; Rogers, 1995).

• Examination of and feedback on progress toward implementation of the change in order to guide student growth, guide teacher growth, and help with teacher comfort related to the change (Darling-Hammond & Sykes, 1999; Duke, 2004; Evans, 1996; Joyce & Showers, 2002; Sarason, 1996).

• Celebration or problem solving as appropriate based on shared results (Fullan, 2001b; Saphier et al., 2006; Schmoker, 2006).

• Recognition of one another's accomplishments and successes (Fullan, 2001a; Kanold, 2006; Saphier et al., 2006; Sergiovanni, 1999), with an emphasis on lateral rather than only top-down recognition (Evans, 1996).

Professional development for significant change itself would have a new look in many schools. It is purposeful rather than opportunistic, coherent rather than fragmented, aimed at transfer into classroom practice rather than at absorption of information, collaborative rather than solitary or private, reflective rather than didactic, informed by needs and results rather than by popularity or availability. It aims to change minds as well as practice. It results in commitment rather than resentment. Although this sort of support for professional development is imperative for second-order change in general, it seems particularly central to the goal of creating classrooms in which students function as a community of learners, with shared responsibility for effective classroom operation, with an emphasis on regard for human commonalities as well as respect for individual differences, with common goals that are achievable in different ways, and with a commitment to providing support for individual and group success.

Differentiation and the Nature of Professional Development

The theme of modeling differentiation will be recurrent. Professional development plans for second-order change toward differentiated classrooms will necessarily have at least a two-pronged intent. First, professional development will need to provide teachers with the knowledge, understanding, and skill necessary to develop and guide academically responsive classrooms. Second, professional development will also need to serve as a laboratory for exploring and living the vision of differentiation so that teachers experience it rather than simply learn about it. In time, professional development to support substantive change toward schoolwide differentiation will be a catalyst for developing a schoolwide culture that reflects what differentiation represents. It's difficult to imagine that classrooms could become pervasively responsive in a setting where teachers are regarded as subservient, where their differences are seen as inconvenient or irrelevant, or where there is diminished enthusiasm for the organic and interactive nature of teaching and learning. Thus ensuring an environment safe for change, developing a professional community of learners, and establishing clarity of focus are, if anything, even more essential to the viability of change toward responsive teaching than for other second-order change initiatives. These attributes not only set the stage for change but also represent the particular change of differentiated teaching.

Ensuring an Environment Safe for Change Toward Differentiation

In a differentiated classroom, the teacher must convey to academically diverse learners the message that the classroom is safe and affirming for each learner. That is foundational to what should follow throughout the year. All students need to believe that they (and their peers) are valued as they are, that they will find purpose in the classroom, that they will derive power through important work, that they are meaningful contributors to the work of the group, and that the classroom will provide both challenge and support for each of them. Each student also needs to know that the teacher owns the success of every individual learner and of the group as a whole. In short, each student needs to develop a sense that the classroom is a place where he or she is known, appreciated, and mentored for success with worthy goals (Tomlinson, 2003). Those are highly reflective of the conditions that make a school environment conducive to teacher trust, risk taking, and recrafting professional practice. Therefore, an environment that is safe for second-order change toward differentiation does the following:

• Establishes and fosters a caring, personal climate in which it is clear that the teachers' varied cultures, genders, experience levels, perspectives, interests, learning preferences, and personal lives are valued, respected, attended to, and seen as having unique contributions to the work of the professional group as well as to the success of a diverse student body.
• Not only shows respect for diverse and divergent viewpoints but in fact invites and celebrates multiple perspectives as a means of broadening the group's understanding of student needs and possible teacher responses and of ensuring that all group members participate in the change process.
• Makes it easy to ask for and receive help by opening access to one another's classrooms; by planning time for small-group and

whole-faculty collaboration and sharing; by providing multiple, trust-worthy, coherent, and readily available sources of information about differentiation; and by establishing a tone of learning through shared inquiry.

• Models a belief that there is no packaged answer to effective teaching, but rather that teaching requires constant learning through interaction with evolving content and consistently changing learners.

• Provides varied learning, coaching, and other support options for teachers to learn about differentiation based on their particular fears, needs, and points of development to ensure that they grow in confidence and efficiency in implementing the principles, processes, and practices of differentiation in their classrooms.

Because differentiation requires teachers to rethink and rework many aspects of their practice, it is particularly important that professional development options not only tie directly *to* the classroom but that, in fact, they take place, at least in part, directly *in* the classroom. Effective coaching in the classroom is particularly important in successful movement toward differentiation because of its multifaceted nature and the degree of change it requires of most teachers. Effectively coached teachers are more likely to practice new skills more often, develop a high level of proficiency in using them, apply strategies more appropriately, display longer knowledge retention about the strategies and better understand their rationale, and explain new models and strategies more fully and effectively to their students than teachers who are not coached (Joyce & Showers, 2002). All of these are important outcomes for defensible differentiation.

Developing a Professional Community of Learners to Support Change Toward Differentiation

Energy, insight, support, peer pressure, inspiration, example, and partnership are all benefits of effective professional communities of learning for any second-order change initiative. For differentiation, the faculty community of learners is also, as noted earlier, a proxy for the classroom community of learners—allowing teachers to experience what they will try to implement in their own classrooms. Another benefit of a strong professional community of learners related to differentiation has to do with the need for varied experiences and talents in addressing the learning needs of academically diverse student populations.

Faculty members of color will bring to discussions understandings about students of color that may be lost on faculty members from other ethnic backgrounds. Some teachers are very effective with classroom management processes that are essential in flexible classrooms, and yet other teachers lack management savvy and cannot move ahead without it. Faculty members who have had strong backgrounds in reading, special education, gifted education, the arts, guidance, and so on have a repertoire of insights and instructional strategies that can no longer be retained for their private practice. Rather, this knowledge, understanding, and skill must be disseminated broadly and effectively. It is really only through shared learning that more teachers can learn to be more things to more students. Professional communities of learners are effective in moving teachers toward more responsive instruction when community members do the following:

• Deal with hard questions and discuss the undiscussable in an atmosphere of respect and safety. For example: Which students in our school are in the foreground of success, and which ones are in the background? What structures in our school make it difficult for some students to succeed? What do we mean by success in this school, and is it a definition that leads each of our students to a productive life? To what degree are we trying to maximize the capacity of each student, and to what degree are we trying to bring them all to a norm?

• Foster nondefensive examination of one's own practice. For example, asking: What do I do to know and understand each student as fully as I possibly can? What do I do to make learning invitational for students? In what ways do I share responsibility for classroom success with my students? To what degree do I accept responsibility for the success of each of my students? How do I try to connect important content with the lives, interests, and concerns of my students? How do I know whether the classroom is working for each student? How willing am I to grow in each of those areas?

• Develop common professional knowledge related to differentiation and to high-quality teaching and learning in general—thus ensuring that teachers and administrators share common vocabulary and principles related to differentiation.

• Develop a shared understanding of differentiation as a philosophy as well as a model for classroom practice and how the philosophy and practices derive from and intersect with our best knowledge of learner development, curriculum, instruction, assessment, and grading.

• Encourage investigation of various instructional approaches that can address the needs of academically diverse students and share findings about how these approaches affect students.

• Provide structures and mechanisms for teachers to share knowledge, skills, insights, materials, and differentiated curricula to maximize teacher time and benefit the full range of learners.

Establishing Clarity of Focus on Differentiation

In a school pursuing second-order change toward defensible differentiation, the umbrella for most professional development and planning time will necessarily be teaching so that each student has maximum opportunities to learn. In other words, the umbrella for all core efforts is differentiation.

Educators can take many approaches to more effectively reach the full spectrum of learners; therefore, it is relatively natural to subsume important initiatives under the differentiation umbrella. For example, primary grade teachers might examine ways to more effectively use the school's reading program to address diverse learners' needs. Middle school teachers might explore ways technology can help them address the varied needs their students bring to school. Teachers in a high school might investigate options for proactively supporting success for a broader group of students in Advanced Placement classes or ways that block scheduling can support teachers in reaching out to a range of students.

All of those examples combine differentiation and other ongoing school initiatives. The key in each of them, however, is that the focus is not on a second or extra topic, but rather on how to think about various aspects of classroom practice to the benefit of a varied student population. Ensuring that differentiation remains the prime focus of teachers and leaders via time, conversation, professional development, classroom observation, and so on is critical to second-order change toward differentiation. Leaders who are successful in maintaining focus do the following:

• Remind the faculty consistently that the goal of the change process is strong achievement and a higher-quality school experience for each individual learner and that it is essential to develop classroom routines that enable the teacher to understand and address the needs of each student in the class.

• Ensure that time and resources are available so that each teacher consistently grows in the knowledge, understanding, skill, and attitudes necessary to address varied learner needs proactively, competently, and confidently.

• Ensure that faculty and staff share a common understanding of the essential elements and principles of differentiation; that the elements and principles are central to the work of the group; that feedback from peers, staff developers, and the principal is based on the elements and principles; and that evidence of faculty and student growth is examined in light of appropriate implementation of the elements and principles.

• Focus small-group and whole-group efforts on addressing problems that will inevitably arise as teachers develop and implement expanded ways of thinking about individuals, assessment, curriculum, and instruction.

• Make sure individual and group successes related to implementation of differentiation are shared and celebrated in ways that build both knowledge and collegiality.

The Nature of Professional Development at Two Schools Learning to Differentiate

Despite the considerable differences between Conway Elementary and Colchester High, several common themes related to the nature of staff development in the two schools are evident. In both settings, principals ensured that the environment was safe for change, developed strong professional communities of learners, and maintained a determined focus on differentiation throughout the change process. Key to success in both settings was also the long-term presence of professional development assistance that was continuous, close to the classroom, and in sync with the vision of the principal. Because this latter element also affected the three other elements, we'll begin an exploration of the nature of staff development in each of the two sites with a discussion of the role of the staff developer and then follow with illustrations related to safety, professional community, and focus.

The Nature of Staff Development at Conway

The Conway faculty began its journey of change toward more effectively differentiated instruction with a number of important positives. The stable nature of the group meant that most faculty members knew one another well. In addition, they saw themselves as continuous learners and had the confidence of their community. Nonetheless, the principal knew that even in a professionally and personally positive setting, she was envisioning change that would call on teachers to reconstruct how they thought about and went about their work. Central in Lane Narvaez's understanding of such a degree of change was that she could not be both the school leader and its staff developer. From the outset, Narvaez knew that success at Conway would call on her to anchor and energize the vision for change and simultaneously would require ongoing work with someone who shared the vision and knew deeply the content of differentiation and the process of professional development. Narvaez knew that only with such a person in place could the faculty feel safe in making the necessary changes, form a productive professional learning community, and remain focused on the tasks at hand.

The Staff Developer at Conway

Narvaez understood differentiation well at the outset of the change initiative and continued to extend her understanding as her staff grew in its understanding. Nonetheless, she knew she needed a partner in the change who could provide the sort of intensive knowledge, understanding, and skill her staff would need as it accepted the challenge of second-order change.

Early in the process, she invited a veteran educator and staff developer to be a part of the long-term commitment to change toward quality differentiation at Conway. The person who would become her partner in leading for change was Kay Brimijoin, who had studied and researched differentiation and had an established record of providing support for professional growth toward differentiation at other sites—including public school and university settings. She had been an elementary teacher for 14 years, a district leader for 10, and had just become a university faculty member at the outset of the collaboration; thus her general knowledge of schools was broad and multifaceted.

In exploratory conversations with Brimijoin, Narvaez found their views about differentiation and professional development were a solid match. Had that not been the case, the principal would have sought assistance from other sources. As they met and ultimately began detailed planning for the work at Conway, they agreed that the second-order change would require professional development with the following attributes:

- Staff development would model the principles and practices of differentiation.
- Staff development options would be differentiated in response to participant needs.
- The staff developer and principal would delineate specific goals for teachers (noted in Chapter 4), knowing that goals would be modified to some degree by teacher needs.
- Staff development would enable teachers to make personal sense of the principles and practices of differentiation (versus transmission of information about differentiation).
- Staff development would include an emphasis on reflection regarding transfer to the classroom.
- Participants would be aware of specific expectations for classroom implementation.
- Staff development would enable teachers to address the needs of the full spectrum of learners in the classroom.
- Coaching in the classroom by Brimijoin would be a regular feature of professional development.
- The process would emphasize individual teacher growth in effective differentiation as well as growth of the faculty as a whole.
- Classroom observations made by the principal between staff developer visits and ongoing faculty conversations guided by the principal would emphasize articulated staff development goals.

Early in her work with faculty members, Brimijoin explained that their work together would encompass six key elements (the first five proposed from the work of Joyce & Showers, 1995): theory, demonstration, practice, feedback, coaching, and facultywide reflection. The goal was to help teachers weave a fabric of the why, what, and how of differentiation. The staff developer would explain theory and research behind a particular differentiation strategy and model it. Teachers would then apply what they had learned in their classrooms. This would be followed by scheduled classroom visits in which the staff developer would observe teachers implementing the various strategies and provide immediate feedback and coaching.

The faculty agreed that coaching and follow-up should involve all teachers, including special-area teachers. Volunteers signed up for initial coaching sessions. Remaining teachers were assigned to slots during the later days of Brimijoin's six visits to Conway during the first year. Beginning early in the work of the group, the principal and staff developer also began conducting whole-faculty reflection sessions after observation and coaching sessions.

A similar process has continued, even as this book is being written, with Brimijoin and the faculty for six years. The sustained presence of an effective professional developer with a deep knowledge of effective classroom practice in general and differentiation in particular has been central to the success of the change initiative at Conway. Her ability both to lead and to follow the lead of the faculty has contributed profoundly not only to the growth of teachers in effectively differentiated classroom practice but also to a sense of safety for change, a dynamic professional community of learners, and a focused change effort.

Safety, Community, and Focus at Conway

The goal Narvaez set for the Conway faculty was an ambitious one. She wanted each faculty member to differentiate instruction at an expert level in the classroom. Such a high goal, she knew, would require an environment safe for growth.

For a sense of safety to endure in the school during the change process, the two leaders would have to establish confidence and trust with the teachers. Early on, they assured teachers that monitoring their growth toward effective differentiation and the feedback they received as part of professional development were separate from their career evaluation process. Furthermore, the lead staff developer had no role in the career evaluation process at Conway. Both leaders continued to express a belief that an absence of missteps in applying new learning suggested an absence of growth. Their goal was extensive growth, and they were prepared to learn from errors and successes along with the teachers.

Brimijoin's first visit to Conway occurred during a two-day faculty retreat. The block of time focused on professional development in a setting outside school was conducive to concentrated work as well as social time together. During this visit, as teachers began to get a sense of the nature of the staff developer, they presented her with two important tests of safety.

First, some veteran teachers raised some points of skepticism regarding the initiative. Narvaez had alerted Brimijoin that this might occur with a faculty that rightfully saw itself as expert. Further, Brimijoin's extensive background as an educator prepared her for probing questions. She acknowledged the value of the questions, indicated that she would share her thinking about the questions with them, and noted that over time, individuals and the group would no doubt discover their own answers to the questions. Her open and nondefensive tone established her willingness to explore issues and entertain divergent perspectives on important issues. Her ability to speak to the questions signaled a level of knowledge about the topic that was reassuring of her competence to guide the work of the group.

A second test of safety came at the end of the first staff development visit. Brimijoin was scheduled to meet with Conway parents to introduce them to her work with the faculty. Several teachers came to her as emissaries for the group to determine what she planned to say to the parents. Faculty members wanted to ensure that parents gained a common understanding of differentiation that would support their growth toward differentiation. They also were afraid parents might leave the meeting with the expectation that teachers would be overnight experts in differentiation. Again, rather than being defensive or dismissive, Brimijoin thanked them for expressing their concerns, told them she'd be appreciative if they could spend some time with her helping her develop the presentation, and noted that their knowledge of the community was an important resource for her. Not only did the encounter result in a parent meeting that addressed the needs of the parents, teachers, and initiative leaders, but it also sent a strong signal that the new staff developer was respectful of the school context, aware of their strengths, and eager to be collaborative with the faculty.

Another indicator of environmental safety that Brimijoin and Narvaez established initially and consistently nurtured was that faculty would find ample support for what they were being asked to do. The pair of leaders not only explained their commitment to long-term assistance and the cycle of their work (theory, demonstration, practice, coaching, and feedback) but also began to reveal resources that would support their work. The principal would make available time for within- and across-grade-level collaboration—including classroom observations and peer feedback as well as shared planning time. Brimijoin had stories about differentiated classrooms, examples of differentiated lesson plans, and videos of differentiation in action to share with them. There would be varied options for professional development—including grade-level curriculum planning, across grade-level curriculum mapping, exploration of targeted instructional strategies, and in-depth analysis of assessment results. These opportunities would be differentiated for the faculty, which included large groups of highly experienced and novice teachers. The Conway Professional Development Committee served as a filter for sharing and analyzing the results of regular faculty surveys to help chart the direction of staff development options and differentiation of those options to address faculty needs. The survey information combined with frequent written teacher reflections helped inform the work of the principal and coach.

Periodic whole-group staff development enabled faculty to develop a common framework for thinking about differentiation, common vocabulary of differentiation, and a shared theory- and practice-based rationale for differentiation. Classroom work allowed the staff developer to build on the strengths of individual teachers while attending to their particular targets for growth. Whole-group sharing after each round of classroom work invited group reflection and problem solving, built trust, celebrated growth, and nurtured collaboration. In all settings, an emphasis on student outcomes, reminders about schoolwide goals for differentiation, and attention to fidelity to the model ensured persistent focus of everyone's efforts. Chapter 4 will examine the content of the Conway professional development cycle in greater detail.

Throughout the differentiation initiative, the principal joined the faculty as an active learner in all professional development sessions. This participation signals to the faculty that the principal is a part of the community of learners and finds the learning process valuable. In addition, what the principal learns in the sessions informs her classroom visits, enables her to continue guiding and supporting staff in the absence of the staff developer, and provides important information for her work with the staff developer in creating learning options suited to the needs of individual teachers and the group as a whole.

From the earliest experiences Conway teachers had with professional development for differentiation, and continuing to the present, teachers have consistently found a caring and nonevaluative climate that welcomed multiple perspectives on shared goals; ensured abundant help for the journey; helped participants remain focused on essential knowledge, understanding, and skill related to teaching in general and differentiation in particular; and proactively recognized and attended to the differing personal and professional needs of staff.

The Nature of Staff Development at Colchester

Unlike Conway Elementary where staff began the journey toward more responsive teaching with a positive school climate, a high degree of collaboration, solid student achievement, and community approval, Colchester High staff began in a much more discouraging place. A negative (if not dangerous) school climate, fragmented faculty, low achievement for a significant proportion of students, and a distrustful community provided Colchester Principal Joyce Stone with—at best—a challenging framework for change. Nonetheless, she had inherited a faculty with a number of teachers who had been at the school in earlier days when it had a strong community reputation and a faculty known by the community for innovation and commitment to students and school. One Colchester veteran teacher explained, "While this was a time with the earmarks of failure, it had not always been so at Colchester. There was a previous history of trying and tweaking things to get things right. That doesn't mean we always did, but Colchester had been a school with a sense of excitement and innovation." Stone was smart to see that history and the steady group of strong teachers and to invest in it. Once she righted the ship, she had members of her crew that were seasoned and talented and ready to work with her.

Stone realized that the faculty would have to reclaim its past strengths and that staff development would be integral to the success Colchester students and staff needed and desired. Ensuring safety, community, and focused efforts for her faculty would be essential to positive and extensive change. The principal would guide vision for change at Colchester and would ensure the availability of multiple avenues for professional growth toward effective differentiation. At the same time, teachers would need knowledgeable, accessible, and steady guidance to ensure application of differentiation in the high school classrooms. The sources and structures at Colchester would look quite different from those at Conway but would be equally pivotal in the success of the differentiation initiative.

The Role of Collaboration at Colchester

Early in the Colchester change process, some teachers knew that the new Colchester principal was contemplating detracking the 9th grade as a way to propel movement toward differentiation. A member of the newly established Leadership Team and a teacher leader shared with Stone that although teachers felt the move was right philosophically, it would be overwhelming for the 9th grade faculty as a whole. Willing to listen to teacher voices, the three of them developed the idea of piloting a detracked 9th grade humanities class the following year as a way of addressing the school's dichotomous academic offerings that typically resulted in low-track classes for students from low-economic backgrounds and high-track classes for students from affluent backgrounds. Brad Blanchette, the teacher leader who helped develop the idea of the pilot class, shared his reflections that Stone "had nurtured a 'kitchen cabinet,' the members of which she had emboldened to speak their minds. She accepted our advice even though it represented a significant slowdown. She didn't hesitate to take our advice when we made a cogent argument or reject it when we didn't."

Stone recognized the pilot experiment as potentially important in helping the faculty understand how differentiation might play out in their classrooms and what its benefits to students could be. She eagerly supported the pilot teachers in attending some intensive, high-quality off-site professional development on differentiation. In that context, the pilot teachers began to develop differentiated curriculum for a differentiated humanities class in which a full spectrum of Colchester students would come together to learn.

Sharing Stone's vision, the Leadership Team had adopted the slogan "Equity and Excellence" as the signal of a new direction at Colchester. The heterogeneous, differentiated humanities class would be a test case for the viability of the slogan.

At the end of a highly successful pilot year, the teacher leader and member of the Leadership Team once again went to Stone with a plan. This time, they asked her to continue the pilot class for another year, allowing the pilot teachers to loop—or move up to 10th grade—with their humanities students. At the same time, they suggested that she ask two other teachers who were veteran teachers but completely inexperienced with differentiation to create a second 9th grade pilot class. Once again, Blanchette said, Stone continued to listen to trusted practitioners even though it meant delaying her goal.

The two teachers who were more experienced with differentiation immediately began to mentor their 9th grade counterparts. In addition, Stone provided an intensive summer professional development opportunity for the four pilot teachers. In this way, she began a powerful proliferation of the principles and practices of differentiation.

Stone noted that it was important for her to have a vision for sweeping change at Colchester and to develop a systematic plan for such change. Given the acute problems in the school when she became principal, however, and the acute nature of the change she envisioned, it also made sense to her to execute the plan in a stepwise fashion. Stone conducted frank and often difficult conversations with the faculty about the general health of Colchester—and about the need to change structures such as tracking to improve the prognosis for the school's students and staff. Meanwhile, the early innovators began to study and apply the ideas of differentiation in the school's own setting. As Stone laid a foundation for change, the humanities teachers began to develop a chain of informed practitioners who came to represent both the feasibility and the practicality of Stone's vision. Blanchette explained that Stone had spent two years figuring out who her innovative teacher leaders were: "When it was time to move ahead, she had two important things in place—teachers whom she almost imperceptibly had advanced into teacher leader status, and the same teacher leaders who supported her when the faculty became edgy over what Joyce expected of us as individuals and a group."

In time, Stone said, the experiences of the initial practitioners of differentiation attracted other teachers to the idea and created a critical mass of energy in a positive direction. Ultimately, the detractors either joined up or moved on. She worked to help reluctant teachers grow and to realize their growth when it happened. She also continued to provide consistent, high-quality learning opportunities related to differentiation for teachers as they continued to develop interest in an application of the principles and practices of differentiation. Some of the professional development opportunities were carefully selected, intensive, off-site options. Increasingly, however, the Colchester practitioners of differentiation assumed roles as professional developers and classroom coaches at Colchester. As the latter approach to professional development became a reality, Stone provided release time for Colchester's key leaders in differentiated instruction to work collaboratively with colleagues both in and out of their classrooms. Most recently, a part-time teacher liaison position enabled a Colchester teacher who fully differentiated his own classroom to work with teachers in their classrooms, plan and provide differentiated staff development, and represent to the principal and Leadership Team the barriers and concerns about differentiation the teachers identified. The structures used to direct and support professional development at Colchester will be discussed further in Chapter 4.

Safety, Community, and Focus at Colchester

As Stone set out to make Colchester a school that was physically and affectively safe for all members of the diverse student community, she also understood the importance of creating a safe environment for teacher growth and change. "In an odd way," she explained, "the negative circumstances in the school called for us to create a highly positive vision as a counterbalance." She talked directly with the faculty about the need for a sense of professional safety in the school and ways they would work together to ensure it.

Key to developing an environment of safety was establishing a professional learning community with multiple emphases on shared vision, shared voice, and shared learning. The intent was to ensure that professional development focused on the school vision of differentiated, heterogeneous classes leading to improved learning for each student but also took into account the varied experience levels, content specialties, and perspectives of a diverse high school faculty. The use of multiple structures to build faculty confidence and competence in differentiation is an example of distributed leadership (Duke, 2004; Spillane, 2006; Spillane et al., 2001). Distributed leadership recognizes that leaders for second-order change exist at every level of the organization, will be required at every level of the organization, and must be recognized and nurtured at every level of the organization. Several newly created structures at Colchester promoted teacher learning that considered teachers' voices and personal learning needs as well as the organization's need for distributed leadership. Each of the following structures helped establish an environment open to teacher voices in an atmosphere of respect and safety, which in turn contributed to the faculty's sense of a community working toward a common goal:

• The Leadership Team, composed of teachers and administrators, developed and continued to refine plans to ensure that all students had equitable access to excellence. The team met weekly for about 90 minutes to deal with current challenges in the school and, perhaps even more importantly, to look ahead—to keep an eye on the horizon. Team leaders represented the five department clusters at Colchester. They were the teacher members of the Leadership Team and were important to success because they bridged change between teachers and administrators. The team leaders did not function as traditional department heads, presiding over balkanized states. Rather, they provided leadership for the school. As members of the Leadership Team, team leaders had voice and responsibility equal to that of the principal and other administrators. They communicated the voice of their teachers, and when they returned to their departments, it was their obligation to move forward the decisions they made as a group. In the early years of the change process at Colchester, the team leaders understood that open discussion was welcome but that decisions would require the principal's blessing. As the school experienced success, and consequently, as the principal evolved in her leadership style, it became standard procedure that the Leadership Team deliberated and made decisions with no one voice having more weight than another. When a new superintendent questioned who made the final decisions in the school, the team leaders responded without hesitation, "We do."

• Learning circles were the first step in creating and institutionalizing a true professional learning community in the school. Learning circles provided low-preparation, low-threat opportunities for teachers to join together around topics in which they had a particular interest—for example, assessment and differentiation, promoting tolerance and respect in the classroom, or understanding students' learning profiles. Learning circles became the entry point for more profound and lasting collaboration that would follow.

• Collaborative work groups were outgrowths of learning circles. These departmental structures enabled faculty members to establish a short-term, measurable goal based on examination of student work and instructional changes to improve student learning. Stone relinquished one faculty meeting per month so that collaborative work groups could meet—a decision that met with excellent outcomes in terms of teacher support and work. The groups worked in three cycles during the school year. They identified goals based on improving student achievement, made corresponding changes in instruction, and assessed how the changes were working with students. Then they reported their progress and findings to the principal and their team leaders.

• Friday forums were called when very specific concerns emerged and required a resolution. Such issues did not necessitate a full faculty meeting, but the Leadership Team felt it was important to get input from some faculty. Anyone could attend a Friday forum.

Attendance was not mandatory, but faculty members understood that a decision would likely be made on the topic as a result of the forum.

• Grade-level facilitators were teachers who facilitated the collaborative work groups at their grade levels. They received a small stipend for this role.

• The Professional Development Committee established a range of professional development options based on the school's vision and the needs of its teachers.

• Teacher mentoring paired new teachers with experienced teachers for their first two years at Colchester to provide support, guidance, and training—including in the differentiation initiative.

• Curriculum work in the summer and Saturday seminars during the school year provided nominal compensation for teachers to work on curriculum and differentiation. These opportunities acknowledged and supported the intensive attention to curriculum often required outside the school day.

• Best-practice faculty meetings kept the focus on teaching and learning, starting with Stone's first one in 1999. In these meetings, Stone, the teacher liaison, and other teacher leaders consistently articulated the vision for differentiation, reviewed progress, introduced new learning, monitored progress, adjusted subsequent plans based on findings, and celebrated successes.

• *The Tuesday Times* is a school newsletter published once or twice weekly (purple paper makes it immediately recognizable) to handle all operational communications with faculty. Such nuts-and-bolts information is never handled at faculty meetings, which instead focus on the classroom. Using faculty meeting time solely for professional development rather than for handling routine information netted a total of 15 additional staff development days in the first six years of Colchester's change process.

Change toward differentiation at Colchester took place in a more stepwise and incremental way than at Conway, where the whole faculty was ready to move forward together toward differentiation. At Colchester, more minds had to be changed, more obstacles had to be removed, and more entrenched instructional practices had to be challenged. However, staff development was also a critical engine for change at Colchester. In this complex high school setting—as in the elementary setting—the principal led with a steady and persistent vision of improved student learning. She enabled the vision to evolve into a reality within a caring environment that was respectful of and responsive to individual differences. Teachers then were able to discuss difficult issues with professional respect. The role of the teacher liaison was also critical in establishing an environment more open to than resistant to change. In that environment, teachers and administrators developed a common understanding of differentiation, found ample help for the change, put structures in place to support teacher collaboration, shared successes, and regularly examined results of the initiative on student learning.

Lessons About the Nature of Staff Development for Change

Conway Elementary's staff developer and Colchester High's teacher liaison were second-order change facilitators. They were trusted by the principals and teachers, and they were pivotal in promoting change toward differentiation, proposing adaptations to the change process along the way, assisting teachers in implementing change, and helping assess the effects of change. Change-oriented principals on the whole tend to incorporate a second change facilitator in their work (Duke, 2004).

In both school settings, staff development practices reflected guidance from landmark research on staff development (Joyce & Showers, 2002). Principals at the two sites ensured safety for change, built professional learning communities, and maintained focus on differentiation as they provided staff development that had the following characteristics:

• Was shepherded by strong and cohesive school leadership.
• Supported collaborative decision making.
• Maintained emphasis on differentiation to benefit student learning.
• Ensured a common frame of reference for differentiation.
• Provided assistance suited to the scope of the change required for differentiation.
• Provided multiple pathways to achieve desired goals.
• Attended to the needs of individual teachers as well as of the group.
• Ensured transfer of new knowledge about differentiation into classroom practice.

• Established enduring and self-renewing structures to ensure refinement of teacher knowledge, understanding, and skill related to differentiation over time.

• Examined the effects of the classroom change.

Chapter 4 will explore the content of staff development for second-order change toward effectively differentiated classrooms and the structures that support dissemination and application of that content. The scope of learning and change required of teachers who make significant progress toward differentiation absolutely requires focused professional development that takes place in an environment of safety and collegial learning.

4

The Content of Professional Development for Change Toward Differentiation

Although most principals understand the necessity of quality staff development to support teacher change, planning the content of such staff development over an extended period of time is a venture into uncharted territory. How much of the planning should be done by the principal? By a staff developer? By teachers themselves?

When staff development is focused on schoolwide differentiation, where is the starting point? Does staff development assume that whatever curriculum is in place is best left in place as staff members focus on differentiating whatever it is that teachers teach, or must there be a shared conversation about curriculum as well? Should staff development begin with an emphasis on assessment, or does that come later? What about the role of the classroom learning environment in differentiation? What about teacher–student connections? Where to begin? Surely teachers can't do everything at once while students require constant attention.

Is there once again a need to think about a leader modeling what he or she commends? Is there a "curriculum" for staff development leading to classroom differentiation? What role would assessment play in staff development? Must staff development be differentiated for teachers who clearly differ as a group? And what about the learning environment and professional development? Principal–teacher connections? Where to begin?

And is there a need to provide support for parent understanding of differentiation? How does a leader ensure that students understand and contribute to classrooms designed to work for them?

Planning for Key Areas of Content Focus in Professional Development

Planning for the content of professional development is critical to its success but often receives little attention (Joyce & Showers, 2002)—almost as though attending to a vision and schedule for change used all the available energy. There are, of course, many directions that the content of professional development might take depending on the needs of students and staff in a school. Nonetheless, there is a good bit of agreement on what should constitute the focus of professional development in schools where educators desire second-order change. Interestingly, much of what has been written about the content of such professional development sounds a good deal like what has been written about differentiation. The broad categories of student focus, rigorous curriculum, assessment to inform teaching and learning, flexible instruction, and classroom management subsume much of the expert advice about school change and important targets for staff development content. Further, experts caution that educators' efforts in these areas must encompass the needs of all students in the school or they are likely to fall short of aspirations (Fullan, Hill, & Crevola, 2006; Schlechty, 1997). Thus in essence, the content of professional development for second-order change involves the core and interrelated areas of learners, curriculum, instruction, and assessment (see Figure 4.1).

Focus on Students

Professional development for second-order change is unambiguously aimed at student learning (Danielson, 2006; Glickman, 2002; Sarason, 1996; Taylor et al., 2006) and will continually draw teachers back to the question of students' varying needs, ways of addressing those needs, and student outcomes. Such staff development is predicated on a belief that what teachers learn is directly connected to what students learn—and that student learning should be the engine that drives teacher learning (Sykes, 1999). Student-focused staff development will assist educators in developing the knowledge, understanding, and skill to do the following:

• Own responsibility for the success of each student (Schmoker, 2006; Taylor et al., 2006) through a belief that the primary sources of variance in student achievement are within the control of the teacher and the school (Schlechty, 1997; Schmoker, 2006; Taylor et al., 2006).

Figure 4.1
The Content of Professional Development for Quality Differentiation

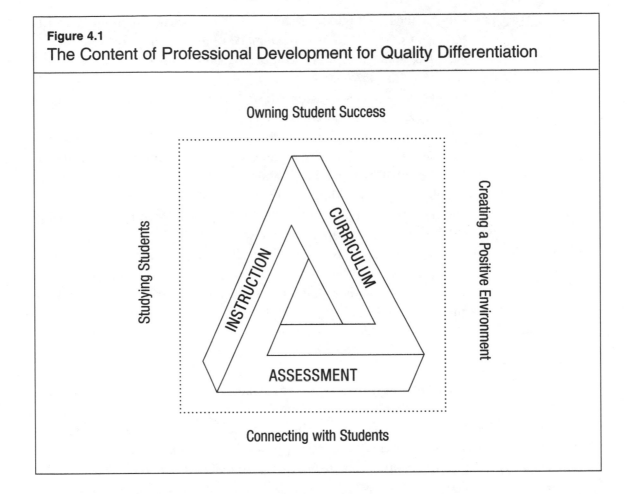

Owning Student Success

Studying Students

CURRICULUM

INSTRUCTION

ASSESSMENT

Creating a Positive Environment

Connecting with Students

• Develop persistently deepening knowledge about individual learners, including their economic backgrounds, ethnic and racial communities, interests, ways of learning, and readiness levels (Darling-Hammond & Sykes, 1999; Fullan et al., 2006; Goodlad, 1990; Powell & Napoliello, 2005; Safer & Fleischman, 2005).
• Connect with students in ways that support and motivate learning (Fullan et al., 2006; Sarason, 1996).
• Build positive climates for learning in which each student feels known and appreciated (Danielson, 2006; Saphier et al., 2006) and where teachers move from accepting students to elevating them (Joyce & Showers, 2002).
• Develop productive mind-sets about students and their learning, including beliefs that learning is effort based, that quality and craftsmanship in work are more important determiners of success than speed, that every student is worthy of the best educational

experiences a school has to offer, and that no student should be written off or overlooked as being in need of teacher support (Saphier et al., 2006; Schlechty, 1997; Schmoker, 2006; Taylor et al., 2006).

Related to a focus on students is a pervasive admonition against fixed-ability grouping and tracking. The importance of teaching in heterogeneous settings is prevalent because high-quality curriculum and instruction are not distributed equitably in tracked settings and that separation of students by perceived ability transmits messages to students and teachers alike that diminish expectations for many learners (Joyce & Showers, 2002; Sergiovanni, 1999). If the goal of schools were—as it should be—to provide an elite education for the great majority of its students (Fullan et al., 2006; Schlechty, 1997; Schmoker, 2006; Taylor et al., 2006), there would be no need to divide them based on expectations for performance. Further, pullout classes that are often used to address the particular learning needs of students have proven unsatisfactory because they are difficult to implement well, disrupt classroom continuity, and fragment services for students who need them (Joyce & Showers, 2002).

A school's staff cannot hope to achieve high-level learning for all students if it neither aims to do so nor believes it to be possible. Therefore, a vision for student learning that drives school improvement efforts recognizes all students' intellectual potential and charges the school with setting conditions for realizing that potential (Danielson, 2006).

Professional development with student-focused content guides the teacher to determine what motivates a student to do his or her best. The teacher also develops practices that tap into that particular motivation (Schlechty, 1997).

Quality of Curriculum

The quality of what students learn (and of what will be differentiated) is a potent factor in student success. Perhaps Schlechty (1997) best captures the goal of focusing professional development on curriculum as well as the importance of quality curriculum in the teaching and learning enterprise: "In sum, the business of schools is to produce work that engages students, that is so compelling that students persist when they experience difficulties, and that is so challenging that students have a sense of accomplishment, of satisfaction—indeed, of delight—when they successfully accomplish the tasks assigned" (p. 58). The absence of a powerful curriculum amplifies the difficulty of teachers' and students' jobs. The challenges are magnified when an emphasis on high-stakes testing leads teachers to study collections of standards rather than a curriculum that provides context and meaning for the standards (Sykes, 1999). Professional development with a content focus on curriculum will help educators develop the knowledge, understanding, and skill necessary to do the following:

- Work from a deepening and authentic knowledge of the content of the curriculum they teach, including content-specific pedagogy (Danielson, 2006; Darling-Hammond & McLaughlin, 1999; Powell & Napoliello, 2005; Sparks & Hirsh, 1997; Sykes, 1999; Wiggins & McTighe, 1998).
- Develop curriculum that centers on the essential concepts and understandings of a content area versus rote learning and exposure to a large amount of information (Danielson, 2006; Wiggins & McTighe, 1998).
- Develop work that ensures that students learn what they should learn—that is, tasks that align with key goals to ensure student understanding and ownership of content (Sarason, 1996; Schlechty, 1997; Wiggins & McTighe, 1998).
- Create curriculum that is relevant to students' lives (Sarason, 1996; Schlechty, 1997).
- Develop curriculum that actively engages students in doing and producing in order to learn (Sarason, 1996; Schlechty, 1997).
- Develop curriculum that helps students see the structure of the disciplines, how ideas are related, and how they can use the ideas in varied settings, as well as "evaluating, even challenging, the knowledge claims embedded in the discipline" (Earl, 2003, p. 34).

Curriculum of this nature and quality cannot be scripted (Fullan et al., 2006; Schlechty, 1997) but rather requires that teachers create knowledge that responds both to the nature of the subjects they teach and to the lives of the students who should learn it. On the other hand, such curriculum cannot be without structure and clarity about what will create engaged learners who learn to grapple with important ideas and use important skills (Schmoker, 2006; Wiggins & McTighe, 1998).

Professional development must help teachers link what they learn about students with what they learn about curriculum. Then teachers are equipped to enter students' worlds as a means of linking them with content. Schlechty (1997) notes, unless reform is coupled with providing students with access to profound knowledge through work that is engaging, compelling, and satisfying, there is little chance the reforms will produce the results they promise.

Quality of Assessment

Assessment is the conduit between curriculum and instruction. In regard to differentiation, effective assessment is closely linked to day-to-day operations and decisions of the classroom. It lets teachers know where students are relative to essential learning goals. Differentiation, suggests Lorna Earl (2003), is making sure the right student gets the right tasks at the right time in order to learn. If a teacher has clear content goals, sees via assessment where students are in a progression toward those goals, and understands what each student needs in order to continue growing, differentiation is no longer an option but is an obvious response. Assessment as a focus of professional development should help teachers do the following:

- Know students' starting points in the various segments of study and know how to know those starting points (Fullan et al., 2006; Sarason, 1996).
- Determine the instructional focus based on where students are throughout a learning progression and what they need next in order to grow (Danielson, 2006; Earl, 2003; Fuchs & Fuchs, 2002; Fullan et al., 2006).
- Guide students in understanding sequences of learning, understanding their progress in those sequences, and accepting increasing responsibility for their progress (Danielson, 2006; Earl, 2003).
- Use multiple sources and forms of assessment to achieve the best possible sense of student knowledge, understanding, and skill (Danielson, 2006; Sykes, 1999).
- Use classroom assessment data to monitor the impact of the change initiative on student outcomes (Sykes, 1999).

Effective assessment practices help teachers be simultaneously on the dance floor and in the balcony (Fullan, Hill, & Crevola, 2006)—in other words, to be actively engaged in teaching but also in monitoring learning. Such assessment is critical in aligning student needs and learning goals. The goal is no longer to teach a unit and then see who got it, but rather to understand student progressions toward learning goals throughout a unit and adjust teaching as necessary to guide each student to success.

Quality of Instruction

Instruction turns curriculum plans into classroom reality. It connects students with important knowledge, understanding, and skill. Danielson (2006) says,

> The quality of teaching is the most important factor that influences student learning. Other components, of course, play a role, from the quality of the curriculum to the policies and programs for students. But it is in the quality of instruction where all the elements come together in an alchemy that students remember for years. Therefore, no matter what else educational leaders . . . do, they must not neglect the skill of teachers in this core responsibility. (p. 97)

Professional development that focuses on quality instruction provides teachers with the knowledge, understanding, and skill necessary to do the following:

- See students as individuals (Danielson, 2006; Fullan et al., 2006).
- Use assessment data to modify instruction in ways that support student growth and success (Danielson, 2006; Earl, 2003; Schmoker, 2006).
- Teach in response to individual needs (Danielson, 2006; Earl, 2003; Fullan et al., 2006).
- Communicate clearly with students (Danielson, 2006).
- Engage students with important content (Danielson, 2006).
- Develop a broad repertoire of instructional strategies through which they can effectively address individual needs as well as content requirements (Darling-Hammond & McLaughlin, 1999; Fullan et al., 2006; Hawley & Valli, 1999; Joyce & Showers, 1995; Powell & Napoliello, 2005).
- Create a flexible but orderly learning environment (Danielson, 2006).

It is important to expand on this latter component because in moving toward effectively differentiated classrooms, classroom management is likely to be an issue for many teachers. Teachers may take part in as many as 200,000 classroom exchanges a year (Huberman, 1983). They face a huge press for immediacy and concreteness of action and for adaptation to a constantly changing and unpredictable environment with numerous interruptions and distractions. In this context, teachers must think about complex lesson goals and multiple lesson materials and props (Fullan, 2001b; Kennedy, 2005). A predictable outcome for teachers who stay in the profession is that they learn to value running a tight ship. This approach translates to the teacher doing most of the work and providing little opportunity for variance based on learners' needs—perhaps even for exploration of ideas. Changing this pattern is a complex and daunting undertaking. If we expect teachers to connect more students with more-ambitious curricula, professional development for second-order change toward differentiation will have to help teachers develop new and more flexible ways of thinking about and orchestrating a classroom. It will also have to help them unlearn old practices (Darling-Hammond & McLaughlin, 1999).

One source (Educational Research Service, 1992) describes four kinds of learning environments: (1) dysfunctional learning environments with a constant struggle for order, (2) adequate learning environments with a basic level of control but still a significant number of distractions, (3) orderly, restrictive learning environments with high structure and where the class runs smoothly but where there is little flexibility and a narrow range of instructional approaches, and (4) orderly, enabling learning environments where the classroom runs smoothly with a higher degree of flexibility and a broader range of instructional approaches. In the latter category, teachers are more likely to emphasize student understanding and consistently find opportunities to address the needs of diverse learners.

The Content of Professional Development to Support Differentiated Instruction

Professional development content aimed at broad and deep change toward more academically responsive classrooms certainly mirrors the more generic guidance presented in the previous section of the chapter. It requires high-quality attention to how teachers think about students and the learning environment, curriculum, assessment, and instruction—including classroom management.

School leaders (including teachers) and staff developers should assess the needs of individual teachers and the faculty as a whole in these areas—building on teacher strengths and ensuring support to correct deficits in any areas. Examining the status of differentiation in classrooms through walkthroughs as a form of pre-assessment (see, for example, Downey, Steffy, English, Frase, & Poston, 2004), surveying teachers to determine their comfort levels with key elements of differentiation, and having discussions with grade-level or subject-area groups can provide a starting point for making decisions about content needs for professional development.

The advice of experts that leaders and staff developers think big and begin small (Guskey, 1995) is pertinent. In time, it is necessary to address all of the key component areas through effective professional development that ensures transfer into the classroom. Starting with an emphasis on all the areas, however, is overwhelming. It is important to target first the areas of greatest need or interest. At the same time, it is important to remember that all of the areas are interrelated and teaching about them in isolation is not effective either. Therefore, it is wise for leaders and professional developers to think in terms of foreground issues and background issues. They should emphasize elements of particular importance at a given time but consistently guide teachers to understand the relationships between elements that are in the foreground of emphasis with those that are in the background.

Among competencies that are ultimately important for effective and defensible differentiation are the following, stated in terms of observable indicators (adapted from Tomlinson & McTighe, 2006):

Related to Students and Learning Environment
• The teacher demonstrates a belief that each student is capable of learning the most important content and makes the belief visible through high expectations and high support for each student.
• The teacher makes consistent attempts to know and understand students' backgrounds—including aspects related to culture, language, economics, race, ethnicity, and experience.
• The teacher makes consistent attempts to connect with each student and communicate that the student is known, valued, and supported.
• The teacher treats each student and the class as a whole with dignity and respect.
• The teacher encourages multiple perspectives on topics and issues.
• The teacher works consistently to establish a learning environment that feels safe to each student and demonstrates mutual respect.
• The teacher balances attention to and emphasis on the needs of individual learners and the group as a whole.

Related to the Curriculum

• Curriculum and content goals reflect state standards but are not limited to them.

• Units and courses reflect careful, coherent design with an emphasis on students understanding and being able to apply and transfer what they learn.

• The teacher articulates what students should know, understand, and be able to do at the end of a lesson, sequence of lessons, unit, and course.

• Students are clear about learning goals and about what is required of them for success with those goals.

• All students work with the same essential understandings as the core of the curriculum and do so at high levels of thought.

• All students consistently work with respectful tasks that are equally important—that is, focused on essential understandings at high levels of thought—and equally interesting.

Related to Instruction

• The teacher demonstrates flexibility with all classroom elements (e.g., time, space, student groupings) to increase the success of each student with essential content.

• The teacher ensures a variety of ways for students to take in and explore the essential content—including multiple texts and resources, multiple modes of teacher presentation, the teacher working with students in small groups, and peer partners—based on students' readiness, interests, and learning profile needs.

• The teacher ensures a variety of ways for students to make sense of essential understandings and to master essential knowledge and skills based on students' readiness, interest, and learning profile needs.

• The teacher ensures a variety of ways for students to demonstrate what they know, understand, and can do (products) based on students' readiness, interests, and learning profile needs.

• The teacher purposefully employs flexible grouping to ensure student opportunity to learn in response to readiness, interests, and learning profile needs.

• The teacher regularly seeks to connect important content with students' backgrounds, experiences, and interests.

• The teacher clearly articulates what success looks like in tasks, products, and assessments through rubrics, checklists for quality, and student exemplars.

• The teacher helps students set personal goals for growth in addition to achieving goals established for the class as a whole.

• The teacher provides appropriate constructive feedback to students to reinforce and build competence, self-management skills, and autonomy.

• The teacher uses varied instructional strategies to address students' readiness, interests, and learning profiles, and thereby support maximum student success, and to help students understand the essential nature of the disciplines.

Related to Classroom Leadership and Management

• The teacher consistently and effectively ensures that students understand and contribute to classroom philosophy and practice that emphasizes each student growing as much as possible and support for each student to do so.

• The teacher is comfortable and effective in efficiently providing multiple sets of task directions.

• The teacher is comfortable and effective in managing distribution and collection of classroom materials necessary for student work.

• The teacher comfortably and efficiently manages varied room configurations to allow for individual, small group, and whole-class work.

• The teacher comfortably and efficiently ensures that students work silently and with conversational voices as indicated by task requirements.

• The teacher comfortably and efficiently assigns students to working groups and monitors the effectiveness of individuals and the group as a whole in completing assigned tasks.

• The teacher comfortably and efficiently assigns and monitors anchor activities for students who finish assigned tasks early.

• The teacher effectively uses a variety of strategies to monitor and keep track of student progress in a variety of classroom configurations.

• The teacher creates classroom routines that ensure flexibility and structure in the classroom and that enable students to work effectively and efficiently in a variety of configurations.

• The teacher shares responsibility for effective operation of the classroom with students and ensures that students know what is expected of them in varied contexts, how they should support one another, and how they can play a meaningful role in the success of the class.

Related to Assessment

• Assessments are tightly aligned with the unit's essential knowledge, understanding, and skill.

• The teacher routinely pre-assesses students prior to the start of a unit to determine their status with the unit's essential knowledge, understanding, and skill.

• The teacher consistently uses a variety of formal and informal ongoing or formative assessments to follow student progress with the unit's essential knowledge, understanding, and skill.

• The teacher provides a variety of ways for students to show what they know, understand, and can do at the summative assessment stage.

• The teacher regularly seeks ways to understand students' interests and learning preferences.

• The teacher consistently uses pre-assessment, formative assessment, and summative assessment data related to readiness, interest, and learning profile to inform instructional plans in the near term and to communicate more effectively with students and parents about student progress.

• The teacher views assessment as a vehicle to teach for success rather than predominantly to judge students and helps students develop the perspective of assessment as a vehicle to support their effort and achievement.

• The teacher helps students become increasingly proficient in assessing their own growth toward important goals.

• The teacher seeks input and feedback from students on how the class is working for them and ideas for making it more effective.

• The teacher becomes a student of his or her own teaching—analyzing the degree to which his or her particular applications of differentiation are addressing the needs of each learner.

These elements and indicators sound a great deal like good teaching. In fact, professional development for academically responsive classrooms should prepare teachers not to do an extra or extraneous thing called "differentiation" but to be more effective in knowing the students they teach, accepting responsibility for the success of each of those students, developing increased sophistication with the content they teach, and developing flexible classroom routines—based to a significant degree on ongoing assessment information—to achieve the goal of maximum growth for each learner in their charge. It is certainly important for professional development content to help teachers understand the pedagogical common sense of differentiation and its benefits for their own professional growth as well as their students' academic success.

Staff Development Content in Two Schools Learning to Differentiate

As with other aspects of leadership for change, the principals at Conway Elementary School and Colchester High School engineered staff development for differentiation that varied in evident ways. Nonetheless, common themes were also evident between the two schools. At both sites, staff development was thoughtfully planned, long-term, tied to classroom implementation, responsive to teachers' differences and needs, and reflective of best practices in staff development in general and staff development leading toward differentiation in particular. In both instances, the principals and staff developers were attentive to elements of differentiation related to student affect and learning environment, quality of curriculum, flexible instruction, classroom management, and assessment to inform instruction—and to the interrelationships of the elements. The similarities and differences between the sites are instructive.

It is not possible in a brief space to recount all—or even much—of what transpired in varied staff development contexts at Conway and Colchester. What follows are illustrative excerpts of multiple-year, multiple-setting staff development programs. They are illustrative of the care and clarity that ultimately enabled two faculties to make second-order change in classroom instruction that benefited a broad range of students in their schools. Referenced materials in the appendixes provide a somewhat more detailed look at the nature of staff development in the two schools.

Staff Development Content at Conway Elementary

From the outset, Principal Lane Narvaez had three imperatives in mind for staff development to support differentiation at Conway. First, she knew that plans for professional development would have to be for the long term; she understood she was planning for years, not months. Second, she wanted 100 percent of her faculty to be involved in the initiative at a 100 percent level. Because she knew that transfer of staff development principles and practices into classrooms occurs at higher rates when all teachers on a faculty are involved (Joyce & Showers, 1995), all classroom teachers and special-area teachers would be involved in every aspect of staff development. Third, coaching and feedback with Brimijoin would follow all group sessions where instruction, demonstration, and modeling the fundamentals of differentiation occurred. Again building on research, she understood that use of expert debriefing and feedback was more likely to lead to second-order change in teacher practice (Bransford, Brown, & Cocking, 2000). In time, peer coaching would evolve, but in the beginning Narvaez felt it was essential for everyone to build a solid foundation of understanding with an expert to diminish the likelihood that teachers new to the practice of differentiation would share their inevitable early misconceptions with one another.

In the beginning, then, and throughout the next two years, staff development at Conway revolved around four key and interconnected structures—whole-faculty staff development sessions, in-classroom coaching, debriefing between the coach and a teacher, and whole-faculty debriefing. Over time, additional and equally interwoven elements became a part of staff development. These included principal observations of teachers and debriefings, grade-level working sessions, and peer coaching. When a particular topic or strategy was the focus of a staff development session, Brimijoin ensured that faculty members saw how it was connected to other essential elements of differentiation.

Whole-Group Staff Development Content

Whole-group staff development proved particularly important during the early years of the Conway differentiation initiative as it served to define the rationale and provide supporting research for differentiation, helped teachers identify a conceptual framework of high-quality curriculum, and created a common understanding and vocabulary of differentiation. Whole-group staff development at Conway focused largely on correlated readings, discussions, demonstrations, hands-on application, and critical review of written and video examples of differentiation.

Whole-group staff development sessions were designed to help teachers increase their understanding of the philosophy and application of the key elements of differentiation and develop competencies necessary to implement aspects of differentiation in their classes. Classroom coaching and observation, then, focused on the particular practices and strategies introduced in whole-group sessions. In addition, however, coaching and individual debriefings inevitably raised issues, ambiguities, and concerns that needed addressing in upcoming whole-faculty debriefing sessions and sometimes in future whole-group staff development sessions.

In whole-group staff development, Brimijoin consistently modeled what she wanted teachers to do in their classrooms, making certain to address multiple key elements of differentiation in each session. For example, she would begin a session by showing participants what she wanted them to know, understand, and be able to do (KUD) by the end of the session. Thus, she used a KUD focus that she would continue to commend for their teaching. She used pre-assessment information to help her plan and tailor the session. The pre-assessment information was often gathered at a previous session via coaching or derived from the Professional Development Committee. She used videos of teachers differentiating instruction to help teachers identify the big ideas of differentiation and to discuss how those big ideas related to their own work—thus building in relevance. She explained and then modeled particular instructional strategies such as tiered lessons; learning contracts; assignments focused on role, audience, format, and topic (RAFT); and interest-based approaches. She always provided time for teachers to work with the strategies in ways that suited their particular readiness, interests, or learning profile needs. Questions about and strategies for classroom management of differentiation were folded into demonstrations and discussions so that thinking about management became a part of planning for differentiation of any type.

When it was evident that Brimijoin needed to adapt her plans to attend to the needs of the group or individuals in the group, she did so and explained to the group how and why she was making changes. She guided participants in analyzing the session—including their individual responses to it and reflection on how the session addressed their own understanding of differentiation.

An Example of Whole-Group Staff Development Content

Early on, in a two-day whole-faculty session, Brimijoin led the teachers through an inductive development of key principles of differentiation by having them reflect on the needs of students in their classrooms during the previous year. She introduced to them the important connection between quality curriculum and quality differentiation, discovered that they were overwhelmed with the idea of designing curriculum around concepts, and changed her approach as a result. She shared examples of differentiated lessons created by other teachers, which allowed the group to apply and test out the principles of differentiation they had generated earlier in the day. The group then watched a video of differentiation in action to reinforce the principles of differentiation.

The group focused on the strategy of tiering, developing a common definition of the strategy by looking at examples. Brimijoin assigned teachers to various work groups in which they encountered tasks developed to respond to different readiness levels, interests, and learning preferences. She then guided the group in a discussion of how the strategy might be used across grade levels and subjects.

Over the two days, she introduced other instructional strategies by having participants work with them in various differentiated formats, sometimes providing (or developing with participants) simple rubrics that could be used across differentiated tasks. Participants often had opportunities to plan for use of the strategies in their own classrooms and to share their plans with others. Brimijoin also taught participants a strategy called an I-graph for engaging their students in discussions about differentiation. In an I-graph, students use a graphing format to depict their particular learning strengths and needs. This enables students to "see" their own profiles as learners and to realize that, as a group, they differ in their learning needs.

At the end of the session, she returned to the importance of teaching for understanding and of emphasizing the key essential understandings in differentiated assignments. Participants synthesized the theory and strategies they had explored by generating big ideas about how differentiation might empower students and enrich teaching at Conway. Brimijoin explained how coaching sessions would help teachers transfer what they had learned into classroom practice. Finally, she asked participants to provide written reflections on the session that would help her know them better and plan for them more effectively.

An early doubter concluded that the session was "a class act." A primary teacher said she was excited to realize that she sometimes did differentiate for her kindergartners and remarked, "Now I need to do it better." An upper elementary teacher confessed that she had been skeptical about the idea of differentiation and said, "I know it's going to be hard, but I can't wait to begin working on this with my students." Two 1st grade teachers invited Brimijoin to coach them first: "We think we are differentiating some, but we aren't sure. Lots of times we have our kids doing different activities, but we make sure they all do all of them. We aren't sure if this is right, or how to change it if it's not. What do you do with 1st graders when you can't be right there with the group that's working?"

The session introduced, modeled, and explored the importance of affect and learning environment in differentiation; the key role of quality curriculum in effective differentiation; the connections among assessment, curriculum, and instruction; the need for teacher flexibility in attending to varied student needs; and strategies for addressing readiness, interest, and learning profile. The content of most whole-faculty staff development sessions, while spotlighting some elements of differentiation, continued to help teachers weave a fabric of differentiation rather than examining isolated elements.

The Content of Coaching Sessions

Coaching at Conway followed a three-step process. After accepting the invitation to participate in coaching, the teacher prepared a differentiated lesson that Brimijoin would observe. In the classroom, Brimijoin served as an active observer, interacting with students, asking for clarifications, being a second pair of hands for the teacher when needed, and taking notes on a coaching tool she developed called a Lesson Analysis Summary form (see Figure 4.2). After the class, Brimijoin conducted a dialogue with the teacher, attempting to schedule the conversation as soon as possible after the observation.

The Lesson Analysis Summary provided a structure for the conversation. Brimijoin typically began by asking, "What did you like about the lesson?" The teacher's answer provided a segue into analyzing the lesson in general and its differentiation in particular. The conversations focused on the lesson's KUDs, how the teacher planned them, what the teacher differentiated, how she differentiated it, and why she differentiated it as she did (Tomlinson, 1999). Brimijoin emphasized particular elements depending on the needs of the teacher and schoolwide emphases. The analytical dialogues helped the staff developer and teacher in several ways: rehearsing and articulating the key vocabulary and principles of differentiation, monitoring understanding of particular strategies, and pointing the way to next steps. Brimijoin was careful to confer status (Cohen & Goodlad, 1994) when a teacher clearly understood and effectively applied a strategy. She posed questions or framed statements that helped a teacher correct misunderstandings or misapplications. Over time, such dialogues helped a staff developer determine patterns of strength and weakness for the faculty as a whole as well as for individual teachers.

Coaching sessions typically lasted for about an hour, with 30 to 40 minutes of teaching and observation time and about 20 minutes for the

Figure 4.2
Lesson Analysis Summary Form

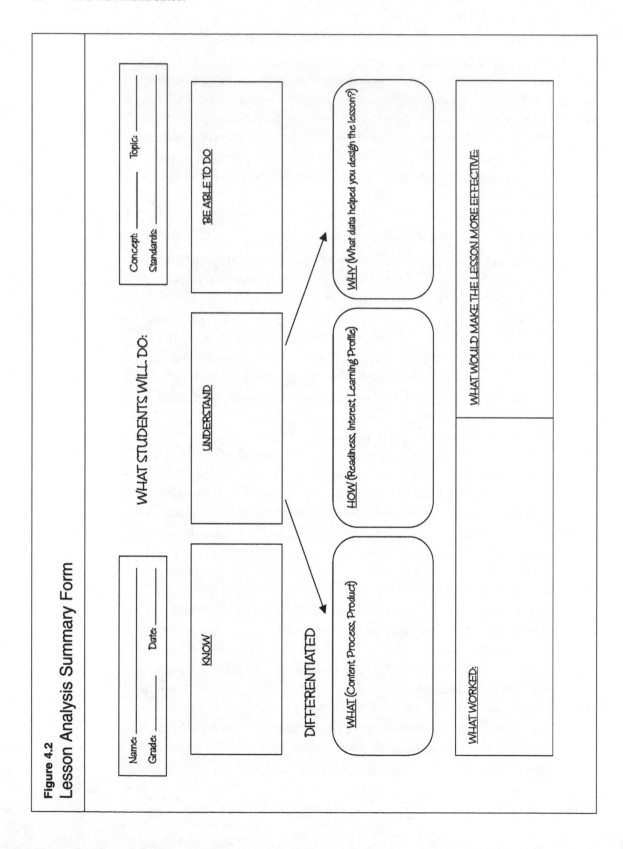

post-teaching dialogue. Narvaez signaled to teachers the importance she placed on coaching by providing coverage for teachers' classes while Brimijoin conducted postobservation dialogues with them.

An Example of the Content of Coaching Sessions

Figure 4.3 is an example of a differentiated lesson plan completed by Cathy Jacobs, a 4th grade teacher, prior to an observation. Jacobs volunteered for Brimijoin to visit her classroom for a coaching session very early in the Conway change initiative. The lesson dealt with skills application for multiplication.

The teacher began the lesson with a whole-group review of why it matters to know how to multiply. Several students pointed out the need to multiply when calculating amounts for purchases, and the teacher used their example as a link to the upcoming lesson. It was near Thanksgiving, and the teacher asked the class questions about buying groceries for the holiday, probing to see how multiplication would be used in calculating cost per pound or quantity per person. She had collected ads from local newspapers and explained to the class that everyone would work with the ads to make decisions about a holiday meal. She also explained that as they worked with the ads, their tasks would be a bit different based on their own next steps in becoming better with multiplication. Even though students would be sitting in groups, she explained, they would need to complete their work individually. However, they could ask for assistance from others in their group. One student in each group was appointed to read the task directions to the group and make sure everyone knew what to do. Students in the green groups calculated the amount spent on specified items (for example, five cans of soup). Students in the blue groups calculated the amount they could spend on six items listed for them if they had a total of $50 to spend.

Students rearranged themselves into groups as the teacher moved among groups to make sure they were settling in and focused on their work. Brimijoin noticed that students in the green groups were often unclear about what math principles they needed to apply. The directions were not clear to them. The teacher moved among the uncertain students trying to push their thinking—for example, asking them to use estimation to see if their reasoning seemed correct.

In time, some students in the blue group stalled because they kept overshooting their budget. The teacher worked with them to help them apply problem-solving skills to their work. Some students in the blue group, however, finished quickly and asked the teacher what to do next.

Figure 4.3

Differentiated Lesson Plan Created Before a Classroom Observation and Coaching Session

Differentiated Multiplication Application Task

The students have learned the skill of multiplying one or two digits by one digit. They are grouped according to readiness. Because we are near the Thanksgiving holiday, I thought that the children could make a math connection with planning as they anticipate this special time with family and friends.

Skills: Multiplication computation
        Problem solving

There are two groups that will look through grocery ads as they prepare a menu for Thanksgiving dinner. Each group will receive a different task to complete based on their readiness:

- **Green group**: Students will be given a list of items to purchase. They will have to find the price of those items by multiplying the number of items by the cost. If they finish, there are additional items for them to purchase.
- **Blue group**: Students are given a list of items and a limited budget of $50. They have to calculate how much of each item they can afford, staying within their budget.

Task Cards for the Green and Blue Groups

Green Card

Name: _____

Thanksgiving Dinner

Part 1:

You are in charge of the shopping for Thanksgiving dinner. Your parents asked you to buy the following items. Using the newspaper ads to plan your list, how much would you spend if you bought:

SHOW YOUR WORK

a. a Schnucks turkey that weighs 8 pounds? _____

b. 2 boxes of Kraft Stove Top stuffing? _____

c. 2 cases of Pepsi? _____

d. 3 packages of Freshlike vegetables? _____

e. a Schnucks spiral sliced ham that weighs 5 pounds? _____

How much did you spend all together?

What are some other items that your family might need for that day?

Figure 4.3 —(*continued*)

Differentiated Lesson Plan Created Before a Classroom Observation and Coaching Session

Part 2:
If your parents send you back to the store, how much would you spend if you bought these additional items for Thanksgiving:

SHOW YOUR WORK

a. 6 cans of Campbell's soup? _____

b. 9 pounds of sweet potatoes? _____

c. 4 cans of Libby's pumpkin? _____

d. 6 packages of Chinet plates? _____

e. 14 cans of Shasta soda? _____

Blue Card
Name: _____

Thanksgiving Dinner
You have $50 to spend on Thanksgiving dinner. Using the newspaper ads, decide how large a quantity of each of the following items you can afford:

SHOW YOUR WORK

a. a Honeysuckle turkey _____

b. Del Monte vegetables _____

c. Ocean Spray cranberry sauce _____

d. Freshlike vegetables _____

e. Kraft Stove Top stuffing _____

f. sweet potatoes _____

How much did you spend all together?

Other items you think your family might need for that day if you have money left:

g. _____

h. _____

i. _____

j. _____

k. _____

Your new total:

In the end, some students had been finished with their work for a while and others needed additional time to complete the task.

Figure 4.4 is the Lesson Analysis Summary form that Brimijoin completed during the observation. The form served as a guide for a postlesson conversation between Brimijoin and the teacher of the math lesson.

As the postobservation discussion began, the teacher knew that the content was essentially the same for all students because all were working with quantities and prices of food. What she differentiated was the process, she said, because some were determining cost related to quantity with budgetary limitations and others were calculating cost related to quantity with no limitations. As the two talked, the teacher said, "There really wasn't much differentiation, is it?" Brimijoin agreed and asked how the teacher might have created a more advanced version of the task for the students in the blue group who breezed through the assignment. It took the teacher very little time to realize that if she had given students a budget of $50 to plan a holiday meal with no specified items, the work would have been more appropriately challenging for the skills of some of the students.

The teacher was able to explain that she had differentiated the lesson largely on the basis of student readiness, which ongoing assessments indicated to her varied considerably in regard to student comfort with applying the skills of multiplication. She had also considered that some students who had practical and kinesthetic strengths would benefit from the use of real-world tasks that required some movement as they sorted ads. She also felt that the task would provide additional formative assessment information for her on student progress with application of multiplication skills.

She talked about a student whom she had assigned to the blue group because she felt that he would benefit from a greater level of challenge. She planned to reposition him with a green group if he became frustrated with the more advanced task. Both Brimijoin and the teacher determined that the student had handled the assignment well, and the teacher said it was helpful to her in understanding upcoming decisions about assignments for him.

Brimijoin and the teacher talked about what needed more work in the lesson. The teacher reflected that she could have reduced confusion about the directions by taking more time at the beginning to model how she wanted students to work through the tasks, sharing examples with them, and checking for understanding. Brimijoin suggested that a rubric

Figure 4.4
Example of Lesson Analysis Summary

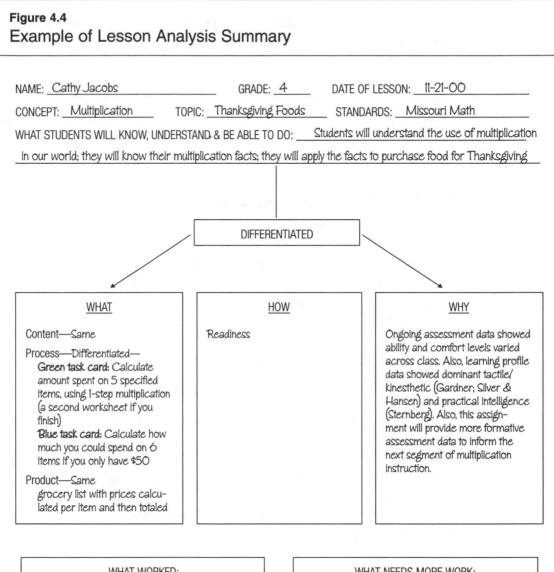

NAME: _Cathy Jacobs_   GRADE: _4_   DATE OF LESSON: _11-21-00_

CONCEPT: _Multiplication_   TOPIC: _Thanksgiving Foods_   STANDARDS: _Missouri Math_

WHAT STUDENTS WILL KNOW, UNDERSTAND, & BE ABLE TO DO: _Students will understand the use of multiplication in our world; they will know their multiplication facts; they will apply the facts to purchase food for Thanksgiving_

DIFFERENTIATED

WHAT

Content—Same

Process—Differentiated—
Green task card: Calculate amount spent on 5 specified items, using 1-step multiplication (a second worksheet if you finish)
Blue task card: Calculate how much you could spend on 6 items if you only have $50

Product—Same
grocery list with prices calculated per item and then totaled

HOW

Readiness

WHY

Ongoing assessment data showed ability and comfort levels varied across class. Also, learning profile data showed dominant tactile/kinesthetic (Gardner; Silver & Hansen) and practical intelligence (Sternberg). Also, this assignment will provide more formative assessment data to inform the next segment of multiplication instruction.

WHAT WORKED:

Everyone was completely engaged! "Even special needs kids were on task the whole time." They really loved the "responsibility" of planning and calculating for a family event. C. was excited about the response of a student she had challenged. She put him in the blue group knowing it would be a stretch, but he excelled. She was pleased with his thinking, and this gave her valuable information for the next multiplication assignment she would craft.

WHAT NEEDS MORE WORK:

C. said, "This really isn't much differentiation, is it?" Some in blue group breezed through—could have specified no items but limited budget and created a third tier. More modeling at front end of lesson on how to check for understanding. Probably needed to focus learning goals on estimation. A rubric for the grocery list would have helped—a generic one for all 3 tiers would have defined goals.

or checklist defining what students should have on their final grocery list would have clarified and streamlined the lesson. Brimijoin also reiterated that a more advanced-level task would have been more effective for some of the students.

This session with Brimijoin is just one example of the coaching teachers received. Conway's principal also served as an active and consistent coach for teachers as they learned to differentiate in their classrooms. Appendix A (see p. 191) provides an example of a coaching session between Narvaez and a new Conway teacher.

Content of Whole-Faculty Debriefing Sessions

Narvaez and Brimijoin followed the coaching visits with whole-faculty debriefing sessions. They had three goals for the debriefings. First, they wanted faculty members to share successes in order to validate their work and see the coaching process as nonevaluative, instructive, reflective, and helpful. Second, they wanted the meetings to provide a forum for reviewing, clarifying, and refining the essential principles and practices of differentiation. Third, they wanted to join the faculty in establishing patterns of success and patterns that pointed to next steps in the learning process.

From the beginning, the whole-group debriefing sessions were affirming for teachers and increased their willingness to volunteer for coaching at Brimijoin's next visit. The positive and constructive nature of the meetings was particularly important for doubters, helping to allay their concerns about what they perceived as overwhelming in the application of differentiation. The sessions also helped build a sense of community among teachers as they saw themselves as learners, focused on improving their professional practice. Sessions typically ended with teachers providing written reflections, which served as a thought-consolidation process for faculty members and ongoing assessment information for Brimijoin and Narvaez.

An Example of the Content of a Whole-Faculty Debriefing Session

During the whole-faculty debriefing after Brimijoin observed the math teacher, the teacher described her "talent spotting" with the student who effectively handled an advanced task for the first time. She explained how her analysis of ongoing assessment information had led her to think the student might be able to handle a more advanced task. She had also used her observations to make future decisions about the boy's work in math. Likewise, other teachers whom Brimijoin had observed and coached on the previous day shared what had worked in their classes and what needed more work. Figure 4.5 represents a chart Brimijoin created during the session to reflect what the teachers shared and to help point the way to future work.

Figure 4.5
A Reflection Chart from a Conway Whole-Faculty Debriefing Session

What Worked	
Talent in students is growing.	Behavior problems reduced.
More engagement—students focused on the intent of a task.	Increased interaction between teacher and students across the entire class.
What Needs More Work	
Fine-tuning differentiation. Doing a better job of matching student learning needs with tasks.	More conversation with students about rationale for differentiation. Students do not understand why they are doing different tasks.
A better match between curriculum goals and learning activities.	Time for teachers to create varied tasks and materials.

Examples of written reflections from teachers at the end of whole-faculty debriefing sessions are strongly linked to classroom practice—sometimes focusing on what they learned from coaching sessions and sometimes what they drew from the whole-faculty sharing. For example, a teacher wrote, "I saw that I should have planned fewer groups for my first attempt at teaching a differentiated lesson. The students needed more scaffolding than I could provide [to so many groups]. The students were fully engaged in the activities, but some groups didn't completely follow the directions because they needed more guidance." Later in the year, a teacher reflected, "Several positive aspects [to differentiation] that I have realized are more variety in application of concepts, more choices for the students, more opportunity for success by children at all the different skill levels, more opportunity for children to expand the application of concepts as they demonstrate success, more challenge for the children who have a very clear understanding of concepts presented."

Additional Staff Development Structures at Conway

As was the case at Colchester High, distributed leadership was evident at Conway Elementary. Staff development leadership roles evolved over time to ensure that leaders were recognized and developed at all levels of the organization. In addition to staff development leadership provided by Brimijoin, the following emergent groups also played pivotal roles in ensuring that everyone on the Conway faculty learned to differentiate instruction at a high level—and did so consistently in their classrooms:

- The principal provided regular classroom observation and coaching in differentiation. She conducted 65 observation and coaching sessions in the first three years.
- The Professional Development Committee, a standing committee composed of teachers, gathered qualitative data after each visit from the staff developer, analyzed the data, and shared summaries with the staff developer, suggesting content for the next visit.
- Grade-level planning teams, composed of all teachers from a grade level, planned differentiated lessons, shared materials, and visited peer classrooms to determine how to refine lessons. They also played a key role in providing staff development for teachers new to Conway.
- Peer coaching evolved in the third and fourth years of the differentiation initiative among members of a grade-level team. Peer coaches observed one another's classes, jointly planned lessons and units, viewed lessons in colleagues' classes and shared analysis to improve lesson design, and became critical friends in regard to design and implementation of differentiation.

Over time, professional development plans became increasingly personalized for teachers as Brimijoin and Narvaez gained insights into particular needs and as circumstances at Conway called for individualization. For example, Brimijoin worked extensively in one-on-one settings with the school's media specialist, who wanted to differentiate her instruction of students in the library, while working collaboratively with teachers to reinforce grade-level standards. Brimijoin also worked extensively with a kindergarten team that, during year three of the initiative, was composed of virtually all new teachers.

In addition to the multiple avenues for staff development within Conway, Narvaez sent key teachers to national-level professional conferences on differentiation each year. These opportunities not only further professionalized the teachers but also provided chances to learn from high-quality presenters and to take stock of their own development via exchanges with other attendees.

In the fourth year of the differentiation initiative at Conway and years following, many teachers assumed roles as professional developers for teachers beyond their faculty. They began presenting their work at state and national conferences. In addition, they assumed major responsibility for formal and informal presentations to a steady stream of teachers and groups that came to Conway to observe and learn from the faculty's experience. At the writing of this book, more than 200 teachers and administrators had spent a day observing differentiated instruction at Conway. All of these factors contributed to the continuing growth of the Conway teachers in understanding and application of differentiation as well as in skills of professional leadership. Appendix B (see p. 202) shows the evolution of deep understanding about differentiation in the Conway faculty.

Helping Parents Understand Differentiation at Conway

Helping parents understand differentiation was an integral part of information sharing at Conway. Before the first staff development retreat on differentiation, Narvaez met with parents to explain what differentiation was, why it mattered for student learning, and why the approach was of interest at Conway. During the retreat, as noted earlier, Brimijoin met with parents to answer their questions and to ensure that teacher concerns were addressed with parents as well. Over the years of the Conway differentiation initiative, the principal presented a minimum of two parent workshops on differentiation each year. She and the teachers also presented examples of differentiated lessons to parents.

Further, each teacher talked with parents about differentiation in parent conferences each year. Parent understanding of and trust in differentiation were also greatly aided by the firsthand observations of the very large group of parents who volunteered at Conway. In time, the Conway Parent Association paid for some of the consultant visits to Conway because they wanted to contribute to appropriate academic challenge for their students.

Staff Development Content at Colchester High

If the change process at Conway Elementary is the narrative of a strong leader and highly professional staff working in tandem to make an excellent school even better, the Colchester High narrative tells a very different story. At the outset of the change process toward differentiation, it was a school in disarray. Conway Elementary faculty and staff began the change initiative with virtually all members willing and ready to learn about differentiation, but that was far from the case at Colchester High. The content of Colchester's professional development was linked with the school's evolutionary and revolutionary changes. In general, the content of staff development for second-order change toward differentiation involves the three stages of change proposed by Michael Fullan (1991): (1) preparation for change, (2) implementation of change, and (3) continuation of change. His fourth stage, outcomes, will be the focus of Chapter 5.

Staff Development to Prepare for Change at Colchester High

As noted, Colchester High was a school in need of change. In August 1999, when Joyce Stone became principal, the school was reeling from years of budget cuts and morale-busting community relations. The previous year had ended with numerous bomb threats, a pattern of poor student discipline in the school, and the resignation of 26 teachers. The exodus was prompted by a district teacher buyout and by teacher discontent with the school environment. The school year began with no guidance counselor, no department heads, two inexperienced assistants, and Stone. Bill Rich, who was a Colchester teacher at the time and is now Colchester's teacher liaison, noted, "Teachers did what teachers often do in these situations. The most resilient ones retreated to their classrooms and did the best they could on their own. Too many, though, succumbed to the understandable temptation to throw up their hands and commiserate. It was a time of helplessness."

The underpinning of Stone's early work was her vision of a school in which all students had full access to high-quality curriculum and instruction. From the outset, she knew that she would have to help the faculty grapple with the school's long-standing grouping practices that demonstrated expectations of excellence from some students and teachers, while accepting far less from others. It was a system that separated not only students but teachers. She recognized that to change the system was to cross social and political fault lines that ran deep not only within the school, but within the community as well. She understood that challenging deep devotions to grouping students would be complex and that even a finely developed and carefully implemented process commending changes in the grouping process would meet with stiff resistance.

Although Stone's personal inclination would have been to move quickly toward detracking students in favor of heterogeneous grouping, she knew she had to begin a process of carefully preparing staff and parents for such a change. Staff development would have to begin where teachers were, not where she wanted them to be.

Further, there were no funds for staff development. Therefore, staff development would have to happen from within the school, and it would have to happen slowly.

By the end of her first year at Colchester, Stone had begun working with the faculty and school board to help them understand the implications of tracking for teaching and learning at Colchester. Rich noted, "Even the teachers most resistant to detracking had their conscience pricked when Stone presented to them the clear correlation between students' socioeconomic status and their placement in academic tracks." To that end, Stone did research in neighboring high schools and used that information to convince the school board that the school could not move forward without a broader base of leadership that included teacher leaders committed to the vision. By the end of the year, not only did the school board provide an infusion of funds for books and resources to support quality curriculum and instruction, but they also funded four team leader positions. The team leader positions—eventually five of them—became the core of the school's Leadership Team. The team leaders would play the roles once filled by department heads as well as becoming a powerful engine in planning the mechanisms and content of staff development.

In addition, Stone early on began the practice of focusing all professional development days on differentiation as well as inviting faculty members to propose particular topics related to differentiation for those sessions. From the first day of her principalship, she established best-practice faculty meetings (two meetings per month), which preserved all faculty meeting time for considering differentiation and related topics rather than for distributing information. *The Tuesday Times*—a weekly informational newsletter—gave faculty operational information about their school. In best-practice faculty meetings, teachers presented examples of how they were differentiating instruction and discussed important questions related to teaching, learning, and differentiation.

Also from the earliest days, Stone regularly spent time in classrooms throughout the school so that she was fully cognizant of all faculty members' classroom practices.

Stone recognized that rushing substantial shifts in grouping and teaching practices would rob the faculty of time they needed to come to terms with the necessity for change and to build readiness to address it. She therefore studied her faculty to identify early innovators—skilled and resourceful teachers who were willing to try out new ideas. When she discussed her thinking with two experienced and respected teachers, they prevailed on her to slow down or risk failure, as noted in Chapter 3. They suggested a pilot program to phase in differentiation, and she accepted their proposal. While continuing her own program of reading and learning related to differentiation, she provided her pioneer teachers with high-quality staff development—including books, videos, and a summer institute on differentiation. These resources helped the teachers solidify their foundational understanding of differentiation and overhaul their curriculum for the pilot course.

As noted in the previous chapter, the first-year pilot was so successful that the class and teachers stayed together, looping to 10th grade for a second pilot year. In addition, Stone asked two other teachers to develop and teach another pilot—providing those two teachers with the same high-quality staff development in preparation for their new roles. During the second summer of the change initiative, all four pilot teachers attended a summer institute on differentiation and worked jointly on their classroom plans—a collaborative mentorship that continued through the second pilot year at Colchester.

In the meantime, data from the first pilot itself became an important source of staff development for the Colchester faculty. The first pair of pilot teachers had carefully surveyed students and parents throughout the year, and results were clear. Overall, teachers, parents, and students felt the differentiated pilot class was a better approach to teaching and learning than the grouped approach—including students who would have been in the honors track. In addition, test data showed that students in the heterogeneous classes were faring as well as, and often better than, students in the tracked classes. Stone was a regular visitor in the pilot classes—learning about differentiation with and from the students and teachers and playing the role of substitute teacher in those classes as needed.

The principal shared all the pilot data with faculty at the end of both years and structured yearlong faculty conversations around the data, thus providing information and a forum necessary to slowly shift faculty perspectives. By the end of the second year of pilots, with similar data accumulated and shared with the faculty, the stage was set for all 9th grade classes to be detracked for the next year and taught in differentiated classrooms. The slow, steady approach to exploring differentiation had paid off, giving validity and credibility to the reasoning behind substantial change. Further, four Colchester teachers who now had first-hand knowledge of, understanding about, and skill with differentiation could provide in-house support for other teachers who were about to begin a new journey in their classrooms.

Also by the end of the second pilot year, students were comfortably using the language of differentiation, and there was a list of parents who wanted their students in the differentiated classrooms. Stone, however, did not use parent requests to assign students to the detracked classes. Assignment continued to be made randomly from structured cohorts of students to ensure a representative distribution of students in all classes.

Even though some Colchester faculty members might still have been skeptical about the idea of differentiation, none could say they had been rushed into the change. It was evident to faculty that this principal was different and so was the change initiative. They had led a schoolwide visioning process in which teachers had considered together—carefully and respectfully—their beliefs, values, and vision for the school. The idea of differentiation was not going away. Rich said, "We didn't know the term then, but 'second-order change' had begun."

Integral to the success of the preparation phase of second-order change toward differentiation at Colchester was Stone's inauguration of the Leadership Team. This group consisted of five teachers who supervised the school's five content clusters (1) science and health; (2) humanities (English and social studies); (3) math, business, and technology; (4) support services (special education and physical education); and (5) art, music, and world languages), the school's two assistant principals, and the principal. Over time, the Leadership Team—particularly the five team leaders—assumed increasing responsibility for implementation of differentiation at the department level, supporting teacher needs, helping to provide staff development, and keeping the vision for differentiation before the departments. Other key roles of the Leadership Team, such as coordinating curriculum work groups and planning Saturday seminars, will be discussed later in the chapter. The team leaders "grew into program managers, nurturers of quality curriculum, teachers of teachers, and keepers of the vision for differentiation," Stone said: "The Leadership Team has worked diligently to create a vibrant and accountable professional learning community." To support the Leadership Team in building its leadership capacity, Rich arranged for a week-long intensive training session conducted by the National School Reform Faculty. This experience provided the group with tools and strategies for guiding change and over time continued to shape how the Leadership Team conducted its work and how team leaders worked with their departments.

Stone's role as an instructional guide was consistent throughout the change initiative. She regularly visited classrooms, talked with teachers about their work, collected and analyzed work samples, and provided structures to help ensure that Colchester administrators and faculty had a common language related to differentiation and a common understanding of its goals. Figure 4.6 is an example of a simple principal-developed guide for teachers to focus attention on what classroom elements (content, process, or product) they plan to differentiate based on particular student needs (readiness, interests, or learning profiles).

Figure 4.7 includes a pre-observation form completed by Colchester teachers prior to a principal observation, once again working for a common language and focus related to differentiation.

Note that the language reflected in Figure 4.8, which is a rubric used by the principal in formal classroom observations, is aligned with the language and focus of the documents in Figures 4.6 and 4.7. Thus teacher preparation for classroom observations and the observations themselves became an important part of professional development at Colchester, working for a shared understanding of the concept and for fidelity to the differentiation model during implementation.

Staff Development to Implement Change at Colchester

As differentiation became a reality for the 9th grade team and an impending one for other Colchester faculty members, they needed expanded staff development to support the new reality. In other words, additional support for effective implementation of differentiation had to grow along with the increasing push for change. Several positions, practices, and structures were pivotal in the success of the transition from conversation to practice. They were the following:

- The role of the teacher liaison.
- The summer institute on differentiation.

• The growth of the Professional Development Committee.

• Emphasis on Colchester as a professional learning community.

The Role of the Teacher Liaison. Even though Stone emphasized her role as instructional leader over her role as building manager, it was clear that she could not do all that was needed to craft quality staff development and build trust among teachers. Stone therefore developed a teacher liaison position for Colchester. This person would continue to teach for part of each day but also would spend part of each day working with and on behalf of teachers toward implementation of differentiation.

Figure 4.6
Teacher Reflection Guide Focusing on Key Elements of Differentiation at Colchester

Use this template when planning or looking back at a lesson. Remember, you do not need to differentiate content, process, and product every time you differentiate. Similarly, you do not have to adjust for readiness, interests, and learner profile every time you differentiate. Regularly using this template, however, will help you develop a sense of how you tend to differentiate. This process may feel clumsy at first, but after a while you will become nimble at adjusting content, process, and products according to students' readiness, interests, and learner profiles.

Content
Check that which applies:

☐ N/A   ☐ Readiness   ☐ Interest   ☐ Learner Profile

Describe how the content is adjusted:

Process
Check that which applies:

☐ N/A   ☐ Readiness   ☐ Interest   ☐ Learner Profile

Describe how the process is adjusted:

Product
Check that which applies:

☐ N/A   ☐ Readiness   ☐ Interest   ☐ Learner Profile

Describe how the product is adjusted:

Figure 4.7
Pre-observation Form for Colchester Teachers

Pre-observation Date _____ Teacher _____ Class _____

To be completed by the teacher.

1. List the general purpose of the learning activity and what the observer should know about the students.

2. What are the specific objectives of the activity being used?

3. Which strategies related to differentiation are you using in this lesson?

4. How will you assess the success of this lesson and student learning?

5. Is there other relevant information the observer should know?

Pre-observation Conference Date   _____
Post-observation Conference Date   _____

Observation Confirmed _____ **Date** _____ **Room** _____

She hired Bill Rich, one of the early pilot teachers, as teacher liaison. In many ways, the teacher liaison is the linchpin of staff development. Stone explained, "I could not possibly overstate the importance of his role and talent in that capacity. He became the coarchitect of the CHS vision and implementation of differentiated instruction. He became the go-to person. He had his thumb on the pulse of the school, and through him, so did I. People would go to him for help who might not have come to my door for it. He came to understand the school behind the principal's closed door and still remained out and about as a teacher and team leader."

A teaching colleague at Colchester explained that Rich's deep personal belief in differentiation, his persistence, his continuing support for teachers, and his belief in his colleagues were instrumental in the school's change: "Without this positive, consistent, and ongoing role, I don't think we'd get change. I think we'd get episodic bursts of doing something new." His work was designed to ensure teacher knowledge, input, and focus on differentiation. Fused with teacher leadership from a growing number of groups, this work was pivotal in the degree and pace of change at Colchester High.

In the role of teacher liaison, Rich helped plan and manage the school's professional development. He worked with the principal and team leaders to establish a Professional Development Committee that provided valuable feedback and buy-in related to staff development. He assisted teachers in finding opportunities to learn about differentiation that matched their needs, and he provided feedback on their work. He sometimes provided feedback to teachers who sought his assistance. Appendix C (see p. 206) provides an example of written feedback from Rich to colleagues who were working to establish more academically responsive classrooms. It highlights a focus on students, uses of assessment to guide decision making, and quality of instruction.

Rich also provided structures and supports for staff development that allowed Colchester teachers to assume increasing leadership roles. For example, he provided a guide for teachers preparing to lead a discussion with colleagues of an article on using assessment to support student learning. He also prepared a discussion guide for the leaders to use with participants in a staff development session. These resources helped the teacher leaders prepare and ensured a similar focus among discussion groups.

Figure 4.8
Rubric for Observing Colchester Teachers' Use of Differentiated Instruction

	Highly Skilled	Practitioner	Apprentice	Novice
Differentiates Content	• Consistently organizes learning (content) around concepts or themes that are highly relevant, coherent, and powerful. • Consistently differentiates content through such means as multiple texts, supplementary print resources, contracts, and compacting.	• Frequently organizes learning (content) around concepts or themes that are highly relevant, coherent, and powerful. • Differentiates content frequently but sometimes offers content inappropriate for the student's learning level.	• Occasionally organizes learning (content) around concepts or themes. • Differentiates content from time to time but offers content inappropriate for the student's learning level.	• Rarely organizes learning (content) around concepts or themes. • Rarely differentiates content.
Differentiates Student Activities	• Consistently designs student activities that are concept or theme driven, are purposeful, and balance critical and creative thought. • Consistently differentiates student activities through work such as multiple intelligences tasks, graphic organizers, simulations, and complex instruction.	• Frequently designs student activities that are concept or theme driven, are purposeful, and balance critical and creative thought. • Differentiates student activities on a regular basis.	• Occasionally designs student activities that are concept or theme driven, are purposeful, and balance critical and creative thought. • Differentiates student activities occasionally.	• Rarely designs student activities that are concept or theme driven. • Rarely differentiates student activities.

Figure 4.8—(continued)
Rubric for Observing Colchester Teachers' Use of Differentiated Instruction

	Highly Skilled	Practitioner	Apprentice	Novice
Differentiates Student Products	• Consistently assigns products that are concept or theme centered, require students to apply all key skills and understandings learned in unit, and solve real problems. • Consistently differentiates student products such as those with criteria negotiated with instructor, tiering, independent studies, graduated rubrics, complex instruction, etc.	• Frequently assigns tasks or products that are concept or theme centered, require students to apply all key skills and understandings learned in unit, and solve real problems. • Differentiates student tasks or products often.	• Occasionally assigns tasks or products that are concept or theme centered, that require students to apply all key skills and understandings learned in unit, and that solve real problems. • Differentiates student tasks or products occasionally.	• Rarely assigns tasks or products around concepts or themes. • Rarely differentiates tasks or products assigned to students.
Differentiates Assessment	• Consistently employs a variety of assessments before, during, and after a unit of study to determine differentiated activities and to measure student learning. • Continually links students to appropriately varied resources (human, material, and technical) that students need to complete assessments.	• Uses various assessments to modify some activities and to measure student learning during and after a unit of study. • Frequently links students to appropriately varied resources (human, material, and technical) that students need to complete assessments.	• Only uses assessment to measure student learning at the end of a unit of study. • Occasionally links students to appropriately varied resources (human, material, and technical) that students need to complete assessments.	• Rarely uses assessments to determine or measure student learning. • Rarely links students to appropriately varied resources (human, material, and technical) that students need to complete assessments.
Teacher as Mentor	• Promotes individual and student growth through continual feedback and modeling. • Acts as a resource person as well as an evaluator.	• Frequently provides feedback from observations and modeling but inconsistently connects this to students' growth. • Frequently is a resource person and an evaluator of students.	• Occasionally observes students to provide feedback and modeling. • Occasionally acts as a resource person and evaluator of students.	• Rarely observes to provide feedback or modeling. • Rarely acts as a resource person and evaluator of students.

Use of Differentiated Staff Development. Rich recalled that before Stone became principal at Colchester, there were two types of staff development. The first occurred when a teacher lifted the lid of a copy machine and found a promising lesson left behind by a peer. The second happened when experts from far away came to share quips and wisdom on designated professional development days while new teachers assiduously took notes and veterans graded papers.

Then things changed at the high school. Before staff development days, Stone and the Leadership Team pre-assessed teachers to gauge their interest in key concepts and practices of differentiation. For example, topics might include concept-based teaching, using assessment to inform instruction, instructional strategies for differentiation, or building classroom community.

The next inservice day, then, would offer a menu of options based on faculty input. First, the faculty would meet for a brief overview of how the process would work. Then everyone would go to workshops conducted by colleagues and in which they had expressed an interest. At the end of the day, the faculty would come back together to complete exit cards (see Figure 4.9) that evaluated the session and asked what support teachers would need to begin applying what they had learned. In many cases, the exit cards provided information useful in planning upcoming staff development options (see Figure 4.10). From the earliest such experiences, teachers began to express a keen desire to ensure that staff development days at Colchester did not revert to the old ways.

Hosting a Colchester Summer Institute on Differentiation. This weeklong course was attended by approximately 25 Colchester High teachers from a range of content areas. Previous summer staff development opportunities had been off-site and had focused on strengthening early innovators. The Colchester Summer Institute provided a time for a broader group of teachers to expand their understanding of differentiation and develop a differentiated unit that they would implement in the fall. Follow-up allowed participants to present their work later in the year and discuss with colleagues what the implementation process was like for them and their students.

Growth of the Professional Development Committee. Because Rich believed that teachers should play an increased role in their staff development, he reenergized the Professional Development Committee to help ensure quality staff development that attended to the school's mission to establish heterogeneous, differentiated classrooms and to teachers' needs for skill in leading these classrooms. The group's role

Figure 4.9
Sample Exit Card for Surveying
Staff Understanding and Needs

Name: _____

Exit Card

This morning our faculty looked at the questions that emerged from the exit cards we completed during our last look at differentiated instruction. One question asked whether or not there is a contradiction between standards and differentiated instruction. What do you think?

What are the three most significant insights you had today about differentiated instruction?

What D.I.-related questions would you like to see addressed the next time we gather to consider differentiated instruction?

in the staff development process continued to grow. The Professional Development Committee consisted of teachers and administrators who volunteered to work with the principal and teacher liaison in overseeing the staff development process. They conducted and analyzed faculty surveys about staff development and played a decision-making role, along with the Leadership Team, in staff development opportunities at Colchester. Rich noted that the presence of thoughtful skeptics in the group was important.

Emphasis on Colchester as a Professional Learning Community. In the fourth year of the change process, Stone and Rich began focused work on establishing a professional learning community (Kruse, Louis, & Bryk, 1994) at Colchester. They began by surveying the faculty about their perceptions of the school's climate of trust and respect, opportunities to influence decision making, systems and structures that promoted collaboration, and administrators that supported teachers. Although the school leaders had not consciously attempted to create a professional learning community up to this point, faculty responses to the survey

---

Figure 4.10
Staff Development Day Station Options

Station 1: *Strategies for Differentiating Instruction* (Room 101)
Because differentiated instruction is a way of looking at our teaching and not a set method, there is not a recipe for how to do it. If you believe, however, that all your students may learn even if they have different interests, readiness levels, and learning styles, several techniques emerge as particularly helpful.

During our *Strategies for Differentiating Instruction*, we will review just a few techniques showcasing content, process, and product differentiation.

Station 2: *Learning Styles and Multiple Intelligences* (Room 103)
We all know that students learn in different ways. We also know that each individual is intelligent in a variety of ways. The *Learning Styles and Multiple Intelligences* station will examine a few ways to approach students' unique ways of learning, look at our own learning profile, and consider the implications on planning with differentiation in mind.

Station 3: *Using Concepts to Differentiate Instruction* (Room 105)
The more one reads about differentiated instruction, the more one comes across references to concept-based instruction. Teaching from a conceptual framework makes differentiating easier and helps students make deeper connections with content by focusing on the powerful ideas that underpin our content. What are concepts? Why should I consider adjusting my content into a conceptual framework? How can I shift my instruction toward a more conceptual approach? This station will consider these questions and more.

Station 4: *ASCD Videotape: Setting the Groundwork for Differentiated Instruction* (Room 107)
This station will view an ASCD videotape that really sets the groundwork for understanding differentiated instruction. This video is the first in a series of five. You have seen the third tape. Working back to the fundamentals of differentiated instruction, the video answers the following questions:

   What are the fundamental components of differentiated instruction?
   How does the teacher identify and address individual student needs?
   How does differentiated instruction benefit students, teachers, and the school as a whole?
   What are the factors that make it difficult to differentiate instruction?
   What might we do in the near future to support more differentiated instruction?

---

suggested that, indeed, such a progression had begun. Most faculty were ready to work together to provide the best possible learning experience for all students. They wanted to deprivatize their practice. Detractors still existed, but it seemed evident that they were few and that innovators were growing in leaps and bounds. As a step toward purposeful strengthening of a Colchester professional community of learners, learning circles and collaborative work groups began.

Rich explained, "Somewhere along the way, we reached a tipping point where we were no longer simply reacting to circumstances; instead, we were proactively anticipating the needs of the school." He recalled that because of the turmoil at Colchester in the early phases of change, it was necessary to address basic human needs for safety, security, and belonging before asking teachers to project a vision for their future work. To have moved faster, he said, would have been hollow at best and downright damaging at worst.

Staff Development to Continue Change at Colchester

By 2004, it appeared evident at Colchester that the faculty was moving as a team toward effectively and defensibly differentiated classrooms. Turning a corner, however, does not constitute the completion of the journey. At this point, Stone, Rich, and the Leadership Team began to emphasize structures that would deepen the understanding and application of differentiation for all faculty members by developing the capacity of teachers to lead their colleagues. Among the structures developed and enhanced to institutionalize differentiation at Colchester were the following:

• **Inauguration of learning circles.** One part of teacher voice in professional development at Colchester was the creation of learning circles. These groups evolved at the urging of the Colchester teacher liaison, who felt additional teacher ownership in differentiation would be necessary if change toward differentiation were to spread beyond early innovators. Teachers proposed learning circle groups and topics based on their interests and perceptions of need in the school. Some learning circle topics dealt directly with differentiation—for example, use of assessment, uses of teacher advisory groups to better understand and connect with students, and teaching based on learning styles. Other learning circle topics did not directly relate to differentiation—for example, conflict resolution. An early principal's choice for a learning circle, strategies for improving student reading skills, did not make the final cut and was therefore not on the agenda. Learning circles began to meet during one of the two monthly best-practice faculty meetings. At the end of the year, each learning circle reported out recommendations for action based on its study. Recommendations then went to the Leadership Team for final action and often affected processes and procedures in subsequent years.

• **Addition of collaborative work groups.** After learning circles researched, discussed, reflected, and made recommendations on key topics and issues, they made presentations on their work to the full faculty and recommendations to the Leadership Team. The Leadership Team, in turn, made decisions about whether and how to implement the recommendations. Responses to implementation varied considerably, for example, folding the recommendations into an existing initiative, employing a task force, taking the recommendations to student government, or addressing them in collaborative work groups. In addition to their connections to learning circles, collaborative work groups served to keep the focus on student work—sharing, examining, and adjusting. They became an avenue to ensure quality curriculum supported by effective instructional strategies and ongoing and differentiated assessment. Their work strengthened practice in many facets of the school and its classrooms.

Through much of the initiation, implementation, and continuation phases of change toward differentiation at Colchester, several ongoing staff development mechanisms continued, including the following:

• Providing common language and formats to guide teacher work toward differentiation. (Appendix D [see p. 212] illustrates use of a Know-Understand-Do lesson-planning format used widely in curriculum planning.)
• Regular attendance at high-quality summer institutes on differentiation by key teachers.
• In-common reading and discussion by the faculty on topics such as addressing the needs of low socioeconomic learners or professional communities of learning.
• Summer curriculum work on differentiated units.
• Expansion of a professional library with materials on differentiation.

Helping Parents Understand Differentiation at Colchester

For some parents of high school students, the idea of detracking is a hot-button issue—especially for those parents who fear their students will lose status and opportunity. Throughout Stone's tenure as principal at Colchester, she never missed an opportunity to share with parents and the community the Colchester vision for an effectively differentiated school and the research that supported the vision. She made regular presentations to parents and offered books and articles to those who inquired about differentiation. At the end of presentations, she used exit cards to gather parents' questions and comments. She reviewed the exit cards and wrote letters to those whose cards seemed to call for a response. Appendix H (see p. 223) is an example of a communication from Stone to Colchester parents, which she addressed to students and community members as well.

As teacher liaison, Rich also had frequent communication with parents about differentiation. His role was especially valuable because he represented the credibility of a highly respected teacher. Rich recalled a conversation with one parent who was persistently skeptical about differentiation. She attended numerous parent presentations on differentiation, expressed her concerns and questions with respect, and corresponded with Stone about her concerns. She talked about her appreciation of the opportunities she had to receive a hearing and of the thorough and thoughtful answers she received from Stone. Even though she never did come to agree about the school's direction, she could not fault the process. There were ample and ongoing opportunities to participate in meaningful dialogue with school personnel and other parents.

Lessons About the Content of Staff Development for Change

Different as Conway Elementary and Colchester High were at the outset of the change process, the content of staff development in the two schools shared important commonalities. In both settings, staff development for teachers centered on response to student needs, the importance of quality curriculum as a foundation for quality differentiation, the role of diagnostic and ongoing assessment in informing differentiation, and the imperative of developing effectively managed classroom communities of learners in which teachers and students worked together to benefit each member of the community. In both schools, the content of staff development for teachers mirrored effective classroom differentiation, modifying content, process, and product based on teachers' readiness, interests, and learning profiles. Perhaps most importantly, the content of whole-group staff development for teachers was closely linked with transfer to the classroom and was reinforced by attention to classroom application of key principles and practices of differentiation.

Also important was the work that leaders and teachers in both settings did to proactively address students' and parents' needs to understand and contribute to differentiation. At Conway and Colchester, professional development for teachers was linked with ensuring student and parent acceptance and support of the school vision, as well as teacher acceptance and support.

5

Monitoring and Evaluating Change Toward Differentiation

If the prospect of a major change initiative is unsettling to teachers, it is no less so for the school principal who risks tension and accepts the stress and uncertainty of leading for change. Principals who are willing catalysts for change toward more academically responsive classrooms feel a sense of responsibility for the students in their school and for the teachers they ask to risk change.

Principals who lead for change ask themselves, "How will I know whether the actions we are taking have the kinds of benefits we envision for them?" "What kinds of information can I gather to answer that question?" "When should I begin to study what we are doing?" "How often?" "What is it exactly that I should evaluate?" "What kinds of evaluation should we use?" "Who should do the evaluating?" "Is the goal of evaluation judgment of our efforts or refinement of them?" "How should we use what we learn through evaluation?"

In leading a change initiative for differentiation, principals in many settings may also wonder, "Is there a parallel between assessment in a differentiated classroom and assessment of our movement toward academically responsive classrooms?" "How can one teach us more about the other?"

Evaluation as Part of the Cycle of Change

Second-order change is complex, messy, uncertain, labor intensive, and long term. When a leader asks colleagues to undertake such change, it is the leader's obligation to determine whether the proposed change is working. Second-order change is also potentially promising in terms of outcomes for students, educators, and schools—but only if leaders and implementers develop increasing understanding of the initiative. Thus it is also important for a leader to take the lead in ensuring that those involved in the change have access to information that will inform their understanding of it, ultimately benefiting students, whose welfare is the focus of second-order change (Joyce & Showers, 2002). In both instances, careful monitoring of a change initiative can inform the change process and should help ensure that more positives and fewer negatives result from that initiative. In other words, evaluation is both a consequence of undertaking change and an impetus to change (Duke, 2004).

It is difficult to create a compelling vision for change, more difficult still to enlist the efforts of others to make the change, and yet again more difficult to ensure that the change takes place in classrooms across a school. Achieving implementation can become so exciting that it blinds us to the truth that, in fact, implementation was not the goal of the change initiative, but rather a means to the goal of benefiting students. Only through careful and persistent evaluation can we know either whether implementation of the change initiative is occurring in ways that suggest fidelity to our knowledge of best practices or whether consequences of implementation are positive or negative and for whom (Rogers, 1995).

In thinking about evaluating change initiatives, leaders for second-order change should consider (1) purposes of evaluation, (2) kinds of evaluation, (3) key principles of evaluation, and (4) uses of evaluation data.

Purposes of Evaluation

Evaluations can serve many purposes. They can be directed at improving the quality of processes and practices in a change initiative, modifying the elements of a change initiative, making a case for additional funding for the initiative, or determining how a change initiative affects students or teachers—to name just a few possible evaluation goals (Duke, 2004). Leaders may wish to focus evaluation efforts on various goals at various times, but it is important to predetermine the goals of evaluation efforts and to plan with those in mind. The nature of evaluation goals will shape the kinds of evaluations a leader pursues.

Kinds of Evaluations

Purposes of evaluation should shape the nature or kind of evaluation a leader undertakes. Duke (2004) suggests considering the following aspects of evaluations:

• **Diagnostic, formative, or summative.** Diagnostic evaluations take place prior to the beginning of a change initiative to determine the need for change, the readiness of individuals to undertake change, or the capacity of the school to support change. Formative evaluations take place as the initiative occurs to determine whether processes and implementation are occurring as intended and to assist leaders and implementers in improving their work. Summative evaluations take place after implementation (or at designated times in a long-term initiative) to make judgments about the initiative.

• **Process focused or product focused.** Process-focused evaluations attempt to discover whether various processes (e.g., professional development, classroom implementation) are taking place as intended. Product-based evaluations look at effects of implementation.

• **Goal based or goal free.** Goal-based evaluations seek to determine the degree to which stated goals are being achieved. Goal-free evaluations look more broadly at what is taking place as a result of an initiative with the aim of determining a range of consequences of the initiative—including unintended consequences.

• **Qualitative or quantitative.** Qualitative methods are well-suited to describing complex classroom situations and interactions. Quantitative methods provide numerical answers to questions and may result in more precise but less explanatory insights.

• **Episodic or continuous.** Will evaluation take place only occasionally at specified times (episodic), or will it be seen as an ongoing endeavor designed to provide a steady stream of feedback to inform the change process (continuous)? The latter seems preferable both from the standpoint of the teacher and for purposes of ensuring positive change.

• **Internal or external.** Internal evaluations are conducted by school personnel; external ones by outside consultants. Internal evaluators are familiar with school culture and personnel, are easily accessible, and tend to be low-cost evaluators. External evaluators can bring an element of objectivity and credibility that is sometimes more difficult to achieve with internal evaluators. It may be that internal evaluators are particularly appropriate for formative evaluations, and external evaluators for more high-stakes, summative evaluations. Sarason (1996) suggests that external feedback may be more likely to determine student growth, whereas internal feedback may be more attuned to teacher comfort.

Key Principles of Evaluation

Whatever decisions are made about purposes and kinds of evaluations, the evaluations are more likely to be sound if they adhere to some key principles of effective evaluation (Duke, 2004; Schlechty, 1997):

• Evaluations should be carefully planned around clear purposes. Among evaluation questions that might be asked are (1) Who is participating in what professional development experiences? (2) What is happening to the content they learned in the professional development experiences? (3) Are participants studying the effects of implementation on students? (4) What do people involved in the initiative think about their experiences (Joyce & Showers, 2002)? Clear evaluation purposes will result in the selection of methods more likely to elicit desired information than ill-focused evaluation will. It is also ethically important for those who will be affected by evaluation data to understand why evaluation is taking place and how it might affect them. It also benefits evaluation results if those who are evaluated have input into how, when, and under what circumstances evaluations will be conducted and into how evaluation information will be used.

• Evaluation data should include relevant baseline information. In understanding whether change is occurring as a result of a change initiative, it is very important to have clear data on what practices were like before the change process began.

• Evaluation data should be collected from multiple sources. Individuals' and groups' responses to a change may vary, and teachers may implement its components differently in their classrooms. Parents, teachers, and students may experience a change quite differently. Students who struggle in school may have different experiences with a change than do students who perform well academically. Focus group discussions may yield different insights than individually completed questionnaires. Confidence in evaluation findings is highly dependent on gathering information from several data sources.

• Evaluation plans should provide for collecting varied types of data. Observations, interviews, questionnaires (open ended or closed response), document reviews, test scores, disciplinary data, attendance records, and many other data sources can provide useful and varied perspectives on impacts of a change initiative.

Uses of Evaluation

It is more likely that evaluation data will serve a positive purpose if leaders plan for use of the data prior to collecting it. For example, formative evaluation is of little use unless data derived from it inform planning for subsequent professional development, become a means of furthering conversations among grade-level or department teams, or help a leader determine how to make more targeted classroom observations. Even positive summative information loses its punch unless it is shared appropriately with varied stakeholders in a way that addresses their interests, concerns, and responsibilities (Schlechty, 1997). It is also critical that leaders ensure that use of evaluation data occurs at times and in ways that are likely to be productive for rather than destructive to individuals and the change process.

Monitoring and Evaluation to Support Growth Toward Differentiation

Monitoring and evaluating growth in differentiation and its results at the school level provide an important opportunity for leaders to model what they ask teachers to do in differentiated classrooms. That is, their charge is to set clear learning goals that focus on understanding and application, work persistently toward the goals, and consistently and selflessly examine formative and summative data to see what's working and what's not—and to adjust as necessary to ensure success.

Change toward more academically responsive instruction is demanding of teachers and simply cannot occur smoothly and seamlessly throughout a school. It is critical for leaders to seek out and celebrate successes, but it is equally important to be on the hunt for misunderstandings and misapplications. Systematic monitoring and evaluation are key in both.

Synthesizing the principles of evaluation and the goals of change toward defensibly differentiated classrooms, leaders for such change should do the following:

• **Carefully articulate the goals of second-order change toward schoolwide differentiation.** Know and make known the nonnegotiables of defensible differentiation. In addition to informing staff development, these essentials should be the focus of evaluation. Although it is not feasible that all of the goals will be achieved quickly, painlessly, or simultaneously, they are and should remain the targets of change. A school is more likely to achieve the desired outcomes if leaders and faculty members monitor how effectively staff development supports teacher application of the goals, the degree and fidelity of teacher implementation of the goals in the classroom, and the effects of implementation on students and teachers. Planning backward (Wiggins & McTighe, 2007) from the outset of a change initiative provides for alignment of essential goals, efforts to achieve the goals, and evidence of the degree to which goals are being achieved. Figure 5.1 is a sample classroom observation form that articulates a set of goals for effective differentiation. It was used as a summative evaluation instrument three years into a district change initiative toward differentiated instruction. No one should expect teachers to attain competence in most or all areas in the short term. Nonetheless, early delineation of long-term expectations such as the ones specified in the form provides a compass for staff development, formative monitoring of growth, and summative evaluation.

• **Collect baseline data on students and faculty.** Because the goal of a second-order change initiative toward differentiation is positive change for students, it is important to have a clear sense of where students are at the outset of the initiative. Certainly baseline test scores are one useful indicator. Baseline scores that are disaggregated by category (e.g., low economic, ethnic group, low achievers/special education, English language learners, students identified as gifted) will enable monitoring of growth by category over time. Test scores, however, cannot and should not tell the whole story of change (Sergiovanni, 1999). Leaders should think carefully about other indicators of success (or lack thereof)—for example, rate of discipline referrals, attendance rate, patterns in students dropping out of school, student engagement in class, student satisfaction—and should collect baseline data in those areas as well. Further, it is important to collect baseline data on faculty and to what degree their classrooms show key indicators of differentiation (e.g., teacher connections with students; learning environments that are both safe and challenging; a sense of classroom community; clear curriculum goals; ongoing assessment to inform instruction; attention to variance in student readiness, interests, and learning profiles; shared teacher/student responsibility for effective classroom operation; flexible use of classroom elements to support learner needs; effective classroom management to support attention to varied learner

Figure 5.1

Classroom Observation Form for Summative Assessment of Differentiated Instruction

School: _____   Grade: _____   Subject: _____   Period/Time: _____

Teacher: _____   Date: ____/____/____   Observer: _____

I. Context/Goal Setting	Strong	Some	None
1. Established clear **learning goals** (knowledge, understanding, skills).			
2. Linked new subject matter to **prior learning** and/or **experience**.			
3. Most students appeared aware of and **understood** the learning goals.			
4. Provided **rubrics or other guides** to focus students on goals.			
5. **Closed the class** with a focus on goals/meaning of lesson.			

Comments:

II. Student Assessment	Strong	Some	None
1. Implemented and used results of **pre-assessment** to adjust the lesson.			
2. Implemented assessment **during lesson** to gauge understanding.			
3. Attended to **student questions/comments** during lesson.			
4. Implemented assessment at **end of lesson** to gauge student learning.			

Comments:

III. Attention to Individuals/Building Community	Strong	Some	None
1. **Talked** with students as they entered/exited class.			
2. Connected with **individual students** during class.			
3. Helped develop awareness of one another's **strengths/contributions**.			
4. Involved whole class in **sharing/planning/evaluating**.			

Comments:

Figure 5.1—*(continued)*

Classroom Observation Form for Summative Assessment of Differentiated Instruction

IV. Instructional Practices and Classroom Routines	Strong	Some	None
1. Varied **student groupings**: individual, pairs, small groups.			
2. Used **multiple modes of instruction**, with emphasis on active learning.			
3. Made **flexible use** of classroom space, time, and materials.			
4. Communicated **clear directions** for multiple tasks.			
5. Provided effective **rules/routines** that supported individual needs.			
6. Displayed effective classroom **leadership/management**.			

Comments:

V. Positive, Supportive Learning Environment	Strong	Some	None
1. Demonstrated **respectful behavior** toward students.			
2. Demonstrated **sensitivity** to different cultures/ethnicities.			
3. Acknowledged/celebrated student **strengths/successes**.			
4. Fostered active participation by a **broad range** of students.			
5. Made students **comfortable** asking questions/requesting assistance.			
6. Emphasis on **competition against self**, not other students.			

Comments:

VI. Quality Curriculum	Strong	Some	None
1. Lesson targeted one or more state **learning standards**.			
2. Lesson focused on **important ideas**, issues, or problems.			
3. Tasks emphasized **thought/meaning versus drill and practice**.			

Comments:

Figure 5.1—(*continued*)

Classroom Observation Form for Summative Assessment of Differentiated Instruction

VII. Preparation for and Response to Learner Needs	Strong	Some	None
1. Showed **proactive preparation** for a variety of student needs.			
2. Attended appropriately to students who **struggle with learning** (LD, ELL, reading, etc.).			
3. Attended appropriately to students with **physical/behavioral challenges**.			
4. Attended appropriately to **advanced** students.			

Comments:

VIII. Evidence of Differentiation	Strong	Some	None
1. **Content:** e.g., materials of varied readability and/or interest, multiple ways to access ideas/information.			
2. **Process:** e.g., tiering, contracts, compacting, readiness-based small-group instruction, different homework, choices about how to work (alone, pair, small group), tasks in multiple modes, variety of scaffolding.			
3. **Products:** e.g., product assignments with multiple modes of expression, with choices about how to work (alone, pairs, small groups), opportunity to connect learning with individual interests, variety of assessment tasks, variety of scaffolding.			

Comments (example of differentiation based on readiness, interest, and learning profile):

1a. Did the lesson meet the needs of learners at **all achievement levels**? (✓ one only)

☐ (1) Yes   ☐ (2) No

1b. If no, toward what **type/s of student** did the lesson seem geared? (✓ all that apply)

☐ (1) Below basic   ☐ (2) Basic   ☐ (3) Proficient   ☐ (4) Advanced

Examples:

Source: This instrument was created with Carol Tomlinson by Strategic Research Associates. Used with permission.

needs). Classroom walkthroughs (Downey et al., 2004) can provide one source of schoolwide baseline data on such elements. (They are not, however, intended to diagnose or track the performance of individual teachers and should not be used for that purpose). Figure 5.2 provides an example of a walkthrough format useful in determining schoolwide baseline patterns related to key elements of differentiation. Figure 5.3 shows a streamlined version of the format used by school leaders to pre-assess schoolwide practices related to two principles of differentiation, allowing observers to focus their attention more specifically. Note that it is not necessary to observe for all categories and that the absence of an objective does not suggest a negative lesson.

In addition, it may be useful to gather baseline data regarding teacher attitudes about elements of differentiation and about their sense of how their classroom practice aligns with goals of differentiation. Figure 5.4 provides one illustration of a form designed to gather such baseline information. (It's useful to know that teachers may feel like their practice is more nearly aligned with the principles and practices of differentiation at the outset of an initiative than after they come to understand what differentiation "looks like." For that reason, using a similar format to assess teacher beliefs and practices partway through a change initiative may provide results that look like backward movement. Probing teacher responses may reveal that teachers are beginning to understand differentiation in a much more realistic way than was the case earlier.)

• **Use multiple data sources and multiple types of data.** It's important, of course, to collect monitoring and evaluation data that provide information about how movement toward differentiation affects students. It's also important to understand the effects on teachers, how parents understand and experience the changes, and perhaps how other stakeholders understand the approach as well. Thus it will be necessary to collect data from all those sources at varied and repeated times. In addition, however, data gathered from students, teachers, parents, and classroom observations can serve as useful triangulation for one another, clarifying patterns and raising concerns. Well-designed surveys—both limited response and open response—can be useful, but so can report cards, attendance records, classroom observations, parent communications, teacher reflections, individual and focus group interviews, and a host of other sources of insight. The analogy of collecting photo albums versus single snapshots of growth over time (Wiggins & McTighe, 1998) is apt.

• **Use diagnostic, formative, and summative information to direct planning for staff development, to guide focus of resources, and to chart growth.** Even a great plan to increase the knowledge, understanding, and skill of learners and to provide for transfer and application of new content is diminished if it doesn't match the needs of the people who are supposed to learn and use the new things (Tomlinson & McTighe, 2006). Simply put, it's important to pre-assess to understand where teachers are as the initiative and its various components begin in order to tailor plans for individual teacher needs. It's

---

Figure 5.2

Example of Walkthrough Checklist to Assess Schoolwide Differentiation Patterns

Teacher: _____   Grade level: _____

Subject: _____   School: _____

Respectful Classroom Environment	+/-	Ongoing Assessment and Use of Assessment	+/-	Powerful Curriculum	+/-
Teacher calls on students equitably. Teacher interacts respectfully with all students. Routines and rituals are in place to assist each learner in feeling a sense of belonging and value in the class. Teacher helps students appreciate and affirm both their similarities and differences in learning, culture, background, and interest. Varied viewpoints on knowledge and classroom issues are sought and honored.		Teacher makes continual efforts to know and understand each student as an individual learner. Assessments contribute to teacher knowledge about readiness, interest, and modes of learning. Teacher consistently adapts instruction based on findings from both formal and informal assessment. Teacher develops assessment options to ensure that each student has an opportunity to show what he knows, understands, and can do related to a topic. Assessment includes the expectation that students will think about and use the knowledge, understanding, and skill.		Curriculum is based on key concepts, principles, and skills to help students understand the purpose of the discipline. All students work with rich and important ideas and essential skills at levels of difficulty that are appropriately challenging for individuals. Activities, discussions, materials, and products call on students to think at high levels and to grapple successfully with complex problems, ideas, issues, and/or skills. Teacher is passionate about content. Teacher teaches for success.	

Figure 5.2—(*continued*)

Example of Walkthrough Checklist to Assess Schoolwide Differentiation Patterns

Teacher: _____   Grade level: _____

Subject: _____   School: _____

Interest and Engagement of All Learners	+/-	Wide Range of Approaches	+/-	Clear Articulation of Criteria for High Quality	+/-
Teacher helps students to make connections between their lives and what they are learning. There are a variety of materials that deal with key ideas and skills and reflect a broad range of cultures and interest. Students have choices about how to express their learning. Curriculum and instruction infuse technology to deepen understanding. Students show persistence when confronted with problems and difficult tasks.		Teacher helps students recall what they know, understand, and can do and build on that knowledge, understanding, and skill. Teacher uses student interests, experience, and concerns to develop course, content, questions, tasks, and products. Students approach content, activities, and products in different ways while focusing on essential concepts, principles, and skills of the lesson. Teacher uses whole to part and part to whole to help learners understand how each learning experience relates to larger goals of the unit and year. Teacher uses both whole-group and small-group instruction to ensure that students understand ideas and skills at appropriate levels of challenge and support. Teacher adjusts question complexity and provides scaffolding to ensure successful participation and success. Directions are given to students in a variety of ways so that each learner has access to and understands goals for the activity or product. Teacher coaches for individual growth and success.		Tasks and products call on students to produce at high levels of quality. Teacher clearly communicates goals and purposes of the lesson. Teacher helps students effectively self-assess and reflect on goals as learners. Teacher consistently helps students build skills of independence as learners. Teacher encourages students to work for quality and provides support and guidance for doing so.	

Source: Virginia Beach City Public Schools, Virginia. Reprinted with permission.

important to use ongoing formative assessment to understand the growth of and roadblocks for individual teachers as the initiative continues in order to create professional development opportunities and interactions that maximize the growth of each individual teacher. It's important to use summative assessment at critical points during the initiative in order to assess the degree to which the initiative is working for teachers and for students and to know how to redirect efforts ahead (Tomlinson, 1999, 2003; Tomlinson & McTighe, 2006). Lorna Earl (2003) reminds us that if we have clear learning goals and we continually work to see who is and is not attaining (and surpassing) those goals, then differentiation is no longer an option. It's just a logical response to what we clearly see. That is as true in supporting teacher growth as in supporting student growth. In fact, in the instance of second-order school change, there should be a direct link between teacher outcomes and student benefits.

• **Use product- and process-focused evaluation.** It's important to know outcomes or products that result from a differentiation initiative (e.g., *what* is changing for teachers and for students). Product data can answer questions such as "Which teachers are generating lesson plans that accurately incorporate differentiation strategies we've practiced in earlier staff development sessions?" "How many classrooms demonstrate consistent and appropriate use of flexible grouping?" and "Which groups of students are meeting and surpassing grade-level science goals?" To understand the outcomes (or lack of them) and to plan more effectively to reach stated goals, it will likely be necessary to study *how* things are working (or not) for students and teachers along the way. Process data can answer questions such as "How did teachers understand the key ideas in today's staff development session?" "How are teacher planning teams assisting in implementation of differentiation?" "To what degree do teachers feel supported in their work to differentiate instruction?" and "How are students feeling about differentiated assignments?"

• **Use goal-based and goal-free evaluation data.** It is important to continue to examine growth and change in terms of the non-negotiables of differentiation. For that purpose, both formative and summative assessment should be goal based. On the other hand, it's virtually always useful in settings rife with human complexity to ask, "What else is going on here?" Casting keen eyes in search of the unexpected can help leaders spot misunderstandings, develop new insights, and discover better ways of solving problems. For that reason, searching beyond goal-based questions is advisable.

Figure 5.3

Modified Version of Walkthrough Form Focused on Two Principles of Differentiation

Room: _____   Grade level: _____

Time: _____   Subject: _____

Powerful Curriculum	+	–	Comments
Curriculum is based on key concepts, principles, and skills to help students understand the purpose of the discipline. All students work with rich and important ideas and essential skills at levels of difficulty that are appropriately challenging for individuals. Activities, discussions, materials, and products call on students to think at high levels and to grapple successfully with complex problems, ideas, issues, and/or skills. Teacher is passionate about content. Teacher teaches for success.			

Interest and Engagement of All Learners	+	–	
Teacher helps students to make connections between their lives and what they are learning. There are a variety of materials that deal with key ideas and skills and reflect a broad range of cultures and interest. Students have choices about how to express their learning. Curriculum and instruction infuse technology to deepen understanding. Students show persistence when confronted with problems and difficult tasks. Student-centered instruction • Student to teacher interaction • Student to student interaction			

Figure 5.4

Teacher Questionnaire to Gain Baseline Data on Differentiation Practices

Reflecting on Practices for Differentiating Instruction in Response to Learner Need

Read each statement below. Circle the response that most closely describes the extent to which you use this practice in your classroom. Use the following scale:

(1) never/almost never　　(2) occasionally　　(3) much of the time
(4) very frequently, consistently　　(5) unsure of terms/meaning

	1	2	3	4	5
1. I pre-assess students to plan for their individual needs.	1	2	3	4	5
2. I identify student interests to assist in planning.	1	2	3	4	5
3. I identify students' learning profiles to help with planning.	1	2	3	4	5
4. My classroom is student centered.	1	2	3	4	5
5. I pre-assess for student readiness to help with planning.	1	2	3	4	5
6. I vary the pace of learning for varied learner needs.	1	2	3	4	5
7. I use ongoing assessment for instructional planning.	1	2	3	4	5
8. I differentiate based on understandings/big ideas.	1	2	3	4	5
9. I use a variety of materials other than the text.	1	2	3	4	5
10. I make accommodations for the needs of various learners by scaffolding (e.g., reading buddies, graphic organizers, study guides, New American Lecture).	1	2	3	4	5
11. I provide tasks that require students to do something with their knowledge (apply and extend key understandings and skills as opposed to largely repeating information).	1	2	3	4	5
12. I use high-level tasks for all learners (e.g., application, elaboration, providing evidence, synthesis, examining varied perspectives).	1	2	3	4	5
13. I plan and use flexible grouping.	1	2	3	4	5
14. I ensure that all students participate in respectful tasks.	1	2	3	4	5
15. I vary tasks by students' interests.	1	2	3	4	5
16. I vary tasks by learner profile.	1	2	3	4	5
17. I ensure that all tasks and products focus on clearly stated learning goals (KUDs) known by the students.	1	2	3	4	5
18. I allow for a wide range of product alternatives (e.g., oral, kinesthetic, visual, musical, spatial, creative, practical, analytical).	1	2	3	4	5

Figure 5.4—(*continued*)

Teacher Questionnaire to Gain Baseline Data on Differentiation Practices

Reflecting on Practices for Differentiating Instruction in Response to Learner Need

Read each statement below. Circle the response that most closely describes the extent to which you use this practice in your classroom. Use the following scale:

(1) never/almost never   (2) occasionally   (3) much of the time
(4) very frequently, consistently   (5) unsure of terms/meaning

19. The assignments I give differ based on individual (or small-group) readiness, learning needs, and interest.	1	2	3	4	5
20. I meet with students in small groups for instruction.	1	2	3	4	5
21. I use tiering.	1	2	3	4	5
22. I use compacting or other forms of acceleration.	1	2	3	4	5
23. I use student learning contracts to differentiate.	1	2	3	4	5
24. I encourage and support independent study.	1	2	3	4	5
25. I use interest centers/groups to differentiate.	1	2	3	4	5
26. I use RAFTs to differentiate.	1	2	3	4	5
27. I work with students to develop reading proficiency.	1	2	3	4	5
28. I work with students to become proficient in working in small groups.	1	2	3	4	5
29. I use technology as a tool for differentiation.	1	2	3	4	5
30. I provide student choice within defined parameters.	1	2	3	4	5
31. I use Sternberg Intelligences to address learning needs.	1	2	3	4	5
32. I plan for more than one way for students to achieve key learning goals.	1	2	3	4	5
33. I talk with my students about the need for different ways to achieve key learning goals.	1	2	3	4	5
34. I use anchor activities to extend student learning and assist with classroom management.	1	2	3	4	5
35. I use other strategies to address learning needs.	1	2	3	4	5

List:

Source: From *Leadership for Differentiating Schools and Classrooms* (pp. 144–145), by C. A. Tomlinson and S. D. Allan, 2000, Alexandria, VA: Association for Supervision and Curriculum Development. Adapted with permission.

• **Use qualitative and quantitative methods.** Numbers answer some questions about differentiation effectively: "How many students are working above grade level in math three years into a differentiation change initiative compared to the number above grade level at the outset?" "How many more students are taking advanced-level classes than the number five years ago?" "How many teachers are regularly differentiating instruction based on readiness, on interest, and on learning profile as evidenced by classroom observation?" On the other hand, some questions about differentiation will require more narrative answers: "Why is it difficult for some teachers who willingly differentiate based on students' learning profiles to differentiate based on student readiness?" "How do teachers understand and implement the concept of alignment between learning goals, tasks, and assessments?" "In what ways are our teachers using assessment to inform instruction?" "What impacts of differentiation do parents perceive at home?" To understand change toward differentiation as fully as possible, number-based (quantitative) and narrative-based (qualitative) methods can each play important roles.

• **Use continuous rather than episodic monitoring and evaluation.** Although summative evaluation is necessarily episodic, diagnostic and formative monitoring should be continuous. In the classroom, everything students do is a source of insight and can be used by observant and reflective teachers to sharpen instruction. At the school level, observant and reflective leaders use continuous assessment to sharpen plans and processes designed to support positive change. Such assessments may be formal (e.g., surveys, questionnaires, exit cards from professional development sessions, walk-throughs, planned classroom observations, lesson plans) or informal (e.g., conversations, informal classroom observations, listening to teacher work groups, chatting with students in the cafeteria).

• **Use both internal and external evaluation.** Leaders for differentiation learn to be more effective leaders by studying what transpires in their schools (and beyond) as the change transpires. Further, they are best equipped to know such things as the culture of the school, growth patterns in individual teachers, and community norms. In addition, it is internal leaders who will need to learn from formative assessment in order to shape plans for maximum impact. Thus principals, staff developers, and teacher leaders must be active and persistent assessors and evaluators. From time to time, however, the credibility and viability of a change effort are enhanced by experts who can take a fresh and informed look at what is taking place. External evaluators of differentiation initiatives should have strong backgrounds in evaluation, differentiation, and classroom teaching in order to ensure validity of process and findings.

• **Use evaluation findings to inform and support the change process.** Leaders should plan for proactive use of diagnostic, formative, and summative evaluation findings to enhance the change process and its outcomes for students, faculty, and the school as a whole. In many ways, solid monitoring and evaluation data recraft conventional wisdom about change and differentiation to be a manual for success tailored for a particular school setting. Such findings should add considerably to the understanding of a wide range of stakeholders about the what, how, and why of change for more academically responsive instruction. How and under what circumstances insights are shared with various stakeholder groups will vary with group needs and responsibilities. Nonetheless, good information effectively shared can build mutual understanding and shared partnerships.

Monitoring and Evaluating Change in Two Schools Learning to Differentiate

Principals at both Conway and Colchester planned for monitoring and evaluating the change process from the earliest days of the differentiation initiatives. In both settings, evaluation data were abundant and were used to inform the thinking and planning of building administrators, staff developers, and teachers. Even though evaluation questions and processes varied between the two sites, it is evident in both schools that the principals invested heavily in understanding the change process they initiated and in using what they learned to lead more effectively. In addition, they shared evaluation findings to plan, help others deepen their understanding of the change process and differentiation, help build a professional community of learners, communicate with the community, and garner resources for their work.

Monitoring and Evaluating Growth Toward Differentiation at Conway

Evaluation at Conway throughout the differentiation initiative was carefully planned around clear evaluation purposes, which included determining the following:

• The efficacy of staff development in shaping differentiated classroom instruction.

• The degree of implementation of differentiation in all Conway classrooms and of fidelity to the differentiated instruction model.

• The ways in which implementing differentiation affected students and teachers.

Further, evaluation at Conway was

• Diagnostic, formative, and summative—that is, leaders collected and used data to determine teacher needs before starting the initiative (diagnostic), throughout the initiative to assist in planning (formative), and at key benchmark points during the initiative to examine effectiveness in reaching goals (summative).

• Process focused and product focused—that is, leaders looked at the effects of the differentiation initiative on teachers and students (product focused) and at ways in which staff development and classroom translation were occurring (process focused).

• Goal based, but seeking additional insights—that is, leaders continued to collect data to determine the degree to which goals of the initiative and of differentiation were being appropriately addressed (goal based). They also, however, continued to pose questions and examine data that led to discovering positive and negative unintended consequences of the initiative.

• Qualitative and quantitative—that is, leaders gathered and used number-based and narrative-based data.

• Continuous—that is, evaluation occurred on an ongoing basis rather than only once or twice a year.

• Largely internal—that is, most of the data gathering and analysis was done by the principal, staff developer, and members of the Conway faculty. Some external evaluation occurred as outside experts visited the school to observe differentiation at Conway and to talk with teachers, students, and parents and as educators from many other schools and districts visited Conway to observe differentiation in action and to discuss what they saw.

Through five years of systematic classroom evaluation at Conway before the differentiation initiative began, Narvaez carefully observed and documented teacher practice, noting areas in which the faculty as a whole and as individuals were attending effectively to students' learning differences and areas that required more responsive teaching that considered student needs. Her observations indicated that the needs of students with special education identification were often addressed by classroom teachers teaming with specialists but that was not the case for students at the high end of achievement, who received services outside the regular classroom. Further, although teachers demonstrated some comfort with modifying instruction based on one particular learning style theory, they were less proficient with addressing students' readiness and interests and were limiting learning profile instruction to a single model.

In addition, Narvaez carefully examined student achievement data before beginning the change process toward differentiation. These test data provided an important baseline for comparing student achievement at key points in the change process. Ultimately, the data indicated positive achievement gains for the spectrum of Conway students as differentiation became standard practice and not just for the high-end students who were a concern at the start. Narvaez consistently shared student standardized test data and discussed them with faculty as a means of monitoring student achievement throughout the change process.

Narvaez continued to use multiple sources of data—quantitative and qualitative—as well as process- and product-focused evaluation. Students, teachers, and parents were regular data sources. Ongoing (not episodic) surveys of all three groups provided consistent feedback to inform the planning process, as did data from systematic classroom observations and from coaching sessions. Data from these sources helped leaders understand how the processes of change (such as staff development, grade-level planning, coaching, and so on) were working and what the effects (products) of change were.

Clearly, diagnostic and formative evaluation tools and methods such as those discussed in Chapter 4 were an integral part of professional development at Conway. Narvaez and Brimijoin also regularly used surveys to help them focus on goals for the change process in general and specific facets of the process in particular. Both Narvaez and Brimijoin also analyzed survey responses with an eye to uncovering unexpected patterns.

Figure 5.5 provides an example of a survey in which students from three grade levels were asked to provide feedback on a differentiated lesson. Principal and staff developer analysis of student responses across classrooms helped shape staff development plans. Analysis of responses for particular classrooms helped Narvaez and Brimijoin with coaching plans and goals and also helped individual teachers have a sense of how their students were understanding and responding to differentiation. The surveys used qualitative and quantitative information, and the faculty analysis of student responses was thoughtful. Teachers used the data to plan individually and for the faculty as a whole. Brimijoin and Narvaez used what they learned to think about next steps even as they initially examined the student responses.

Likewise, Figure 5.6 presents a faculty survey given at the end of Conway's third year of the change process to help faculty reflect on their work with differentiation. Appendix E (see p. 215) presents similar questions used in a teacher survey at Conway. The principal and staff developer analyzed teachers' responses to these goal-based questions to help them understand teacher perspectives more broadly and to plan accordingly.

Throughout the change process at Conway, monitoring and evaluating products and processes were inseparable from decision making. The two leaders provided for and used a steady stream of information from students, teachers, and parents to inform planning, coaching, and whole-group professional development—the latter two then informing subsequent monitoring and evaluation. Student achievement data were consistently examined on a school and grade-level basis. Student perceptions of their experiences with differentiation were frequently monitored at the classroom and grade level. Teachers' readiness for and response to whole-group professional development were monitored as a part of each planning and presentation cycle. Classroom observations were interwoven with coaching. Regular parent meetings and written communication to parents about differentiation encouraged and resulted in parent feedback on differentiation—as did the heavy involvement of parents as volunteers in the school. The two leaders meticulously processed and analyzed data from all sources individually and jointly. They then not only used what they learned to make decisions about next steps in professional development and allocation of resources but also shared insights with teachers and guided them in classroom decision making based on the data.

Figure 5.5

Student Survey to Gain Feedback on Differentiated Instruction at Conway

Student Survey, Grades 3 to 5

Name: _____   Teacher: _____

Grade: _____   Subject: _____   Topic: _____

1. If you had to explain to someone in another class what this lesson was about, what would you say?

2. I am still confused about this after the lesson:

3. I think my confusion is because:

4. I think the best part of this lesson was:

5. I thought that part was best because:

6. The part of this lesson I liked least was:

7. I liked that part the least because:

8. Check one:

   ☐ I worked the whole time (working includes talking with classmates about the assignment and completing the lesson parts. It does not include general conversation off the lesson topic). Please explain why:

   ☐ I got sidetracked. Please explain why:

Figure 5.5—(*continued*)
Student Survey to Gain Feedback on Differentiated Instruction at Conway

9. I think this lesson was:

☐ Too hard even with help.

☐ Hard, but with help I got it.

☐ Hard, but I figured it out on my own.

☐ Easy. I finished early and needed something else to do.

10. Think about what everyone was doing during the lesson. Check what you think happened:

_____ Everyone in the class was doing exactly what I was doing.
If you checked this, please tell why you think so:

_____ Some kids in my class were doing something different than I was.
If you checked this, please check one of the following:

_____ It was all right for others to do something different.
Please explain why:

_____ It bothered me that others were doing something different.
Please explain why:

11. Think about other lessons during this school year and read the list of possible reasons why you stay focused on your work. Then number the reasons that you choose from 1 up to 5, with 1 being the most important.

_____ I was able to make a choice about something I worked on.

_____ I was asked to do my work in a way that is comfortable for me because it was in my learning style.

_____ I felt comfortable with my working arrangement (circle one: on my own, with a partner, in a small group)

_____ I had a good idea of what was expected of me.

_____ I thought the work was just right for me—hard, but not too hard.

Thank you for your help!!

Figure 5.6

Faculty Survey on Results of Differentiation at Conway

Please be as specific as possible with each answer, giving both explanations and illustrations/stories for your responses.

Part I: The Students

How do you think Conway's students have grown as a result of your professional development in differentiation? Please refer to specific struggling, grade-level, and advanced students as you explain.

Have any strategies for differentiation improved student achievement in your classroom? If so, how?

Do you see any relationship between differentiation and student engagement in your classroom? If so, please describe.

Do you see any relationship between differentiation and management problems in your classroom? If so, please describe.

When you differentiate lessons, are students grasping concepts better than when you don't differentiate? Please explain.

Part II: The Teacher

Please list the pros and cons of your work with differentiation from a professional and personal perspective.

Please list the following:

Your greatest areas of confidence with differentiation.

Your greatest areas of uncertainty with differentiation.

Describe as specifically as possible how your understanding of differentiation has changed over time.

How do you feel parents and students perceive differentiation as it is now happening?

Do you believe parent and student opinions about differentiation have evolved over time? If so, what do you think might have influenced that evolution?

Outline a wish list for next steps in staff development or other support for your growth in differentiation.

3rd, 4th, and 5th Grade Teachers

We have been implementing differentiation for three years. Have you noticed any difference regarding students this year in terms of their approach to learning experiences, their motivation, or their expectations for instruction? If so, please explain.

Monitoring and Evaluating Growth
Toward Differentiation at Colchester

As at Conway, the change process at Colchester High was consistently informed by a thoughtful and reflective process of monitoring and evaluating all facets of the school's evolution toward effective and pervasive differentiation. Colchester's evaluation purposes included determining the following:

• The status of Colchester faculty as a developing professional community of learners.
• The efficacy of staff development in shaping a faculty community of learners and differentiated classroom instruction.
• The degree of implementation of differentiation in Colchester classrooms and of fidelity to the differentiated instruction model.
• The ways in which implementing differentiation affected students and teachers.

Evaluation at Colchester also had the following characteristics:

• Diagnostic, formative, and summative—that is, leaders collected and used data to determine teacher needs before the initiative (diagnostic), throughout the initiative to assist in planning (formative), and at key benchmark points during the initiative to examine effectiveness in reaching goals (summative).
• Process focused and product focused—that is, leaders looked at the differentiation initiative's effects on teachers and students (product focused) and at ways in which staff development, professional growth, and classroom translation were occurring (process focus).
• Goal based, but seeking additional insights—that is, leaders continued to collect data to determine the degree to which goals of the initiative and of differentiation were being appropriately addressed (goal based). They also continued to pose questions and examine data that led to discovering positive and negative unintended consequences of the initiative.
• Qualitative and quantitative—that is, leaders gathered and used number-based and narrative-based data.
• Continuous—that is, evaluation occurred on an ongoing basis rather than only once or twice a year.
• Both internal and external—that is, data were gathered, analyzed, and used by the principal, teacher liaison, and Leadership Team to

inform decision making and allocation of resources (internal), and data were also gathered by three outside experts who conducted extensive research on the change process at Colchester over a two-year period (external).

Because of her tenure as assistant principal at Colchester before becoming principal, Stone was well acquainted with baseline data from the school related to student achievement, disciplinary referrals, the dropout rate, and the relationship between economic status and course enrollment. These data not only served as a baseline for analysis of comparable data in all other years of the change process at Colchester, but in fact served as a major impetus for undertaking the change in the first place. In other words, the decision to lead the school toward implementation of effective differentiation was motivated by a data-based need. At the outset of the change initiative, Stone shared the data, which indicated many problems and economic-based disparities, with faculty as a call to action. Throughout the change process, she provided the faculty with annual data updates in a presentation that came to be known as "Ourstory" (see discussion in Chapter 7), guiding the faculty in analyzing the effects of the change process on student achievement, attendance, disciplinary referrals, the dropout rate, and course selection.

Some monitoring and evaluation strategies used at Colchester (such as pre-assessments and exit cards) were discussed in Chapter 4. Appendix F (see p. 217) provides another example of an exit card used by the Colchester teacher liaison and Professional Development Committee to monitor the professional development process and its results as well as to inform subsequent planning.

Similar monitoring processes were a regular feature at Colchester for all facets of the change process and related professional development. Figure 5.7 is a survey designed to monitor the readiness and interest of faculty to move differentiation forward into the Blue House (11th and 12th grades). Rich shared their responses with the principal and with the Professional Development Committee as a means of charting a course to support necessary change.

As teachers grew accustomed to using pre-assessment and ongoing assessment to reflect their readiness levels, interests, and learning preferences, and as they studied the value of assessment as a means of informing instruction, they began to employ assessment-for-learning tools in their own classes. These approaches helped teachers monitor student understanding of differentiation and its effects and guided

---

Figure 5.7

Teacher Survey on Readiness for and Interest in Next Steps in Colchester's Change Process

---

The purpose of this assessment is to gather data that will make upcoming professional development opportunities meaningful and helpful to all of us as we head toward implementing our Blue House vision. Throughout the assessment you'll be asked to rate your readiness and your interest in the topics mentioned. Each of these is on a scale of 1 to 3. In the right-hand column is a place for a brief comment or question, if you have either. It looks like this:

Comment

Readiness: 1   No previous knowledge   2   Some previous knowledge   3   I know this well

Interest: 1   Little to no interest   2   Mildly interested   3   Highly interested

---

Why Should I Differentiate Instruction?

Cognitive Research and Learning Theory

• How People Learn

Comment

Readiness: 1   No previous knowledge   2   Some previous knowledge   3   I know this well

Interest: 1   Little to no interest in learning more   2   Mild interest in learning more   3   Highly interested in learning more

• Vygotsky's Zone of Proximal Development

Comment

Readiness: 1   No previous knowledge   2   Some previous knowledge   3   I know this well

Interest: 1   Little to no interest in learning more   2   Mild interest in learning more   3   Highly interested in learning more

• Constructivism

Comment

Readiness: 1   No previous knowledge   2   Some previous knowledge   3   I know this well

Interest: 1   Little to no interest in learning more   2   Mild interest in learning more   3   Highly interested in learning more

Figure 5.7—(*continued*)

Teacher Survey on Readiness for and Interest in Next Steps in Colchester's Change Process

• Learning Styles

Comment

Readiness:

1	2	3
No previous knowledge	Some previous knowledge	I know this well

Interest:

1	2	3
Little to no interest in learning more	Mild interest in learning more	Highly interested in learning more

Any other questions/comments?

What Is Differentiated Instruction?

Curriculum

• Erickson: Theory of Knowledge

Comment

Readiness:

1	2	3
No previous knowledge	Some previous knowledge	I know this well

Interest:

1	2	3
Little to no interest in learning more	Mild interest in learning more	Highly interested in learning more

• KUD

Comment

Readiness:

1	2	3
No previous knowledge	Some previous knowledge	I know this well

Interest:

1	2	3
Little to no interest in learning more	Mild interest in learning more	Highly interested in learning more

• Habits of Mind

Comment

Readiness:

1	2	3
No previous knowledge	Some previous knowledge	I know this well

Interest:

1	2	3
Little to no interest in learning more	Mild interest in learning more	Highly interested in learning more

Figure 5.7—(*continued*)

Teacher Survey on Readiness for and Interest in Next Steps in Colchester's Change Process

● Wiggins & McTighe: Backward Design

                                                   Comment

Readiness:	1 No previous knowledge	2 Some previous knowledge	3 I know this well
Interest:	1 Little to no interest in learning more	2 Mild interest in learning more	3 Highly interested in learning more

Any other questions/comments?

Assessment

● Formative Versus Summative Assessment

                                                   Comment

Readiness:	1 No previous knowledge	2 Some previous knowledge	3 I know this well
Interest:	1 Little to no interest in learning more	2 Mild interest in learning more	3 Highly interested in learning more

● Affective Assessment

                                                   Comment

Readiness:	1 No previous knowledge	2 Some previous knowledge	3 I know this well
Interest:	1 Little to no interest in learning more	2 Mild interest in learning more	3 Highly interested in learning more

● Transitions

                                                   Comment

Readiness:	1 No previous knowledge	2 Some previous knowledge	3 I know this well
Interest:	1 Little to no interest in learning more	2 Mild interest in learning more	3 Highly interested in learning more

Figure 5.7—(*continued*)

Teacher Survey on Readiness for and Interest in Next Steps in Colchester's Change Process

- Grading

Comment

Readiness:	1 No previous knowledge	2 Some previous knowledge	3 I know this well
Interest:	1 Little to no interest in learning more	2 Mild interest in learning more	3 Highly interested in learning more

Any other questions/comments?

How Do Teachers Differentiate Instruction?

- Teachers can adjust content, process, and product according to students' readiness, interests, and learner profiles.

Comment

Readiness:	1 No previous knowledge	2 Some previous knowledge	3 I know this well
Interest:	1 Little to no interest in learning more	2 Mild interest in learning more	3 Highly interested in learning more

- Comparing Traditional Classroom to Differentiated Classroom

Comment

Readiness:	1 No previous knowledge	2 Some previous knowledge	3 I know this well
Interest:	1 Little to no interest in learning more	2 Mild interest in learning more	3 Highly interested in learning more

- Collaboration

Comment

Readiness:	1 No previous knowledge	2 Some previous knowledge	3 I know this well
Interest:	1 Little to no interest in learning more	2 Mild interest in learning more	3 Highly interested in learning more

Figure 5.7—(*continued*)

Teacher Survey on Readiness for and Interest in Next Steps in Colchester's Change Process

• Vibrant Learning Community

Comment

Readiness:	1	2	3
	No previous knowledge	Some previous knowledge	I know this well

Interest:	1	2	3
	Little to no interest in learning more	Mild interest in learning more	Highly interested in learning more

• Instructional Strategies

Comment

Readiness:	1	2	3
	No previous knowledge	Some previous knowledge	I know this well

Interest:	1	2	3
	Little to no interest in learning more	Mild interest in learning more	Highly interested in learning more

Any other questions/comments?

How Do You Feel About Differentiating Instruction?

• Overall I believe in the philosophy of differentiated instruction.

   strongly agree   agree   disagree   strongly disagree

• I feel confident that I am growing in my capacity to differentiate instruction.

   strongly agree   agree   disagree   strongly disagree

• Sometimes when I learn about differentiated instruction, I feel bad about my current teaching.

   strongly agree   agree   disagree   strongly disagree

• I feel that I am part of a network of colleagues here at CHS who encourage, inform, and support my efforts to improve my instruction.

   strongly agree   agree   disagree   strongly disagree

Any other questions/comments:

teachers in making instructional adjustments. When student input from such surveys was shared within and across departments, data also informed decision making at a broader level. Figure 5.8 illustrates an example of a survey format used to hear student voices about differentiation. Appendix G (see p. 219) contains two additional examples—one designed to monitor student perceptions of the appropriateness of challenge level in a class and the other to reflect student understanding of differentiation as an approach to teaching and learning. In most instances, when teachers analyzed data from such student surveys, they then conducted discussions with their students about the findings and what they suggested in the way of student and teacher response. These discussions were important in building a sense of student–teacher trust, the idea of shared responsibility for classroom success, and a depth of student understanding about differentiation.

In addition to multiple forms of ongoing internal evaluation data at Colchester, a rich source of external evaluation data stemmed from the principal's invitation to three outside experts to conduct research at the school. Two doctoral students with long public school teaching careers and extensive publication and presentation experience in differentiation gathered data for dissertations at Colchester over a two-year period. In addition, the principal accepted Tomlinson's request to conduct research on the school's change process. The three projects examined teacher and student experiences with differentiation, the evolution of the change process at Colchester, and teacher-developed differentiated product assignments for students. Results of these studies were shared with Colchester leaders, providing them with insights about next steps in the change process. They especially focused on staff development needs and classroom applications of advanced challenge for high-end learners, which were linked closely to formative assessment data, and general linkage of formative assessment data to instructional planning.

Lessons About the Evaluation for Change

Perhaps one of the most evident features of the evolution toward differentiation at Conway and Colchester is the careful and intentional integration of monitoring and evaluation with all aspects of the change process. In both settings, leaders persistently acted on the belief that they had not only an obligation to have clearly defined goals for change but also an equal obligation to know whether the school was moving toward the goals in reasonable ways and at a reasonable pace. They also

Figure 5.8
Survey to Gain Student Perceptions of Differentiated Class

Film as Dramatic Literature

Course Evaluation

After reading each statement, please circle the ONE response (Strongly Agree to Strongly Disagree) that best matches how you feel.

After you circle your response, attend to the following:
 a. Explain why you circled what you circled.
 b. Supply one or two examples that illustrate your explanation.

Accepting for the moment that "all people learn best when they succeed at things that are a bit too hard for them," *Film as Dramatic Literature* **has been appropriately challenging for me.**

   strongly agree   agree   disagree   strongly disagree

a.

b.

It is easier for most people to succeed when they are in a community—even a microcosm of a community—that feels safe, friendly, supportive, respectful, and challenging. *Film as Dramatic Literature* **has been such a community for me.**

   strongly agree   agree   disagree   strongly disagree

a.

b.

Film as Dramatic Literature **has offered content and activities that have interested me.**

   strongly agree   agree   disagree   strongly disagree

a.

b.

Every person is different, so every learner has certain ways s/he learns best. *Film as Dramatic Literature* **has offered activities that are varied enough to appeal to a wide range of learning styles.**

   strongly agree   agree   disagree   strongly disagree

a.

b.

Figure 5.8—(continued)
Survey to Gain Student Perceptions of Differentiated Class

Film as Dramatic Literature has opened me up to things that I might not have come up with on my own.

strongly agree   agree   disagree   strongly disagree

a.

b.

Writing well is very important in today's world. *Film as Dramatic Literature* has advanced my writing skill.

strongly agree   agree   disagree   strongly disagree

a.

b.

Mr. Blanchette has graded me appropriate to my readiness (ability) level.

strongly agree   agree   disagree   strongly disagree

a.

b.

For Honors Students

The challenge level for honors students in *Film as Dramatic Literature* warrants the "honors" designation on my transcript.

strongly agree   agree   disagree   strongly disagree

a.

b.

Please add to the back of this page anything you wish to say that hasn't been covered so far. If you *do* write something on the back, please check the box below.

☐

needed to know how the change process and changes themselves were affecting students, teachers, and parents. To that end, leaders in both schools modeled monitoring (pre-assessment and formative assessment) and evaluating at key points (summative assessment) to inform thinking, planning, and decision making. By staying close to teacher and student experiences during the change process as well as by adhering to the essential principles and practices of differentiation, leaders in both schools reduced the number of unfortunate surprises that inevitably occur in second-order change and maximized the likelihood of progress toward the goals of the change initiatives. To that end, both leaders worked from clear goals for change and evaluation; used multiple data sources and formats; conducted careful qualitative and quantitative data analysis that was goal based and emergent (goal free); used diagnostic, formative, and summative monitoring/evaluation of both process and product; ensured persistent (not episodic) monitoring and evaluation; and both privately and publicly used monitoring and evaluation data for affirmation, regrouping, and celebration. Evaluations at Conway and Colchester were not afterthoughts or add-ons, but rather guided the entire process of change.

6

Snapshots of the Change Process at Conway Elementary School

Seymour Sarason was a professor of mine when I was in graduate school. He was a wonderful educator and he always told us to question assumptions. 'There's an assumption,' he said, 'that schools are for students' learning. Well, why aren't they just as much for teachers' learning?' I've never forgotten that.

–Carol Dweck, *Mindset,* p. 195

The first five chapters of this book focus on key principles of change based on research and practical experience and implications of those principles for second-order change toward defensible schoolwide differentiation in regard to leadership, staff development, and monitoring and evaluating change. The first five chapters have illustrated these underpinnings of change with examples from two very different schools that have navigated the change process toward schoolwide differentiation.

To end the book with a bit more of a big-picture look at the two schools, their staffs, the change process in each school, and the challenges of change, this chapter presents a series of vignettes or snapshots of the journey toward second-order change at Conway Elementary School. Chapter 7 does the same for Colchester High School. In both instances, key school personnel have selected what to include in the snapshots and have provided commentary on why these particular moments help tell the story of change toward differentiation in their particular school and how they might be helpful to others who also seek to lead for more responsive instruction in their schools.

Snapshot 1: An Overview of the Evolution Toward Differentiation at Conway

In 1999, Lane Narvaez, principal of Conway Elementary School in St. Louis, Missouri, took stock of where her students and teachers were in terms of performance. For five years, students had been surpassing state averages on standardized tests across all subject areas. Conway had been recognized for outstanding performance in achievement based on state assessments and norm-referenced testing.

In spite of all the good news, Narvaez saw some trouble spots. She wasn't certain the advanced students at Conway were being challenged adequately in their heterogeneously grouped classrooms. In the preceding few years, Narvaez had also seen more special needs students enroll at Conway and wondered if classroom teachers were meeting their needs effectively in inclusive settings. Although the district provided ongoing staff development on learning styles theory and practice, she questioned whether this was enough to help teachers meet the wide range of student needs across language arts, math, science, and social studies—and whether the school's curriculum reflected the best in curriculum design principles.

Early in the spring of 2000, Narvaez decided to attend an ASCD Staff Development Institute on differentiation in the hopes of finding answers to her questions. Based on what she learned at the three-day institute, she began to shape a vision for Conway Elementary that launched a journey to develop faculty expertise in differentiating curriculum and instruction.

Narvaez welcomed input from her staff on how the journey would unfold, but she made it clear from the outset that everyone would be on board. Full participation was nonnegotiable. After careful consideration, Narvaez invited a consultant she had met at the ASCD institute, Kay Brimijoin, to help guide the Conway faculty on their new path. Brimijoin had focused on differentiation as a classroom teacher for 13 years and as an administrator and staff developer for a decade. Brimijoin's profile fit what Narvaez was looking for: an educator who had experience differentiating with her own students, who had experience in helping teachers grow toward expertise in differentiation, and who had an understanding of the needs of advanced learners.

Narvaez enlisted Brimijoin to launch the Conway differentiation initiative in a two-day summer retreat in 2000. During the academic year that followed, Brimijoin provided additional instruction in half-day workshops and observed and coached all regular classroom teachers. In this first year, teachers were mostly at an awareness level when it came to differentiation. Narvaez and Brimijoin assured teachers that professional development would occur in a risk-free environment and recognized that most faculty members were largely beginners when it came to effective differentiation.

At the outset, teachers most frequently designed and taught tiered lessons in language arts or math with activities or products differentiated primarily based on student readiness. Although the staff had seen examples of successful lessons differentiated by interest and learning profile, teachers felt the amount of content they had to cover argued against designing instruction this way. Their mind set was that they didn't have time to spare on differentiating by interest because there was "too much to cover" for state testing.

As Conway moved into its second year of work on differentiation, Narvaez and Brimijoin saw a growing acceptance on the part of teachers that it was OK for everyone in a class to not be doing the same thing. This was a paradigm shift for the faculty.

In year three—most likely as a result of the staff development focus on clarity about essential knowledge, understanding, and skills requirements for units and lessons—there was broad evidence of a sharpening of instructional planning at the school. Lessons became more complex. Multiple elements of differentiation appeared, and teachers began to modify more than the process components of their units. In addition, teachers were differentiating in new ways based on student needs—for example, differentiating content based on readiness, process based on interest, and products based on learning profile.

After observing and coaching every regular classroom teacher at least once, Brimijoin worked in the second and third years with all special-area teachers. In the first year, Narvaez intentionally stayed away from coaching conferences with Brimijoin, wanting to underscore the non-evaluative nature of the coaching process. By the second year, however, teachers often requested that Narvaez observe along with Brimijoin, sometimes even requesting that an observation be counted as a formal evaluation.

In year one, Narvaez required that every teacher design and teach one differentiated lesson. In year two, this increased to four lessons, and in year three, to six lessons. However, teachers had begun to use their planning time more collaboratively and began to share their lessons with their grade-level teams. As a result, the number of lessons for each grade level across the school tripled. All along, Conway's Professional Development Committee worked with Narvaez and Brimijoin to plan whole-faculty instruction based on teacher reflections and individual suggestions. Narvaez consistently checked with individuals and grade levels to determine how Brimijoin's time would be spent on site. As the years progressed, individual coaching was often balanced with grade-level planning meetings where Brimijoin assisted teachers in drafting units of instruction with clear learning goals defined and ideas for differentiation mapped out. After year three, Narvaez and Brimijoin developed teacher surveys, one for teachers who had gone through at least two years of training in differentiation and who had previous teaching experience and one for teachers who were new to the profession. The surveys were designed to ascertain specific professional development needs and to get teachers' insight into how schoolwide differentiation was affecting students' learning and teachers' practices. The answers would also guide Narvaez and Brimijoin on what to provide for further training.

Why Does It Matter?

As differentiation shifted from a predominantly readiness-based approach in years one and two of the change process to providing more interest and learning profile options in the third year, flexible grouping increased.

Classroom observations showed a growing sense of the teacher as the diagnostician of student needs. The instructional clinic became almost institutionalized, with the teacher seen as the provider of emergency services or triage on the spot. Students knew when they needed emergency care and weren't hesitant about asking for help because they might be perceived as somehow less than their peers. Providing different tasks, options, choices, or materials became a common instructional practice across grade levels and disciplines. Differentiation was now seen by students and teachers as the normal approach to teaching and learning. Asking students for feedback on differentiated lessons became routine. Talk about celebrating individual strengths, fairness as getting what you need to succeed rather than what everyone else gets, and tailoring instruction to promote individual success became a common language among teachers, students, and parents.

In addition, teachers began to see the need to rely on each other in new ways. The regular classroom teacher cast the reading specialist, for example, in a new light—as someone who could help find content at students' specific instructional levels. The media specialist became a source of ideas for interest-based lessons. The physical education teacher could suggest ideas for movement options in a lesson differentiated by learning profile, and the art teacher could suggest ideas for visual-spatial learning tasks.

The teacher specialists began to "push-in" to work with a group during a differentiated activity. This was another paradigm shift. Previously, specialists worked in a pullout model with small groups of students. By experiencing instruction in differentiation, the reading teachers realized that they could provide direct instruction to the students in the classroom as well. Classroom teachers responded positively because having another teacher in the room allowed for more individualized attention for all the students. Because the specialists now worked with an entire group of students, some of whom were not officially a part of their caseloads, they were able to assist a larger number of students and came to be viewed as a resource by the entire class. The perception of their roles tended to shift—from helping a few students who were labeled as needing help to being a resource for all students.

Overall, however, the most significant outcome of the decision in 2000 to embark on the journey toward differentiation was that teachers began seeing students as the engine that drives the teaching-learning cycle. They became students of their students. The teachers used assessment to monitor their students' needs every day—and, most importantly, they responded to those needs in increasingly effective ways. From a student perspective, the young learners came to see themselves as unique individuals and were less interested in competing with their peers than in moving their individual learning forward.

A Conway teacher summarized the feel of the school's evolution toward defensible differentiation effectively. "Before differentiation," she said, "I was teaching curriculum. Now, I am teaching students."

Snapshot 2: Coaching at Conway

First-grade teacher Chris Kiely was sitting at a small table down the hall from her classroom with Kay Brimijoin, staff development consultant and differentiation coach for Conway Elementary. Brimijoin had just observed Kiely teaching a 45-minute lesson on the short /u/ vowel sound. Kiely provided a lesson plan, using the template that everyone on the faculty used when Brimijoin observed. Brimijoin referred to the form as she took notes and moved around the room during the observation, not only watching the teacher, but also lending a helping hand.

Kiely had selected this particular day for an observation and would be one of about five teachers whom Brimijoin would visit and consult with during the day.

Seated in the hall, Kiely and Brimijoin discussed what had transpired in the class. About 10 minutes before the wrap-up of Kiely's lesson, a teacher assistant had stepped in, bringing the lesson to a close and guiding students into their next activity. This arrangement allowed Kiely to meet with Brimijoin immediately following the lesson. Despite the challenges of covering teachers' classes for conferences with Brimijoin, Narvaez knew the conferences were valuable. The lapse of even an hour between an observation and a debriefing session with the coach could blur recollections.

Brimijoin began the dialogue with Kiely by using a graphic organizer she created to structure the debriefing process. First she guided Kiely in determining how well she had defined the learning goals of the lesson—what the students should know, understand, and be able to do.

Next, Brimijoin checked to make sure Kiely could describe *what* was differentiated in her lesson—content, process, or product, and *how* it was differentiated—by readiness, interest, or learning profile. Once this was clear, the coach asked Kiely to explain *why* she differentiated the way she did, focusing this part of the coaching conference on assessment. Brimijoin had worked with the faculty for several years to build knowledge and understanding about differentiation, and it was important for teachers to be able to articulate the structure of and rationale for any differentiated lesson. This ability indicated the teacher's readiness to transfer learning from a staff development situation into classroom action.

At this point, Brimijoin asked Kiely to talk about what worked well in the lesson. The coach used her notes from the observation and her experience to expand and elaborate on what Kiely remembered as notable. Brimijoin next helped the teacher dissect her use of differentiation to determine how it supported individual students and helped them access the content. Finally, Brimijoin asked Kiely to talk about how she might improve the lesson and what she might change next time, again sharing ideas Brimijoin had noted during her observation.

The teacher found that she had a better understanding of differentiation than she thought. She explained how she focused the lesson on knowledge, understanding, and skills derived from the Missouri curriculum standards and shared how the assessment data about her students guided her to differentiate the content of the lesson based on readiness levels. Brimijoin's feedback affirmed for Kiely that she was "getting it." In a dialogue with her coach about what worked and what didn't, Kiely found that her hunches about how particular students responded to the lesson were confirmed by Brimijoin's observations and interactions. They shared a laugh about a time halfway through the lesson when every student was so engaged that the two of them were standing in the middle of the room unwanted—a most unusual scene for a classroom full of 1st graders. Again and again during their coaching conference, Brimijoin could reiterate the basic principles of differentiation and show how they were evident or missing by using examples from the lesson Kiely had just taught to her students.

After school the next day, the faculty gathered in the library for a staff development session that began with an opportunity for teachers to share any highlights from the coaching sessions of the past two days. In each whole-faculty debriefing session, Brimijoin encouraged teachers to select any experience or information they felt would help colleagues deepen their knowledge, understanding, and skill related to differentiation. Providing brief annotations of each lesson she observed, Brimijoin then offered teachers a chance to tell their peers what they had learned. Kiely decided to share two aspects of her lesson. First, she told about how she started the lesson on the short /u/ vowel by asking key questions: "Why do we spend so much time trying to learn the vowel sounds in words? What's the point of this?" She described how the students at first had a difficult time coming up with answers because they were not easy or obvious. She related to her colleagues that she worried a bit about how she persisted in getting her students to find the answers but said Brimijoin was very positive about the introduction. Kiely said she was startled by one student's "ah ha!" when he answered, "When you are a grown-up you have to read in your job." Another student added, "Yeah, and in video games, too!" She then shared the conversation she and Brimijoin had about the importance of making learning relevant for students, setting a purpose for instruction, and connecting definitions and terms about vowels to a bigger picture of why they are important to us.

Kiely then told her colleagues that when she taught this lesson again she would adjust the task for the advanced learners by reducing the number of words they had to find before beginning the next step in the assignment. She reflected on her discussion with Brimijoin about how easy it is to make the mistake of asking advanced students to produce more of something rather than asking them to think in depth or expand on an idea. Many of her peers across the room nodded in agreement. The group thanked Kiely for her reflections with applause.

Why Does It Matter?

Analytical and reflective dialogue about the lesson design and differentiation can help the teacher and staff developer in several ways. It helps to articulate knowledge of terms, rationale, and key principles. For example, the coaching conversation may informally assess a teacher's definition of tiering a lesson, demonstrating a solid understanding of this strategy or revealing misconceptions about process or implementation. Coaching can then take one of two paths. If a teacher clearly understands how to design and deliver a tiered lesson, it is a perfect opportunity for a coach to assign status to the teacher. Conferring status affirms knowledge and understanding. It also helps teachers discriminate between a general sense of differentiation and specific examples of effective differentiation in action. Conducted this way, the coaching experience casts a positive light on the attempt to differentiate. Because it is nonevaluative, the resulting dialogue can be prescriptive without being value laden. The focus on teachers becoming better at what they do brings the coaching experience full circle—from a deductive examination of the whole lesson to a meticulous analysis of its parts and then back to a study of the whole lesson measured in terms of student and teacher outcomes, finally blending and refining theory and practice.

During the dialogue with the teacher, the coach may make connections to broader learning goals targeted in ongoing, whole-group staff development. If the dialogue indicates that the teacher has missed the mark in any way, it is an opportunity for the coach to frame questions or statements that, in a constructive way, correct the error. Finally, the analytical dialogue phase of coaching provides the perfect conditions for on-the-spot differentiation as the staff developer tailors instruction for each teacher. In this way the coaching process serves as a springboard for projecting future individual teaching and learning goals.

The after-school reflection session allows the entire faculty to learn about differentiation within their own context and using their own language. Individual teachers are recognized for their successes and for identifying refinements after debriefing with the coach. Teachers who have not been coached sense the nonthreatening nature of the experience and see the benefits of professional growth that can accrue. Everyone grasps a sense of moving forward, of gaining clarity, and of pursuing a worthy vision together.

Snapshot 3: The Emergence of Professional Learning Communities

Rowena Coates, Jill Davis, and Elaine Sattler were seated around the reading table in Davis's classroom during a 30-minute grade-level planning period. All three 3rd grade teachers were reflecting on professional development goals for the year. They knew that their principal and their differentiation coach expected them to support their peers as they analyzed the effectiveness of differentiation in their curriculum and instruction. Peer observation with shared feedback was a goal Narvaez had set for each teacher that year. Having experienced the coaching process themselves, teachers were ready to transfer their learning by applying the coaching model in observations and debriefing sessions with each other.

The three were also thinking about Brimijoin's last visit to Conway when she met with their grade level and addressed their concerns about the time it takes to design and plan a differentiated unit. Brimijoin talked with them about how important it is to "work smart" by sharing expertise, ideas, materials, and resources when designing a curriculum unit intended to match individual needs. They decided to rethink the way they would design and teach their upcoming unit on telling time, taking into consideration their professional development goals related to peer observations.

Davis volunteered to try her hand at clarifying the "know, understand, and do," designing assessments, and differentiating the tasks. When she taught the first lesson in the sequence, she invited Sattler to observe. Afterward, the three discussed what had worked and what needed more work, following the coaching model they had experienced, and they generated valuable ideas for improving the lesson. Very shortly thereafter, Sattler taught the revised version of the lesson while Coates observed, after which all three met together and debriefed once again. They made minor adjustments in timing, materials, and management, and then Coates taught the lesson. As the teacher in 3rd grade with the fewest years of experience, having a carefully honed lesson at her fingertips offered Coates a leg up when beginning this unit with her students. The result was that all three teachers had a well-refined lesson to put in their tool kit for teaching the next year.

In a written reflection, the three teachers explained the value added to their understanding of differentiation through the peer coaching approach:

After we teach a lesson we find it important to share the lesson immediately so that our partners can use it while we are teaching that same skill instead of waiting until the following year. . . . We are finding that differentiation is made much easier and less time consuming because of our strong cooperation and our willingness to share. As a result, our repertoire is continually expanding.

Why Does It Matter?

Teachers discovered a way to systemize lesson development and refinement by combining collaboration, peer observation, and the kind of lesson analysis and reflection that had been modeled in coaching sessions. The process is what Joyce and Showers (1995) refer to as the development of metacognitive behaviors that enable a teacher to make instructional decisions about innovative teaching practices—in this case differentiation—apart from the professional development setting.

A common complaint from teachers is that planning differentiated lessons requires additional planning time. They are right. However, at Conway this grade level found a way to share the work, and they also discussed the value of pooling ideas and capitalizing on individual strengths when designing lessons. Although the main focus of the Conway initiative was differentiation, the professional learning community was a by-product of the work, evolving naturally from the work with differentiation.

Collegial support for differentiation increased dramatically within grade levels after the emphasis on peer observations in the second and third years. After observing, teachers would regularly make changes and discuss these changes with their grade-level colleagues—even when the coach wasn't there. The three 3rd grade teachers ventured into new territory when they collaborated on their redesign of a previously taught unit, and other grade levels followed their lead.

Snapshot 4: Special-Area Teachers and Differentiation

Rae Meyer, Conway's media specialist, had just left a meeting with 2nd grade teachers. Her mind was racing with ideas for making connections with their science unit on honeybees. Meyer had begun linking her lessons to topics that paralleled regular classroom work, offering readings across varied instructional levels and interests, and carefully crafting guiding questions differentiated in response to students' reading readiness levels in order to engage students in research. After crafting initial sets of questions for several topic areas, Meyer brainstormed with Carole Stafford, the gifted education specialist, and Marian Rosen, the technology coordinator, to make guiding questions more challenging and respectful for all students. Meyer discovered that a major dividend of differentiation was improved student behavior in the library. She reported that students were "consistently and totally engaged" when she adjusted instruction based on their interests and readiness. In reflecting on the changes over the past two years, she said, "I feel more comfortable than I ever have. It's a shame I didn't do this years ago. I feel I'm doing a better job and the kids seem to be enjoying it more."

In a small resource room Jean Lovegreen, a special services teacher (reading specialist), was working with two students from Faye Denninger's 5th grade class. During the coming week, Denninger would incorporate literature circles to enrich comprehension and build critical monitoring strategies as the class read *Tuck Everlasting*. Denninger and Lovegreen discovered that, if Lovegreen used small-group sessions to guide inclusion students about making informed choices as they carried out interest-based roles in the literature circles, the students were much more confident and successful and made valuable contributions to the discussions that ensued.

Fourth graders in Nancy Walther's music room were using acquired skills in vocal performance, notation, construction of chords, and instrumental performance to produce songs in class. They were creating their songs as singers, instrumentalists, or composers. In their last class, Walther gave them choice ballots and asked them to rank order the role they wanted based on their interest. She created task cards for each group that focused on the Missouri standards for music. The three roles assigned to students based on their choices called for creating a song from one of three different perspectives. However, the important vocabulary, skills, and understandings related to song production were consistent for all students.

Why Does It Matter?

By making full participation in the differentiation initiative a nonnegotiable for every faculty member at Conway, the principal confirmed the importance of special-area teachers as integral to the work of the staff on behalf of students. Throughout the change initiative, Conway's special-area teachers participated in whole-group staff development, coaching, and observation as much as—and sometimes more than—their regular classroom counterparts.

An interesting pattern that emerged from observation of the special-area teachers was their focus on management strategies and organization of materials to make differentiation effective. Because of tight schedules with one class immediately following another and a caseload of so many students, these teachers collected choice ballots from the preceding day's class in order to specify assignments, created task cards to clarify directions efficiently, provided support structures to economize on time (e.g., glossaries, word banks, charts with directions), practiced routines for self-management, color-coded materials, and used green, yellow, and red cups for keeping track of who needed help. These strategies all served to make differentiation more effective and more manageable as groups of students moved through their classrooms each day.

As special-area teachers shared their successes in whole-faculty reflection sessions, regular classroom teachers began to see them as valuable resources for supporting differentiation. For example, special services teachers helped organize materials, assisted with management, and provided on-the-spot support to help special needs students succeed in the regular classroom. By joining forces to implement differentiation effectively, special-area teachers and regular classroom teachers entered into a rich collaboration, creating a faculty more focused on meeting the full range of student needs than ever before.

Snapshot 5: What the Students Say

Linda Armbruster's 5th graders were all silent, leaning over their desks, concentrating on answering questions. It looked like they could be taking a test on their current science unit, but in reality they were responding to a survey that asked very different questions—it asked for their thoughts and feedback on differentiated curriculum and instruction. All together 181 students in 3rd and 5th grades at Conway responded to surveys after they had participated in a differentiated lesson. On the surveys students responded to rank-order, multiple-choice, and constructed-response questions—formats that were familiar because of state and national testing.

Why Does It Matter?

Student surveys in the third year of Conway's differentiation initiative provided valuable data about differentiation from the learner's perspective. An average of 85 percent of the students could recognize and report that differentiation was going on during the lesson and gave sound reasons for why differentiation made sense to them. Eighty-eight percent of 5th graders in one class stated that it was OK for other students to be doing something different. The vocabulary the students used made it evident that their teachers were talking explicitly with them about the rationale for differentiation. The fact that students were developing a vocabulary and understanding of differentiation along with the teachers constituted an additional and unanticipated layer of staff development outcomes.

In looking at what students said they liked best about the lesson, their responses pointed to activities or process. Seventy-two percent said that choice, comfortable learning profile, or comfortable working arrangements contributed to their ability to stay focused on the task. The students' words emphasized the importance of offering options, the link between interest and motivation, and how state-tested content could be explored in ways that were personally productive.

Results from the student surveys indicated that teachers were developing a learning environment that supported differentiation, helping their students understand why instruction should be modified, and fine-tuning learning profile and interest differentiation. Three-fourths of 5th graders in one class reported being stretched by their lesson, and almost 80 percent of the 3rd graders said their lesson was challenging.

As they analyzed responses related to student engagement in their classes, teachers asked critical questions: Was the work too easy, too difficult, or did the workload need to be more appropriate for individuals or groups? This analysis led to more careful assessment of the match of tasks to learning needs and more proactive design of meaningful anchor activities.

Survey results from students also helped inform the next steps of staff development. For example, data about the reasons for students being off task pointed to the need to address management of the differentiated classroom in whole-group staff development. Only 38 percent of students in all four classes were able to define the big ideas related to their lessons. These results indicated that teachers had not adequately emphasized the essential understandings related to the topic they were teaching. Clarifying learning goals in curriculum design thus became a critical focus area for staff development sessions.

Results of student surveys confirmed that teachers were building a rationale for differentiation as early as 3rd grade. This meant that teachers who would have these students in upper elementary and beyond would have an advantage—their students would already accept and understand that one size doesn't fit all, and they would be comfortable navigating through the process of differentiated instruction.

Snapshot 6: Parent Meetings and Differentiation

Approximately 30 parents were arriving in the Conway Elementary library for a presentation on differentiation by the principal and teachers. Most of these parents were new to the school, and they wanted to learn more about teaching and learning at Conway. They took their seats at the tables and introduced themselves to each other. Narvaez welcomed the parents and gave an overview of Conway's work with schoolwide differentiation and how this philosophy translated into classroom practice. Amy Denning, a kindergarten teacher, then described a differentiated lesson on patterns that she taught to her students. Materials for activities were on the tables. After explaining the activities and how they were differentiated, Denning asked parents to complete one of the activities. As they worked, there was a lot of conversation and sharing of strategies among the parents—not unlike a kindergarten classroom. Denning then asked the groups how they solved their problems. Parents commented on the number of different ways the groups arrived at their answers and how engaged they were in their activities.

Next, Caroline O'Brien, a 2nd grade teacher, introduced a lesson on telling time. She began with a discussion to clarify the lesson's understandings and how this skill applied to daily life. To help parents visualize the different levels of readiness in the lesson, she asked each group to complete each of the activities. They began with the most basic level and worked upward. The last activity was to create a movie schedule with time between the movies to clean the theater. The running minutes of each movie were given along with the opening and closing of the theater. Some parents commented on the complexity of the task and were surprised that some of Conway's 2nd graders were ready for this activity. At the end of the evening, they left with a better understanding of how and why teachers differentiated learning for their children. Many stayed to ask questions. Some were still working, trying to figure out the movie schedule.

Why Does It Matter?

Whenever a school begins a new initiative it is important that parents are aware that a change is taking place and why the change has been initiated. With such a noticeable change in teaching practice—parents may see different assignments being brought home in the same class—it is much better to be proactive in informing and educating parents about the new process in a positive way. The difference could amount to parents supporting the initiative in discussions with their children versus coming to the teacher upset that their children are being treated differently.

Parents want their children to succeed. However, parents are like most people when it comes to change. They are nervous about changing the status quo, or what is familiar, for something new and unknown. Leading and informing them is a step-by-step process. We gain their support as they see the positive results in their children's learning and enthusiasm toward school. Parents can become strong allies in promoting the philosophy of differentiation.

When teaching a differentiated lesson, we do not always have the luxury of the extra pair of hands needed to support multiple groups of learners and tasks. Narvaez has enlisted the help of parents when teachers need this support in the classroom. With a well-planned differentiated lesson, a parent does not need expertise in educational strategies or content to function in a supportive role. The parent simply needs to understand the task and keep the groups working toward their goals while the teacher is working with other students. At Conway, Narvaez and her teachers have found that this approach applies status to the parents and connects them to the learning environment as partners working toward a common goal.

Snapshot 7: When You Retire, You Don't Really Leave

Rae Meyer, Conway's retired librarian, was teaching a differentiated lesson to 4th graders in the library. Tricia Small, the new librarian, was watching Meyer teach. This was Small's first year as a school librarian, and Meyer had been available to help her with the operation of the library and differentiated lessons. Meyer also introduced Small to all of the Conway library volunteers and described their roles in the library.

Down the hall, Donna Perrey sat in the back of a classroom as Carole Stafford taught whole-group enrichment to a 1st grade class. Perrey was the new teacher, and Stafford was a retired gifted and enrichment specialist. Perrey had many years of experience in gifted education, but she valued learning from Stafford what the Conway program entailed.

The new teachers understood the importance of learning the school and community culture as a means of making a smooth transition for themselves and for the retirees. For everyone, it worked well to have two teachers working collaboratively to meet students' needs for a while.

With more than 70 years of teaching experience between them, Meyer and Stafford helped interview and select the teachers who would replace them. To make a smooth transition, it was important to find teachers who would embrace collaboration, understand the connectivity of their subject area with the total program, and be willing to learn about differentiation and its role in the total school environment.

During the first year of her retirement, Meyer helped to organize the library's parent volunteers and Conway's book fair. She taught Small about the community culture and continued teaching the after-school Junior Great Books program while Small assisted. Meyer taught Small how to coordinate the Favorite Author Program and the Mark Twain Awards Program. Meyer also shared with Small the differentiated lessons she had polished over the past four years. After the first year, Meyer turned over the library completely to Small and volunteered when needed. Meyer's support provided continuity for Conway teachers who had come to see the library as a critical resource in their work with differentiation.

Carole Stafford and Donna Perrey, the new gifted and enrichment specialist, also worked well together. Perrey chose to learn by observing her predecessor delivering whole-group enrichment to grade levels. She also asked Stafford to teach certain lessons and observed her on numerous occasions. Stafford gave Perrey all of her lessons, shared her expertise on differentiation, and collaborated with Perrey in designing new lessons for various grade levels and specific tasks to meet the needs of advanced learners. Perrey used Stafford as a sounding board for the new units she designed, and they collaborated often. Stafford also familiarized Perrey with students' backgrounds to help her understand their learning needs and strengths.

Why Does It Matter?

It was a great benefit to the continuity of Conway's differentiation to have retirees support the new faculty members' understanding of the philosophy and practice of differentiation. It was also a commentary on the positive environment and collegiality at Conway that numerous retirees elected to continue in the school as volunteers. Stafford explained that she wanted to leave a legacy to Conway, and the best way was to pass on knowledge: "I have a respect for the school and its reputation. I spent 30 years here, and I want to help maintain its excellence."

When teachers are part of a close-knit community, they keep their ties to the students and staff. New teachers have mentors who model and teach strategies that facilitate differentiation. This complements and accelerates the work of the differentiation coach with new teachers.

Snapshot 8: Letting Go Isn't Always Easy to Do

Second grade teachers Carolyn Parham, Caroline O'Brien, and Sarah Wieck were meeting in Parham's room the week before school. They decided that it was time to clean out some of the files that had accumulated over the years. Wieck, a third year teacher, and O'Brien, in her fifth year, were reluctant to discard some of the worksheets and lessons that they had either inherited or collected, in case they needed them in the future. Parham focused the conversation on the knowledge, understanding, and skills (KUD) of the grade-level objectives. "If it's not in our curriculum, we need to get rid of it," she said.

As the teachers continued the somewhat painful process, they came across the Johnny Appleseed unit they had once taught. The unit had children measure the circumference of apples, count apple seeds, and graph the colors of their favorite apples. "The kids love these activities," Parham remarked, and then the three asked the key question: "Does this support the 2nd grade KUDs?" Parham was the first to point out that the activities were fluff. The unit needed to go.

Later that year, Parham worked with 2nd grade teachers visiting from another state. They had just begun their study of differentiation and had brought one of their favorite units to get help in writing the KUDs. The unit was focused on economics and taught the concepts of community, scarcity, and opportunity cost. The first lesson compared five versions of a fable. The visiting teachers loved teaching the lesson. "How does it connect with economics?' was Parham's first question to the visitors. It didn't. She suggested that the teachers use the original story as a hook to teach another version that stressed the importance of community and resources. At a grade-level meeting, Parham discussed her experience and the process it took for the visiting teachers to realize that the lesson didn't match the subject-matter KUDs. "It was hard to get them to let go!" she explained.

Why Does It Matter?

Teachers worry about losing time if they differentiate instruction. Here, teachers learned that they could recapture time by asking hard questions about why they taught certain things and whether what they taught aligned with the grade-level KUDs. It's difficult to let go of favorite and successful lessons. The 2nd grade teachers were able to move beyond sentimental favorites by objectively assessing lessons based on designated KUDs. By working as a team, they were able to talk through the decision-making process and let go when the lesson didn't meet their learning goals. They understood what they were doing well enough to help other teachers with the process as well.

Snapshot 9: A Beginning Teacher's First Attempt at a RAFT

Tonee Simmons, a 3rd grade teacher in her first year of teaching at Conway, was in Principal Lane Narvaez's office after school discussing a differentiated lesson Narvaez had observed that morning. Simmons had requested that Narvaez use the observation as a formal evaluation, but they had agreed it would also be an opportunity for her to be coached as she began to apply principles of differentiation that were relatively new to her.

Simmons taught this lesson at the end of a unit on Martin Luther King Jr. The lesson was designed as a culminating performance task, and Simmons thought a RAFT activity—focusing on role, audience, format, and topic—would be an appropriate vehicle for students to demonstrate key knowledge and understanding for the unit.

When she left Narvaez's office after a coaching session with the principal, Simmons was pleased. The coaching conference had confirmed her expanding competence with differentiation. At the same time, Narvaez had posed key questions that revealed ways in which the content and goals in the RAFT would profit from increased clarity and stricter adherence to the basic principles of differentiation. Together they brainstormed revisions, and Simmons felt excited about their work together. She knew that when she taught this unit next year her students would be the beneficiaries of the coaching session.

Why Does It Matter?

An emphasis throughout the Conway change process was persistent linkage between designing high-quality curriculum and defensible use of differentiation to support each student in mastery of essential knowledge, understanding, and skill. Simmons's lesson is an excellent example of how a new teacher, with foundational instruction and follow-up coaching, can design, implement, and then refine a differentiated lesson.

Looking at Simmons's planning, teaching, and reflection for this lesson provides a sort of think-aloud about how to enhance the quality of curriculum and then make decisions about what and how a teacher will differentiate. Appendix A (see p. 191) provides an elaboration of the coaching session for Simmons's lesson as well as versions of the lesson created before and after coaching.

Thinking About the Snapshots

At the beginning of its journey toward second-order change, Conway Elementary School was, by all measures, a very strong school with a highly professional staff. The change process at Conway moved forward in a relatively orderly fashion given that so many educators were attempting to change the way they thought about teaching and learning—as they continued teaching.

Of course, they did have moments of frustration and doubt, instances of head shaking and adjustment, and times of celebration. Throughout the ups and downs of the process, there were certain moments when teachers, the principal, the staff developer, parents, and students knew that something interesting and important was happening. The snapshots presented here represent some of those benchmark moments.

The moments of epiphany will not happen the same way in any other school, but if change is occurring, they *will* happen. Thinking about why Conway staff chose these particular vignettes to represent their pilgrimage can provide points of comparison for other educators examining their own progression toward defensible schoolwide differentiation.

7

Snapshots of the Change Process at Colchester High School

When innovation reaches [a] critical mass and has recruited a range of advocates, change acquires a momentum of its own and moves into the mainstream of discussion, perception, and practice. Much of the resistance that emerges in the early stages of implementation begins to recede.

—Robert Evans, *The Human Side of School Change,* p. 69

As in Chapter 6, this chapter's verbal snapshots are designed to communicate a stronger sense of the nature of change when a school has made, and continues to make, radical change in how it "does school." At the outset of Colchester's journey toward defensible differentiation, the past was represented by a core of longtime, well-respected, innovative, and energetic teachers. The present was represented by a sense of growing turmoil and the realization by faculty and community alike that the status quo was unacceptable. The future was represented by a visionary and determined principal who saw her work not as a job but as a mission to steer a course toward equity and excellence for the full range of Colchester's students. Through Joyce Stone's judicious leadership, the future was also represented by a significant group of teachers who were willing to ask hard questions, face hard answers, and do the uncertain work necessary to find a new way.

Unlike the relatively linear and orderly change process at Conway Elementary, the change process at Colchester High was messy. It always rested on knowledgeable leadership but also had to promote healing where there was hurt, make way for divergent viewpoints, recognize and build on moments of serendipity, and honor the need for individuals and groups to reinvent trust. The snapshots that follow reflect the choices of Colchester personnel as moments that proved telling in the Colchester journey. They provide a flavor of the wisdom, courage, and luck that propelled the journey forward.

Snapshot 1: Decisiveness

For many years prior to Stone's tenure at Colchester, there had been an annual inservice meeting in which middle and high school teachers met to work on issues related to curriculum alignment. Year after year, the meetings proceeded in a similar fashion, with teachers meeting by subject area, mapping on chart paper the units and topics they taught, identifying areas of overlap, and noting gaps in content. Year after year, nothing came of the meetings except an occasional adjustment in teaching made by a conscientious teacher. As assistant principal at Colchester High, Stone was asked to preside over the group. She immediately made it clear that dialogue was only one goal for the day. By the end of the day, she insisted, the group would make decisions that would be acted on and evaluated. Skeptical subject-area groups proceeded through the day as they had for years. At the end of the day, Stone led a surprised group in finalizing decisions as a stunned teacher raised his hand and said, "Are we really going to make these important decisions we've only spent a day discussing?" Stone responded with one word, "Yes."

Why Does It Matter?

Second-order change requires decisiveness. There must be time for conversation, but there is always a time for action. In a school that had for some time lacked a clear sense of direction, Stone's approach foreshadowed a change in the way things would proceed.

As important as signaling action was in the generally purposeless meeting, Stone's follow-up was equally significant. She followed up to make sure the high school teachers were acting in accordance with the decisions. Says Rich, one of Stone's enduring strengths is that she always "inspected what she expected." She made sure individuals did their part. When they did, she was there to celebrate. When they did not, she was there to inquire, and then to support, and finally, if need be, to demand.

Snapshot 2: The Sign on the Door

Early in Joyce Stone's tenure at Colchester High, she made references to her obsessive attention to detail. Not long thereafter, she hung a sign on her office door that said, "Meticulous Attention to Detail." It was pointed out to her more than once that, unintentional though it may be, the acronym created by the sign was M.A.D.

In fact, notes one of her colleagues, "She was a force to be reckoned with. Her passion was matched only by her research. Her vision was crystal clear, her research was airtight." And time after time, her meticulous attention to detail in service of her vision resulted in unequivocal documentation in support of a position that made it hard for the School Board or the Colchester faculty to ignore what she shared with them. Sometimes, a colleague says, people would acquiesce because they knew if they resisted she'd spend the weekend preparing a case they simply couldn't poke holes in.

Why Does It Matter?

The way Stone attacked barriers to change in her early days as principal was sometimes difficult to watch, noted Bill Rich, Colchester's teacher liaison: "Now that I've worked with a number of other schools, I've grown to appreciate how change in high schools requires a catalyst that absolutely interrupts business as usual. All change agents must, at times, push the envelope, but it seems to me like high school principals who want to be change agents have to push the whole post office. I've met some very smart high school principals who desire change but are just not willing to shake the system as hard as it needs shaking for fear of being shaken themselves."

Snapshot 3: A Refrain

In her early days at Colchester, Stone was talking with Brad Blanchette, a greatly respected Colchester teacher and leader. She was trying to gain from him an understanding of how things worked in the school and why they worked that way. As he provided answers, her questions became more pointed and indicated dissatisfaction with what she was hearing. "Joyce," he told her, "you have to understand that the reason you can't make sense of it is that the edges do not touch." That metaphor—the edges do not touch—became a refrain for Joyce and those with whom she shared leadership at the school.

Why Does It Matter?

Schools are not especially sequential or orderly places. They are repositories of diverse lives, world views, schedules, and priorities. Nonetheless, a school with a coherent direction must have some edges that touch. Understanding which edges must touch and which can remain loosely coupled is a hallmark of intelligent leadership. Aligning the key edges of the puzzle pieces that were Colchester was vital in bringing about second-order change. Espousing the value of each learner doesn't line up with tracking. Detracking doesn't line up with one-size-fits-all instruction. Teacher buy-in doesn't line up with top-down leadership. Asking teachers to take on a new dimension of work doesn't line up with asking them to do multiple new things or with using available school time for unrelated purposes. The aspiration for quality classroom practice doesn't line up with rejection of research on teaching.

Stone and her colleagues worked to line up edges at Colchester that had become disconnected. Even as they continued the quest for alignment into the future, an observant visitor to the school could see ample evidence of people and practices that were "easy" in their shared educational "skin."

Snapshot 4: Shared Drive

In a procrastination mode while preparing for class one day, Bill Rich began to explore the school's computer network to find places he had not been before. Along the way, he came to a folder called "Shared Drive." When he tried to open it, he received a computer message that he did not have access to the folder. When he checked with nearby colleagues, no one knew what the purpose of the folder was. When he asked Stone about the folder, she explained that it was a place where administrators kept documents and templates that helped them with their duties—calendars, policy statements, newsletters, and so on.

Initially Rich's curiosity was satisfied, but soon he began to question why teachers didn't have a place to keep documents that they revised each year to keep their classes running well. Further, why did he create documents and lessons that no doubt had been created by many other teachers in years past?

Then, the double entendre kicked in. A shared drive was not only a place for people to share documents, but a way to make the hopelessly private practice of high school teachers more public. Shared drive was what was missing in schools—a shared sense of purpose that would make their collective efforts greater than the sum of their parts. Shared drive was a symbol of teamwork.

Why Does It Matter?

Colchester, like many high schools, had no sense of shared drive when the change process began. Rich's moment of illumination became symbolic in his mind and practical as well. On one level, he and his colleagues had to work to move from being static file cabinets to a dynamic shared drive. That called for a kind of team building and teamwork that did not exist and would evolve only as trust and time to share evolved. It also meant a sharing of leadership between principal and teachers—a conferring of status by the principal. It meant everyone had to have opportunities and support to shine—to feel known, appreciated, and mentored. Over time, the school undeniably developed that symbolic sense of shared drive. It is metaphorical of what the school became and continues to become. On a more concrete level, faculty members created a shared-drive folder on the school's network to support and facilitate their active exchange of ideas, which saved time and extended their reach to students.

Snapshot 5: Attila the Hun No More

At Colchester, Joyce Stone initially had to work consistently in high gear to confront problems, challenge ineffective practices, and reverse negative patterns in the school and at the district level. At times, this required a confrontational stance, and everyone eventually recognized that the principal had done a Herculean task of righting the sinking ship that was CHS. Once the gales died down, however, and faculty were getting their sea legs, they became far less tolerant of the principal's top-down leadership style. By Stone's design, the teacher liaison sometimes brought the principal negative news. But in that role, Bill Rich cautioned Stone or shared advice to preserve goals that were imperative for Colchester students. With that intent, one day Rich shared the view that her aggressive leadership style had worked well to right the ship but that she needed to adjust her style to align with new needs. He jokingly observed that her Attila the Hun style of leadership had worked wonders, but that the faculty's needs had changed, and her style of leadership would need to change, too, so she could create the culture of collaboration and shared ownership that she desired.

As is often the case when we hear an unwelcome truth, Stone was initially upset with Rich. Given a few days to reflect, however, she thanked him. Then in typical self-effacing fashion, she alluded to the conversation with faculty members, making it clear that she was committed to adjusting her leadership style to meet their evolving needs. She showed the Leadership Team the drawing of Attila the Hun she had pasted on the back of her school identification tag—a reminder to her and to others that she, too, was working on adjusting her practice.

Why Does It Matter?

At Colchester High, Stone found a sinking ship. Her quick, decisive, and sometimes autocratic leadership served as ballast for the ship and helped resuscitate a gasping crew. Once the ship was righted, however, the school would increasingly need a new kind of leader. Stone faced a difficult challenge that school leaders often fail. She had to adjust her initial style of leadership to meet the demands of a new environment—one in which trust had to be built among members and in which leadership had to be shared broadly in order to develop followers. To make such a change is to allow—and in fact support—people in making decisions that sometimes differ from one's own. It is to know that their mistakes are learning tools. It is to realize that a shared vision rises from many voices.

Stone was able to make the change from a take-charge leader to a shared-power leader. As Gandhi suggested, she was able to be the change she wanted to see in the world. In many ways, she experienced the uneasiness teachers confront when they have to learn to trust and listen to students in their classrooms in order to differentiate instruction. "Won't I be giving up power that's mine?" "Won't they take advantage of me?" "Won't they make bad choices?"

There is a discussion among sports fans about the attributes of the best coaches. Is the better coach the one who befriends and listens to players, working hard to develop a sense of teamwork, or is it the autocratic and passionate coach whose unpredictability and passion fosters anxiety in the athletes to the degree that they would do anything to avoid errors that might evoke the coach's wrath? Notes a Colchester teacher and sports fan, "It depends on the previous coach. After years of a friendly coach, it's best to have an autocrat come and shake things up. After years of an autocrat, it's best to have a friendly coach take over."

Stone learned how to succeed herself. The school first needed a more assertive leader. In time, it needed a mentor. Through her own insights and honest conversations with trusted faculty members, she evolved as a leader in accordance with the changing needs of her faculty. Throughout the process, she stayed true to the core of her initial vision, confronting violations of the mission's core. She continued to push hard and was always willing to render what she demanded. But she learned to trust and to listen, just as she asked her faculty to trust and listen to one another and their students.

Snapshot 6: It's About the Students

There was a knock on the door of Joyce Stone's office, where Stone and the Leadership Team were engaged in an important discussion. A group of students, unhappy about the Iraq war that had recently begun, had come to explain that they were organizing a sit-in to protest the war and that the sit-in would disrupt the school schedule. Stone could have dismissed the students because they interrupted a meeting. She could have cracked down on their efforts because of its potential to create tension in the school. Instead, she asked the students what they wanted to accomplish. They explained that they felt too many of their peers were unaware of or apathetic about the war and they wanted to increase dialogue about the war in the school. Stone listened to the students and talked with them about her experiences in the Civil Rights Movement. Ultimately, she suggested a more effective alternative to a sit-in. In conjunction with student government leaders and with Stone's guidance, this group of students designed, coordinated, and implemented a schoolwide assembly with a panel of professors and an Air Force pilot representing diverse views about the war. Before the assembly, all students in the school were given tiered readings about the war. After the assembly, Stone modified the school schedule so students could meet in their teacher advisory groups to talk about the war. Students in the initial group were elated with their success, and the student body as a whole was appreciative of the opportunity to try to make sense of a highly relevant issue.

Why Does It Matter?

When Stone came to Colchester High, the general sense of discontent that pervaded the school as a whole permeated classes as well. In many cases, students felt neither safe nor appreciated. An important element in changing the course of the school was developing a schoolwide sense of respect and guiding teachers to create such environments in their classrooms. In the sit-in instance and in many others, Stone made sure to model with the students what she asked the teachers to do. She took time to listen to the students and to create a learning opportunity that was substantive and pertinent to them based on their interests.

To facilitate developing a sense of connection and understanding between the high school faculty and students, Stone initiated a teacher advisory program in which students met daily throughout their high school years with the same teacher and a relatively small group of students. Stone herself always had one of these advisory groups, which met in her office. She found that working with students in her teacher advisory group served as an important window into how students saw the school.

In other instances, Stone listened to less weighty suggestions from students who had not found the school inviting for some years. For example, a pep rally with a Jell-O-eating contest was not on her agenda, but she let it happen because she knew it was good for building a sense of community among students.

Throughout the process of change toward differentiation, Stone led the teachers in talking about the goals and challenges of differentiation with their students—just as she did in her teacher advisory group and in many other settings. Including students in the discussion was key to ensuring that differentiation was something done *with* students rather than *to* them. In the fourth year of the change process, Tomlinson visited the school. Stone requested that she address the student body on differentiation. It seemed unlikely that a group of adolescents would care to sit through an assembly on an educational concept, but Stone was difficult to refuse. Because of the investment in teacher–student discourse and partnership regarding differentiation, the high schoolers were, in fact, clearly engaged in the content of the assembly, asking thoughtful questions and sharing mature insights.

Stone gave what she asked others to give. She enacted what she believed. She kept the students in the center of her vision.

Snapshot 7: The Dramatic Reading

No matter how powerful a vision for change is, if it belongs only to the leader, it cannot endure. For some time in the Colchester change process, divisions existed among faculty members about the school's new direction. Although the discourse about differentiation was colored with respect and professionalism, it also involved thinly masked animosities and a sense of dis-ease. In his role as liaison between teachers and the principal, Rich encouraged Stone to survey the faculty to determine their assessment of the state of community among the Colchester faculty. When responses from the faculty survey were analyzed, many were affirming. Some were harsh and even brutal. Rich suggested to Stone that the faculty needed to confront its feelings. Says Rich, "Most people would have read the comments privately, but Joyce boldly had the faculty members hear for themselves what individuals had written."

Rich typed up a narrative script of the comments. Following a presentation of quantitative data from the survey, faculty members sat in concentric circles and listened as predetermined readers read all of the comments aloud.

Why Does It Matter?

Rich explained the significance: "It is difficult to convey the power of the moment. It was a clear indication for the faculty that it was time for us to face one another. The airing of feelings provided a release of sorts in that everyone could now hear what before had been rumbling just below the surface." The very dramatic reading made hidden feelings public. Only then could the faculty begin a meaningful conversation about who they wanted to be, how their perspectives affected their work, and where they could find common ground to move themselves to a better place. The reading also made clear and public that the critical mass of teachers at Colchester supported the change process for differentiation. The detractors were a small minority, and everyone now knew it.

It is interesting, and perhaps not accidental, that Colchester teachers often survey their students about the state of a particular classroom community of learners and share results with the students. Some results make the teachers look good. Some do not. But always the discussion turns to how the group as a whole—teacher and students alike—can act to make their community stronger and more successful.

Snapshot 8: Gallery

Throughout the large room were displays created by the faculty to demonstrate their work toward a designated goal. Teachers and administrators roamed around the room, studying examples of student work and individual or department explanations of strategies, approaches, and procedures they used in addressing the common goal. Each educator carried forms for jotting down ideas they would like to use, implications for future work, and feedback on the displays. These occasions are called galleries, and they have become greatly valued by Colchester's faculty and administrators as a way to share ideas and make public their work and growth. Galleries are announced well in advance—generally at least a semester. Throughout the span between the announcement and the gallery itself, teachers work on the common topic that the upcoming gallery will feature, and they collect samples of their work and of student work that they will ultimately share with their colleagues.

Why Does It Matter?

Galleries can be held on a wide range of topics—for example, using common assessments or integrating nonfiction writing into all content areas in ways that work for all students. Galleries provide a time to talk about what, how, and whom the teachers at Colchester teach, and teachers and administrators learn a lot in the process. Sometimes people learn small things, such as how one department asks students to format their work that seems to be effective. Sometimes they learn big things, such as how two teachers teach a very similar idea in very different content areas such as science and humanities. A lot of cross-pollination goes on, and what teachers see can indicate important next steps for faculty consideration. Galleries also provide a time to visibly see and celebrate teacher and student growth.

Snapshot 9: The Right Answer

A few years into the change process at Colchester, the pilot differentiation classes were clearly successful, and the 9th grade had been detracked. It was time to expand the capacity of the entire faculty to differentiate instruction in their classes. An important step in this direction was the decision to model differentiation for the faculty through differentiated staff development.

Administrators and key teachers pre-assessed faculty members to determine their interest in important concepts and underpinnings of differentiation. The next staff development session provided content for teachers based on their interests, and teachers had options for which sessions they would attend. Teachers weary from previous prescribed and prepackaged staff development sessions found the day highly successful.

Bill Rich had recently become leader of his department and felt it important to build on the success of the differentiated staff development day. At the next meeting of his department, he asked teachers to offer feedback about the day. Their comments were highly positive. They liked seeing their peers emerge as experts who could guide their thinking. They appreciated choices. They were worried that staff development might revert to the old way.

At about that point, Rich noted, a trusted and respected veteran member of the department divined where all this was going and asked a simple question: "Bill, how much preparation time did this inservice require?"

Not quite sure how to answer, Rich asked his colleague to elaborate on the response. "Well," he said, "I don't want to take anything away from what was a terrific inservice, but I'm a little concerned that this kind of instruction might become an expectation for teachers who, frankly, don't have the time to pull this off. Do you think it would be realistic to expect individual teachers to teach this way in all their classes?"

Rich recalls a frightening silence before he answered, which gave the question even more importance. He noted, "How or why I had the presence of mind to answer as I did is still a mystery to me. I explained that he was right. It took more time to plan for differentiation than was reasonable for teachers who taught separately, which was why we would need to begin thinking about how we could work together. It could happen only if we began to think differently about what it means to teach in a high school—to redesign how we work."

Why Does It Matter?

In a way, Rich's answer to his colleague was a stroke of luck—one of those moments when words serve the speaker well. A colleague asked an honest question, and Rich gave him an honest answer. He didn't try to put down or dismiss his colleague's idea. On the other hand, he did not retrench on his sense that if faculty felt invigorated and energized by learning opportunities designed in response to their needs, they owed students the same kinds of opportunities.

In another way, Rich's response was predictive of what had to happen at Colchester. Differentiation could not happen with a faculty of isolated, private practice teachers. They had to learn to think together, to jointly solve problems, to share what they created, to learn from one another. Rich's answer signaled to his colleagues that to reinvent their teaching was a professional obligation and that they could achieve it if they worked together to reinvent how they used their time and abilities.

Snapshot 10: Teachers Leading the Way

At a Colchester staff development day, there was a sense of anticipation rather than resignation among faculty. Colchester teachers were to lead the day's sessions. The leaders were colleagues—Julie, Heather, Di, Brad, Wayland—not imports. The day's learning options were going to be differentiated for faculty based on their interests and needs, and that made a difference. But even more importantly, the contents of the day stemmed from the work of teachers next door or down the hall. It's difficult to dismiss ideas that are commended by peers.

Why Does It Matter?

As differentiation became more acceptable, accepted, and implemented at Colchester, an increasing number of homegrown teacher leaders could share their classroom approaches with colleagues. They had no need to whitewash their experiences or to "sell a bill of goods." They were simply sharing ways in which they had taken risks on behalf of their students—the same students taught by many other teachers in the school. In addition to sounding real to their peers, they were an affirmation that change could happen and could happen to the benefit of students. The teacher leaders understood the school's context—and were likely just enough ahead of colleagues in their development toward differentiation so that what they shared seemed achievable by others on the same journey. Another key benefit to the teacher-led staff development, of course, was a growing number of Colchester teachers who felt competent and confident in leadership roles, expanding their impact within and beyond the school.

Snapshot 11: Ourstory

The Colchester faculty assembled before school started for a PowerPoint presentation by the principal that by now was a part of the fabric of the school year. An adaptation of the word *history,* the presentation was called "Ourstory." It included a statement of the vision of differentiation; evidence of change in the school at classroom, school, and department levels; an analysis of student test scores, attendance, office referrals, dropout rates, and other data since the beginning of the differentiation initiative; goals and plans for the upcoming school year; and other indications of an evolution toward a school that was functioning as a community to ensure equity and excellence for its full range of students. Faculty listened with interest to the principal's annual review of where they had been, what they were becoming, and challenges ahead.

Why Does It Matter?

Stone knew from her experience as an administrator that she needed to become Colchester High School's narrator and advocate, the person who over and over again in as many settings as possible repeated different parts of the school's story so that, over time, everyone knew the story. From this realization, the Ourstory format was born. Although this may sound small, it was key to change in the school. Many school administrators underestimate how often they must broadcast their vision of the school's future. Stone did not. She used every medium available to keep the vision in front of faculty, students, parents, and community, but one of the most powerful was her annual, opening day "Ourstory." Although the presentation evolved each year, it always looked at where the school had been in its journey, where it was as the year began, and where it was going as the year moved ahead. Not only is it critically important for administrators to tell the school's change story over and over again so that new people hear it and experienced folks exercise recall—but it's a good story! It helped people see themselves as players in the change process. As a culture's narrative becomes commonly shared, people act accordingly. When a school's story is one of helplessness and defeat, it shows; likewise, when a school's story is one of progress and achievement, it shows.

Snapshot 12: The CHS Bear

A faculty member stood up at an end-of-the-year faculty meeting holding a teddy bear that had a strange kind of alligator costume on. (The CHS mascot is Champ, the fictitious sea monster of Lake Champlain, so the alligator costume made sense and was very funny.) The teacher explained that where he previously worked, during each faculty meeting the person who possessed the bear would pass it on to a deserving colleague. The exchange of the bear became a small but important ritual of celebration at CHS. Faculty members have shared many poignant and humorous moments when the person holding the bear explained why he or she was passing it along to a particular colleague.

Why Does It Matter?

As the Colchester faculty began to work more as a team—and as a collection of teams—rather than as individuals in private practice, faculty members and administration found ways to reinforce the growing sense of community. The CHS bear was one such mechanism. Over time, the bear collected memorabilia that teachers attached to him from different departments, and he became a humorous-looking creature. He was a visible representation of the changes, challenges, and victories throughout Colchester's differentiation initiative. Notably, the bear ritual allowed individual teachers to decide who should receive the bear. It was not an administrative decision or a team leader decision. The person given the bear would decide who received it next. This practice encouraged teachers to reinforce one another's strengths and ensured that a teacher narrative would remain in the foreground of change.

Snapshot 13: Keeping It Real

When differentiation began to permeate everything at Colchester, a comment by a small group of detractors was making its way through the faculty. The joke was that DI stood for "dumb idea." Rich, who was particularly valuable because he had the ear of the faculty and the principal, was aware of the comment. He noted that often what detractors are saying aloud is what the critical mass is considering privately.

During the same time period, Rich was scheduled to lead a staff development session on differentiation at a faculty meeting. He began the session by making his own joke about hearing that DI stood for dumb idea. He went on to say that if anyone in the group didn't care for the idea of differentiation, or felt threatened by it, or had a beef with it for whatever reason, he wanted to make sure they were informed skeptics. "If you're an uninformed skeptic," he noted, "you'll sound ignorant because you'll sound like you're saying differentiation isn't what's best for teaching and learning." Rich then provided a number of pieces of evidence that effective teaching is what differentiation is all about. He added, "However, if you're dead set against differentiation—for any reason—you can say things like this. 'Of course we all aspire to differentiate instruction. I mean, who can argue against meeting kids where they are and taking them as far as they can go? Whether differentiation is a worthy goal is pretty clear. The real questions are these: Do we have the time necessary to do excellent teaching? Do we have the resources to offer kids what they really need?'"

Why Does It Matter?

One of Rich's mottos as a teacher has been "Keep it real." By that, he means being honest about what's really going on. In that way, he's been able to keep small disagreements, small misperceptions, and small problems from becoming bigger. In his work as teacher liaison at Colchester, he has found that same principle important. It defuses a situation to acknowledge that it exists. It airs the concern and provides an opportunity to discuss it as a group. Many times, handling such a situation with a bit of humor can further de-escalate the problem. It continued to be important for Colchester teachers and administrators to confront their feelings without animosity but also without retrenching and losing forward movement toward more responsive classrooms. As Rich explained, "We needed to allow room for doubt and space for detractors, but no harbors."

Snapshot 14: Celebration Assemblies

When the lights went down in the Colchester auditorium and the curtain went up, the school's student/faculty band—The Substitutes—set an upbeat tone with a late-night television band kind of groove. Lots of hand clapping and wide eyes were evident from the audience. Then a teacher host came out in a tux and began the night as if it were the Oscars. Just like the Oscars, the host announced a category for recognition—for example, New Standards Reference Exam test scores, sports, theater, clubs, and so on—that deserved recognition. He would open an envelope and announce the winner: some group from the school. Then a predetermined teacher would come up and accept a small trophy and say thanks to all the folks who made this possible. The host carried the Oscar theme through the entire assembly. There were lots of laughs and a clear appreciation for the planning required for the event. And the students heard about all of the great things happening at the school—from scholars bowl to varsity football.

Why Does It Matter?

When Stone became principal at Colchester, she did not allow school assemblies at first because the environment was unstable. It took time to build a sense of trust and community where tension and disruption had been the rule. Being able to not only hold an effective student assembly but also herald successes was a significant sign of progress for the school community. From the first Celebration Assembly, the school's administrators and faculty continued the tradition of whole-school meetings that celebrated the school, although they were not always called by that name. An annual Diversity Week whole-school assembly celebrated diversity in the world and then specifically at CHS. An annual end-of-the-year slide show showered kids with images of them and their school and teachers, all set to music that the students liked. As a sense of community evolved, members of student government began working with faculty and administrators to plan and carry out the celebrations. The assemblies became another manifestation of the shared direction, spirit, community, and pride that were once absent from the school and came to typify it.

Snapshot 15: Two Steps Back?

On National Public Radio (NPR) several years ago, Ira Glass told a story on *This American Life* about a teacher who had made some dramatic changes in her classroom as the result of some second-order change that had been going on in her school. The woman's classroom gave testimony to the power of the changes for her students and for her sense of accomplishment as a teacher. Several years later, Glass got in touch with the teacher again and was devastated to learn that she was about to stop teaching because the positive changes that had been made in the school had toppled when the principal retired. Teachers had gone back to closing their doors, teaching privately, and covering facts to prepare students for mandated standardized tests. The reform was dead.

In 2005, Stone announced her retirement from the principalship. Even though her faculty had known the decision was likely, it was nonetheless unsettling for a faculty that had undergone radical change in a reasonably short time.

During an inservice day, some of the school's teacher leaders included the NPR recording. Few dry eyes remained as the Colchester faculty listened and understood that they needed to carry the vision forward without the principal who had guided them thus far. The transition of leadership had begun.

Why Does It Matter?

Rich explained that it's important to keep people's hearts engaged in the change process as well as their minds. Moments like this one served as a sort of group catharsis. The NPR program helped the faculty think about what lay ahead. It also helped cement in their collective awareness that differentiation belonged to *them* and *they* would have to ensure that their good work did not atrophy during another phase of change at the school. It was their vision now, and they had to be keepers of the vision.

Thinking About the Snapshots

As the change process at Colchester began, it was a school in trouble. Teachers, students, and community were restless, discouraged, and often angry. A rich legacy of high professionalism and community respect had seriously eroded. Predictably, old tensions spilled into new tensions. Although it may seem logical that such a time is ripe for change, it's difficult to embrace the idea of reinventing yourself when you're down for the count.

The principal felt that moving toward differentiation was the only way to right the wrongs at Colchester, but the outcomes of Stone's vision were anything but clear to most stakeholders. The Colchester crew did not face a tidy, linear journey. People had to learn to look at one another in new ways, to trust one another, and to trust themselves. Further, budgets were tight, and resources were limited. The way ahead was uncharted terrain.

Much like the head of a family trying to reconcile alienated family members, Stone set out to change minds and practices. Along the way, she had to reinvent herself as she asked faculty members to reinvent themselves.

The progression from a school in trouble to a school of distinction was neither predictable nor placid—but it happened. Its snapshots tell the story of struggle as much as of triumph. In the end, the pictures are hopeful because they reveal courage in action. They yield images of an evolution of hearts and minds—a capacity to let go of old ways of thinking and doing in favor of new ways that become trustworthy only after they are embraced.

It is relatively rare to see a whole school change its psyche and its pedagogy. It is very, very rare to see a high school do so. The Colchester snapshots provide insights into the change process in a high school and into some of the positive outcomes that, in turn, fed the change. As was the case with Conway Elementary, the Colchester snapshots are specific to its progression. Nonetheless, they are both instructive and encouraging to other leaders who, despite starting in a difficult place, can envision something better and have the will to risk going to that new place in the company of peers.

8

Change for Academically Responsive Classrooms: Looking Back and Ahead

---

"You must learn to think of yourself as a writer."

"I'm not good enough," I said.

"No, you're not. But you're getting better. You're doing the hard work. But you must tell yourself that you're a writer. A work in progress. But a writer."

—Pat Conroy, *My Losing Season,* p. 144

We human beings mark important milestones in history—both personal histories and collective ones—with some fanfare. And so it was when we recently entered a new year, decade, century, and millennium. It seemed a moment of change deserving of celebration and introspection. And then life goes on much as it did on the preceding day, which was another millennium.

As we were in the process of exiting the old millennium, changes suggesting a new era were also happening in and around the schoolhouse—perhaps just out of our consciousness. In the last 30 years, the number of students in the United States classified as belonging to a minority group nearly doubled—from 22 percent of the school population in 1972 to 43 percent in 2004. At the same time, white students decreased from 78 percent of the school population to 57 percent. Young people who speak a language other than English at home increased 179 percent between 1979 and 2004, and the number who speak English with difficulty rose 144 percent. The poverty rate has not decreased in the past three decades, and thus 37 percent of students were eligible for free or reduced-priced lunch in the 2004–05 school year. Further, the number of students coming to school from two-parent families decreased from 83 percent to 68 percent during the past 25 years (U.S. Department of Education, 2006).

At the same time, the number of students eligible for special education services has risen dramatically. For example, more than 208 million students are currently identified as having a learning disability, with between 20 percent and 40 percent of these students also diagnosed as having attention or hyperactivity problems. Most of these students spend 80 percent of their school day in general education classrooms (McNamara, 2007).

All schools also serve students who learn quickly and deeply and who benefit academically and personally from teachers and teaching that support them in moving at an appropriate pace, work with materials that are appropriately challenging, and probe meanings at levels that are appropriately sophisticated for their readiness to learn (Kulik & Kulik, 1992).

Even though not so much is written about them, we might assume that our classrooms also continue to include a range of relatively typical students who, at a given moment, neither excel nor struggle academically. Like all other students, they come to us with a plethora of backgrounds, interests, dreams, strengths, and needs.

Whether or not we have marked the changes in the contemporary school population as momentous, the idea of a classroom in which students are relatively alike as learners has gone the way of Model T Fords, record players, and typewriters. At the same time that students are becoming more diverse in their learning needs, it appears imperative for all students to be educated at a level we once assumed was appropriate only for our most advanced learners—at least if our intent is to prepare them for the world in which they will live as adults (Marx, 2000). We may have missed the new student reality as we toasted a new era, but our persistent one-size-fits-all instructional practices make us look, at best, out of step with the world around us.

From Backdrop to Action

Taking stock of the students we serve and of the degree to which our current teaching practices serve each of those students well should be a call to action:

- Who are the students that come to school?
- Which of those students flourish in the classroom?
- Of whom are we expecting too little?
- Who slips under our radar as having unique needs?
- To what degree are fixed instructional groups identifiable by the economic and ethnic status of the students in them?
- What's going on in our best classes? Who has access to that quality?
- What's going on in our weaker classes? Whose children are there?
- Why aren't the best classes the nonnegotiable standard for all students?
- What percentage of students is taught as though we needed to prepare them for a highly productive life?
- What percentage of our students find learning worthwhile, engaging, and personally relevant?
- Who is languishing for lack of persistent challenge?
- What do we believe—what do we *want to* believe—about the enterprise we share, and how do we represent those beliefs to our students?

Answering those questions honestly and reflectively should provide enough fuel to propel a vision of a more compelling and contemporary kind of classroom. Seeking out honest answers to the questions more often than not leads to a vision of differentiation. The vision for differentiation is relatively straightforward. It asks that educators do the following:

- Accept the premise that human variability is normal and beneficial rather than inconvenient or distasteful—in the classroom as in the world beyond the classroom.
- Accept responsibility for maximizing the possibilities of each student we teach.
- Develop classrooms in which teachers actively work to know and connect with their students in order to teach them as effectively as possible.

• Develop classrooms in which all students work together effectively from a base of learning goals that are clear, engaging, authentic, and based on understanding.

• Set learning goals and "teach up" with the expectation that every student can do more than we believe possible when we provide the support necessary for them to do so.

• Check frequently to see who is with us as we move toward (and hopefully beyond) designated learning goals.

• Make adjustments in instruction when we see that students are struggling or that they have already achieved essential goals.

• Build student–teacher partnerships in order to build dynamic communities of learning in which students acknowledge one another's commonalities, respect one another's differences, and support and celebrate one another's growth.

• Create generalist–specialist teams that work collaboratively in heterogeneous settings to ensure equity of access to high-quality curriculum and instruction and to maximum personal growth for each learner.

Those goals seem self-evident—little more than the common sense of teaching. Nonetheless, to many of us, such an approach seems like a formidable task or even a recipe for failure (Earl, 2003). After all, how can we make adaptations for all those students? In the elementary grades, we teach too many subjects. In the secondary grades, we teach too many students. But differentiation isn't about creating a lesson plan for each student each day: "It means recognizing and accepting that each student is a unique individual. It means using what you know about learning and about each student to improve your teaching so that all students work in ways that have an optimal effect on their learning" (Earl, 2003, p. 87).

Right as the goals of differentiation may sound, they are not, of course, easy to achieve. But "easy" is rarely the companion of "worthwhile."

Leaders for second-order change don't expect or aspire to "easy." Nor do they awaken one day with the premise that change for the sake of change is a good thing. Rather, they find it difficult to sleep because they see an injustice that needs to be righted, a hunger that requires feeding, a failing infrastructure that needs replacing. For many students, classrooms that ignore their humanity and individuality are all of these things. Leaders for second-order change toward effective differentiation are bothered by that reality, and they set out to bother others with it as well—to ensure that others come to share their sense of urgency for the change.

Lessons from the Literature of Change and Leaders for Differentiated Classrooms

Perhaps the most important lessons from the literature and successful leaders is that second-order change is possible. What it takes to make substantive change happen in schools is not so exotic or costly that it is out of the reach of ordinary schools (Fullan, 2001b). Although such change is neither common nor simple, it is achievable and worthy of the effort required.

There are many take-away lessons from the literature of change and from the stories being written daily in schools where educators create new ways of thinking about and enacting classroom practice to benefit academically diverse student populations. Among the most valuable are these:

• There is a difference between an administrator and a leader. Leaders for second-order change are necessarily administrators as well, but they are also people of conviction and passion. Their personalities can differ broadly, but they are inevitably sometimes provocative, sometimes inspirational, always risk takers. They mobilize people to tackle substantive problems and to live with ambiguity as they do so. Even though they may apply pressure at times, they succeed because they inspire commitment rather than because they issue edicts. Their leadership works because they help people connect with something deeper, something better, than the status quo (Fullan, 2001a; Sergiovanni, 1999).
• Leaders for second-order change know where they want to lead, and they have a deep knowledge of the change initiative. They know why they want to invest in the change and why it is worth the risk to ask others to make the journey with them. Leaders for second-order change also know the difference between the vision and the journey required to realize the vision. They understand that the vision involves informed dreaming and that the journey will take principled and strategic planning. They know where they want to be, and they plan and evaluate with the end in mind (Wiggins & McTighe, 2007). Such leaders are students and nurturers of the vision and the plan. They are also persistent students of the change initiative and of the change process.
• Leaders for second-order change are neither impervious to nor overcome by complexity. They are not afraid of making mistakes or

of tensions. They don't seek to eliminate differences of opinion but rather to draw on varied voices to help them find shared meaning. That doesn't mean they like being wrong or don't care what others think about them. Rather, they know that change inevitably generates uncertainty, which in turn spawns tensions. They know that looking for missteps offers opportunity to correct them. These leaders do not compromise their core vision while they learn as they go and use persistent evaluation as a vehicle for learning.

• Leaders model for colleagues what they envision in their colleagues' practice. They are what they want others to become. Leaders for effective differentiation respect individual differences—even when those differences are manifest in counterperspectives. Leaders for effective differentiation create environments safe for risking change and conducive to learning from one another. They make it first necessary and then rewarding to engage in inquiry, debate, and observation about what works—and what doesn't—for individual kids. They help teachers find renewed meaning in their professional practice (Sergiovanni, 1999).

• Leadership begets leadership. Leaders for second-order change cannot—do not—go it alone. Leadership for them is not about being a prima donna, but rather about developing an ensemble, a cadre, a team.

• Real change demands real support for the change. It does not happen because teachers hear a presentation on a topic, go to a conference, or read a book together. Deep and meaningful classroom change requires relearning a complex professional practice—on the order of relearning one's fundamental skills after a stunning injury and necessitating a similar degree of support for the relearning. Further, the relearning requires years, not days, weeks, or months of support.

• Staff development for second-order change must alter beliefs, mind-sets, and practices. It must focus on individuals as well as on the group. Plans for staff development have to be coherent, focused on student needs, closely linked to specific content and to classroom practices, embedded in multiple facets of school life, ongoing, and performed by administrators and teacher leaders (Sparks & Hirsh, 1997).

• Elements in schools and classrooms are interconnected. It is not possible to change them one at a time (Sparks & Hirsh, 1997). Nurturing community among faculty increases its likelihood for students. The quality of curriculum, instruction, and assessment are inextricably linked. Looking at, rather than past, the humanity of students has direct bearing on what and how we elect to teach tomorrow. Changing one thing changes others—for better or for worse.

• The process of second-order change does not have a finish line. There is never a time in teaching when an individual teacher, let alone a faculty, can say, "Got it! Nothing else to figure out." The variety of students joins with the complexity of the teacher's job to render impossible a state of "having arrived" as a teacher. Even if that were not the case, new teachers arrive each year along with new mandates and new students—all defying complacency. Sustaining second-order change is as demanding as generating it in the first place. Leadership for second-order change is really about cultivating and perpetuating the highest possible level of professional expertise in the maximum number of educators for as long as expert teachers are needed.

Leaders at both Conway Elementary School and Colchester High School not only understood these principles but were willing to embody them. At Conway, the principal was unwilling to accept that what is good today is adequate for tomorrow. She was not satisfied with accolades, but rather drew purpose from the belief that teachers learning to raise ceilings of expectation and support for a school's highest-achieving students in heterogeneous classrooms would benefit all students. At Colchester, the principal was unwilling to accept as inevitable a school's downward spiral. She was incensed by a setting in which some students were assigned second-class status. She believed that accelerating expectations in high-quality heterogeneous settings would have to replace segregated classes designed for remediation if her school was to be a dream maker rather than a dream breaker for students. Both principals believed that second-order change should better the school experiences for all students.

Both principals, then, aimed to do whatever it took, for as long as it took, to make their visions tangible. The story of change at Conway is almost linear—thoughtful planning, followed by purposeful action, followed by results informing more targeted planning, and so on. The story of change at Colchester is more random and turbulent but no less thoughtful and no less action oriented. Both principals seemed to internalize the rules of change. Both risked sustained application of those rules.

Teacher liaison Bill Rich concluded that second-order change at Colchester High School was rooted in his colleagues' evolution into a culture committed to continuous shared reflection that informed instructional decisions. "It's that simple," he said. Then he paused and added, "and that hard." The Colchester journey, he explained, caused people to look inward for solutions rather than outward for blame or explanations. It caused them to examine beliefs and practices "so buried in the psyche of a school that they can be invisible to the acculturated, and anyone who shines a light on them risks being rejected by the group." It caused them to ask and grapple publicly for answers to hard questions, including the biggest one, "What is the purpose of our school?" They found the courage to ask questions about the degree to which their practices aligned with research about how students learn. They experienced anger, fear, and exhilaration over small but continual successes. The process was—as it always will be—perpetually demanding, difficult, and rewarding. And they are not finished, nor will they be.

A similar synopsis fits the Conway faculty members' journey. They had a leader with a vision. They developed a plan to achieve the vision. The plan changed. The vision did not. They kept at it. They continue to become what they want to be. It's that easy. And that hard.

It is difficult, confounding, and risky to undertake change to ensure that an increasingly diverse student population can be effectively educated in contemporary schools. Yet the real difficulty, experts remind us (Fullan, 2001b; Reeves, 2006), the real risk, happens if we fail to change.

Appendixes

Appendix A
Example of a Coaching Session with the Conway Principal and a New Teacher

Background

Lane Narvaez, principal of Conway Elementary School, consistently maintains an active role as a classroom observer and coach for teachers who are learning and applying the skills of differentiation. Key in the success of the differentiation initiative at Conway has been the principal's attention to individual teacher development and focus on fidelity to the model of differentiation. When new teachers enter Conway, the principal and staff developer provide formal staff development support. In addition, grade-level colleagues work steadily with new colleagues to provide them with knowledge and support to begin the journey toward differentiating instruction. Nonetheless, the process of differentiating instruction is multifaceted and complex, and it is inevitable that plans will need tightening. The following example shows the principal's level of understanding of differentiation as well as her level of involvement with her teachers as they learn and apply the principles of differentiation.

Below is an assignment focused on role, audience, format, and topic (RAFT) that was developed by Tonee Simmons, who at the time was a new 3rd grade teacher. The task was a culminating assignment for 3rd graders at the end of a social studies unit on Martin Luther King Jr.

Version 1, Before Coaching

What students will KNOW:

- Important events in Martin Luther King Jr.'s life that helped change laws.
- What Martin Luther King Jr. wanted to accomplish and why.

What students will UNDERSTAND:

- Martin Luther King Jr. started a movement toward equality.
- People should stand up for what is right, even if it is not the easy way.
- Regardless of our differences, we need to accept and respect one another.
- Our differences make us unique.
- All cultures should have the same opportunities, and we should learn about our differences.

What students will DO (skills):

- Write for understanding and then present and discuss in class.

The RAFT Assignment

Role	Audience	Format	Topic
Yourself	Martin Luther King Jr.	Thank-you letter	Thank you for making my life better. This is why.
Martin Luther King Jr. as a child in 1936	A friend's parents	Friendly letter	I like him because of who he is, not the color of his skin. Why can't I play with him?
3rd grade teacher	The teacher's students	Timeline	Six dates that will teach your class what is important about Martin Luther King Jr.'s life.
High school student	The student's teacher	Essay	Why Martin Luther King Jr. is such an important person and why he has helped so many people.
Yourself	Your family and friends	Poster poem	I have a dream of peace—write a poem and decorate a poster to show your dreams of peace.
Reporter	The public	Newspaper article	"1929–68: Millions Mourn King's Death" What a difference he has made!
Martin Luther King Jr. in 1963	Himself	Journal entry	Am I making a difference, and what will happen in years to come?

To support students in their work with the RAFT, the teacher also created the following directions and rubric to go with the various RAFT strips.

Thank-You Letter

Write a letter to Dr. King thanking him for what he has taught you and telling him how you use his lessons in your life today. Be sure to include at least two reasons you are thankful, and explain to Dr. King why these are important to you.

(A letter format was provided with a "Dear Dr. King," introduction.)

Friendly Letter

While reading our books and watching our video, we learned that Martin Luther King Jr. was not allowed to play with his friends because he was black and his friends were white. His friends' parents did not believe that Martin Luther King Jr. was as good as they were just because of the color of his skin.

(A letter format was provided with a "Dear Mr. and Mrs.," introduction.)

Timeline

Use the given set of dates to make a timeline of Dr. King's life or find your own in the books we have read. Use at least six events in your timeline. Cut out each event and glue it to the timeline or carefully write them directly on the timeline. Be sure to put them in the correct order on the timeline. Helpful hint: Cut out the events and lay them out on the timeline *before* you glue them down and then check to see if they are in the correct order.

After your timeline is complete, write a paragraph explaining why these dates are important to us today. What did Dr. King accomplish? How did he accomplish these things? Do you think Dr. King was successful? Why?

(Twenty separate events were provided for students to select from and cut out for the timeline.)

Journal Entry

You are going to write a journal entry as Dr. King in the year 1963. You have just given your "I Have a Dream" speech and are reflecting on your accomplishments. Put yourself in his shoes. How are you feeling? Are you making a difference in the world? Are your dreams worth so much hardship? Talk about at least one goal you have accomplished and how you think it will affect the future.

(A letter format was provided with a "Dear Diary," introduction.)

Written Essay

You are to pretend you are a high school student and your assignment is to write a paper about Martin Luther King Jr. You need to write one to two paragraphs about Dr. King's life. Include at least two important events that took place during his life and why they were important not just to Dr. King but to everyone around the country. How have these events impacted our lives today? What makes him a hero to so many? (You may include an illustration showing one event. It is your choice.)

(Lined writing paper was provided.)

Poster Poem

Martin Luther King Jr. believed in peace. He believed that everyone should be able to get along with each other. Use the following outline to create a poem of your own describing what dreams you have to better the world and what peace means to you.

I Have a Dream . . .
I have a dream that I will _____.
I have a dream that my family will _____.
I have a dream that my school will _____.
I have a dream that my community will _____.
I have a dream that the world will _____.

Peace . . .
Peace is like a _____.
Peace looks like _____.
Peace sounds like _____, and
it can be _____, but
peace is always _____.

Now, using the ideas above, write your own poem showing how you feel about peace and what you, as well as your family and friends, can do to promote a peaceful and loving community. Put your poem on a poster and decorate it. You can show this to your family and friends to help teach tolerance and encourage everyone to live peaceful lives.

Newspaper Article

You are a reporter covering the shooting and killing of Martin Luther King Jr. Write a newspaper article describing the difference Dr. King has made. Include at least two reasons that Dr. King was so important. What did he do for people? What kind of person was he? Why are so many people mourning his death? How do you think Dr. King would want to be remembered? What do you think the future holds?

(Lined paper with the title "Martin Luther King Jr. by _____" at the top was provided.)

RAFT Rubric

The teacher designed a rubric that was generic across role, audience, format, and topic for all assignments and added one additional indicator linked to the specific task required for each RAFT option. Below is an example of the rubric for the Thank-You Letter:

Rubric for Thank-You Letter
Role: Student followed the role.—**5 points**
Audience: Student's project was prepared for the correct audience.—**5 points**
Format: Student's project followed the correct format.—**5 points**
Topic: Student followed the topic, added creativity, and used correct grammar/spelling.—**10 points**
Student used time wisely in class and participated in class discussions.—**5 points**
Student included at least two reasons he or she was thankful for Martin Luther King's contributions and how this has affected his or her life.—**10 points**

The Principal's Debriefing Conference with the Teacher

During the principal's observation of the teacher's work, it was clear that this new teacher had understood a great deal in a short time and had invested considerable effort in developing a high-preparation differentiated lesson based on the learning styles of her students and supported each task with scaffolding when necessary. Narvaez was specific in drawing out Simmons's sense of her growth and commending her on it.

At the same time, there were predictable ragged edges in the teacher's work—some simply due to learning about teaching in general, others due to the complexities of differentiation. A synopsis of the steps in the postobservation debriefing session is as follows:

1. Seven choices in the RAFT assignment are likely too many for 3rd graders. During the observation, Narvaez had observed students struggling with the number of options in the assignment and the similarities among some of them. Not only do unnecessary choices create confusion for students, but they create extra work for the teacher as well. Narvaez and the teacher decided to eliminate some of the RAFT options.

2. To determine which choices to eliminate, it was important to look at the goals (KUDs) for the RAFT assignment to be sure each task was aligned with the KUDs.

3. Under "Know," the teacher had appropriately listed two fact statements but had not specified the precise content she was expecting her students to master during the unit.

4. The "Understands" incorrectly contained a "Know" (*Martin Luther King Jr. started a movement toward equality*), and the list did not capture a key connection between prejudice and how we see and judge people or between the elimination of prejudice and peaceful means—both essential understandings about Martin Luther King Jr.'s life and work. Through the process of asking essential questions, the principal guided the conversation to capture the broad understandings of the unit.

5. There was only one "Do," but the teacher's RAFT options required multiple skills. A critical realization was that not all of the tasks required writing, yet the "Do" called for it. The first step in revising the "Do" was to decide which key skills were important for students to demonstrate as part of a culminating assessment on this unit. The teacher saw that students needed to draw on prior knowledge gained about the content, they needed to identify and analyze key events in King's life, and they needed to summarize their conclusions in writing. Furthermore, their writing should be grammatically correct with no spelling errors. At this point, the teacher was able to list the exact skills she expected students to demonstrate through the RAFT assignment.

6. With the KUDs revised, the teacher and principal looked at the initial RAFT options. There were problems with some of the original roles. It would be difficult for a 3rd grader to assume the role of King in 1936 and write a letter to parents. It would also be difficult for the students to become reporters because they had not learned anything about newspaper writing. Looking at the new KUDs, the principal and teacher decided that three of the existing options could be kept but

revised and that a new option should be crafted. At this point the teacher understood that each task should focus on key events and their significance and that each would involve a writing experience. She decided not to drop the poster poem activity. Instead she realized it would make an excellent anchor activity, meaningfully linked to much of the content students had explored about Dr. King's life and work.

7. To adjust the RAFT topics, Narvaez encouraged the teacher to keep in mind that each should be rigorous for students—in other words, call on them to think in complex ways and to apply essential knowledge, understanding, and skill. The two rubrics were then revised to reflect the expectations of the new KUD and the RAFT.

Although many of the original RAFT options had pieces connected to the newly defined KUD, the principal guided the teacher in clarifying each task so that it aligned well with the big ideas, key knowledge, and core skills. As a new teacher, Simmons drew on what she had learned in her staff development workshop on differentiation with Kay Brimijoin at the beginning of the year and subsequent coaching sessions with Brimijoin later in the year. Simmons knew it was important to begin her lesson planning by trying to define what students should know, understand, and do (KUD) in the lesson. Her first attempt shows the typical confusion a teacher encounters and creates when trying to design activities with a KUD that is not fully developed. Without clearly defined learning goals, there was no guarantee that every task in Simmons's RAFT would be aligned with the knowledge, understanding, and skills she wanted her students to master. The opportunity for Simmons to be coached by Narvaez made it possible for the teacher to make some critical adjustments on the spot just as her students had completed a culminating assessment. The expertise of the principal gave Simmons guidance, confirmed her growing competence, sharpened her sense of how quality curriculum and differentiation are interdependent, and built her confidence in her ability to make differentiation effective for all of her students.

Version 2, After Coaching

What students will KNOW:

- Elements of quality writing
- Terms: *prejudice, peaceful protest, civil rights*
- Martin Luther King Jr.

—Childhood

—Contributions

–Peaceful protest movement

–Equal rights for everyone

–"I Have a Dream" speech

What students will UNDERSTAND:

• Prejudice can alter how we see and judge people.

• It is possible to reduce prejudice through peaceful means.

• Every individual is unique and worthy of respect.

• Sometimes standing up for what we know is right may be difficult.

What students will be able to DO (skills):

• Gather information and determine key events in Martin Luther King Jr.'s life.

• Analyze the importance of key events in Martin Luther King Jr.'s life.

• Draw conclusions.

• Share conclusions in writing.

• Use correct grammar and spelling when writing.

• Meet deadlines.

Role	Audience	Format	Topic
African American 3rd grader today	Martin Luther King Jr.	Letter	Here are three ways you have made my life better today. Here is how life used to be and why things are better now.
3rd grade teacher	Your students	Timeline	Use the timeline to teach your class the important events in Martin Luther King Jr.'s life and their significance.
Martin Luther King Jr. in 1963	Himself	Journal entry	What have I done, and what does it mean? Am I making a difference?
Publisher	3rd grade students	Social studies book	Choose three important events in Martin Luther King Jr.'s life for this chapter in the new book. Illustrate them and write about their significance.

Below are the teacher's descriptions for the RAFT tasks following post-conference revisions.

Letter

Write a letter to Dr. King telling him three ways he has made life better for you than it was for African Americans before 1955. Compare your life today with that of an African American before 1955. Use the graphic organizer to help you plan your letter.

(A letter format will be provided with a "Dear Dr. King, Your work and peaceful actions have . . . " introduction. In addition, graphic organizers ranging from concrete to open ended will be provided for students to organize their ideas for the letter.)

Timeline

Use the given set of dates to make a timeline of Dr. King's life or find your own in the books we have read. Use at least six events in your timeline. Cut out each event and glue it to the timeline or carefully write it directly on the timeline. Be sure to put each event in the correct order on the timeline. Helpful hint: Cut out the events and lay them out on the timeline *before* you glue them down, and then check to see if they are in the correct order.

After your timeline is complete, write a paragraph explaining to your students why these dates are important to us today. How did Dr. King change the way people treated each other? How did he accomplish these things? Do you think Dr. King was successful? Why?

(Fourteen separate events will be provided for students to select from and cut out for the timeline.)

Journal Entry

You are going to write a journal entry as Dr. King in the year 1963. You have just given your "I Have a Dream" speech and are reflecting on your accomplishments. Put yourself in his shoes. How are you feeling? Are you making a difference in the world? Are your dreams worth so much hardship? Talk about at least three goals you have reached and how you think they are changing the world.

(A diary format will be provided with a "Dear Diary, Tonight I gave my 'I Have a Dream' speech, and as I think about it, there are three goals I believe I have accomplished . . . " introduction.)

Social Studies Book

Your company is publishing a new social studies book for 3rd graders. You are working on the chapter on Martin Luther King Jr. Choose at least three important events in Martin Luther King Jr.'s life. Illustrate each event and write a paragraph that serves as a "caption" describing the event and why it is important.

Revised Rubric

Again, the teacher's rubric is generic across certain shared criteria. On all the revised RAFT tasks, the descriptors for role, audience, format, and using time wisely are the same. The descriptor for topic, however, is customized for each individual task. Below is an example of the rubric for the letter:

Revised Rubric for Letter

Role: Student assumes correct role.—**5 points**
Audience: Student's project is appropriate for the audience.—**5 points**
Format: Student's project is presented in the correct format.—**5 points**
Topic: Student writes about at least three ways Martin Luther King Jr. has made life better.—**15 points**
Student used time wisely in class.—**5 points**
Student uses correct grammar/spelling.—**5 points**

Simmons's Reflection on Her Refined Lesson Plan

As a new teacher, I took to differentiation because I believed that it was the right way to teach in order to reach all learners. I wanted to be the best teacher I could be for my students, but there were so many parts to differentiation that I really didn't understand. I was unable to fully create a differentiated lesson. I thought I was differentiating, but I was missing a few key pieces.

I think that one of the most important things that I learned about creating differentiated lessons was the KUD. In my first lesson, and two previous lessons I created, I thought about what to teach first. I then thought of the activities that I thought would work for each. Lastly, I completed the KUD.

After conferencing with my principal and having some sessions with Kay, I realized that I first needed to create the KUD and go from there. The reason for creating a differentiated lesson is to meet the standards and objectives in a KUD. By becoming more familiar with the KUD and really understanding what each part should include and address, I am better able to make my activities so that everyone is reaching a common goal. After you decide what your students should know and understand, then you can start to decide how to best reach this goal with different types of lessons.

After fully understanding the KUD, this brought me to my next challenge. Every activity needs to be meaningful and directly reflect your KUD. After becoming more familiar with the different types of learning styles, I was better able to narrow my activities down in order to represent each learning style for my revised version. I also included scaffolding in my activities by reading and writing readiness. I looked at what my students' needs were and realized that I was not testing any part of their reading or writing in this particular lesson, but instead was looking for understanding of the subject matter. Because of this, some students were at a disadvantage with the original activities, so I prepared more appropriate formats allowing them to really show me what they had learned.

Little by little I am learning the hows and whys of differentiated lessons. I grasp a little more after each lesson I create, and then I must go back and reflect on how to improve this lesson for next year. I have found that my best resource is my coworkers. I conference with my principal after each lesson as well as my grade level, and together we look at ways to improve lessons and to be sure all the important parts of a good lesson are addressed.

When teachers experience modeling and coaching on quality curriculum design, there are two important outcomes. First, students are more likely to be successful in reaching intended goals, seeing the purpose of their learning, and staying engaged and focused. Second, teachers internalize a system of thinking about how to create a blueprint for instruction that will provide a road map with directions that are absolutely clear. Such conversations professionalize the teaching-learning process and help forge partnerships between teacher and principal toward more effective classrooms.

Appendix B
The Evolution of a Deep Understanding of Differentiation at Conway Elementary School

One of the most difficult obstacles to overcome when beginning staff development in differentiation is staff members' beliefs that they are already differentiating instruction. For example, teachers often explain that they have grouped students by readiness and are therefore differentiating based on student readiness. The reality is that the groups rarely change and what has been created is fixed, not flexible, grouping. The process of staff development for *defensible differentiation* is analogous to peeling away the layers of an onion to get at the core of the how and why differentiated instruction *should* work. Some of the major shifts in teacher learning discovered along the Conway journey may help others as they begin schoolwide differentiation. Key concepts include the following:

• **The Teacher as Facilitator.** It was difficult for many teachers to give up control of classroom learning and turn it over to the students. This was a shift from teachers delivering all instruction to being facilitators in the classroom. Teachers learned that by putting their efforts into the preparation of differentiated activities they were able to monitor the class as the students worked. Students were actively engaged, and the teacher then had time to work with small groups in a clinic format when there were questions or when concepts were unclear.

• **Student Feedback.** The role of student feedback regarding the lesson was another major shift. Teachers had not previously asked students for feedback on the lesson. When they were asked for input, students felt more vested in their learning and teachers received valuable information as to what needed to be changed and which students needed help with the learning objective. The students were acting as mirrors for the teacher—they were telling teachers what to *adjust* for future instruction.

• **Managing Differentiation.** Teachers at Conway learned to use *anchor activities* to help them manage time for working with small groups. These activities anchor students to academically meaningful tasks that students can complete independently, thus allowing the teacher the flexibility to instruct small groups on their assigned differentiated tasks. The activities are also useful when children finish their work at different times. As teachers began to use anchor activities, management issues disappeared. Strategies for managing a differentiated classroom were a part of most staff development at Conway.

• **Peer Observations and Learning.** One of the positive outcomes of schoolwide differentiation was that teachers began to share differentiation strategies and lesson plans and to participate in peer observations. Despite the initial reluctance of teachers to cross the line and go into a colleague's room to observe a lesson, the culture changed, with leadership from the principal. Once teachers accepted mutual observations, this step was key in breaking the ice and produced other benefits. Teachers realized the advantage of having another set of eyes to observe the lesson and how the students worked in their groups. Ultimately, teachers learned to plan together and to share their lessons, realizing that they could multiply the number of differentiated lessons ready to teach at their grade level.

• **Rigor.** To ensure that students at all levels of differentiation received challenging instruction with activities requiring complex thinking skills, Conway teachers gradually rewrote lesson plans and constructed tasks with more rigor in the various curricular areas. In many cases, they scaffolded instruction by providing struggling students with tools or aids to use in more complex tasks. This process shifted teachers' prior concept of flexible grouping to another level and provided motivation to students to learn at a higher level.

• **Pre-assessment.** About three years into differentiation, Conway faculty realized that to know where students were in their understanding of a specific skill or topic, the teachers had to pre-assess for that skill immediately before they taught it—and not just rely on previous formal assessment scores. They developed pre-assessments for many skills and readiness levels, including advanced students, as they came to understand that they could not provide tasks that stretched advanced students without knowing their current ceilings of performance. Using a range of pre-assessments helped teachers design and modify instruction as the lessons and units progressed, providing more challenging material as particular students needed it.

• **Internalizing the Understanding Behind Lesson Design.** Many teachers found it easier to plan lessons around what students should know and do than to express what students should understand (KUDs). Over several years, teachers gradually deepened their own conceptual understanding of their lessons and realized that *understanding* was the key to helping students make personal connections to the subject matter and to retain what they learned. Teachers also learned to address KUD objectives before designing lessons and to align all parts of the lesson (and the differentiated activities) with the core learning goals. This clarity enabled teachers to give up or modify favorite activities that did not effectively address KUDs. They also polished their ability to distinguish between skills and activities. Many Conway teachers learned to discuss the KUDs *with the students* at the beginning of a lesson and to ensure that differentiated lessons contained the same essential knowledge, understanding, and skill for all learners.

• **Curriculum Mapping and Cross-Grade-Level Planning.** In the fourth year of working with differentiation at Conway, teachers began to learn about curriculum mapping—planning grade-to-grade alignment of curriculum areas. Teachers worked together to map out learning goals by subject and grade-level objectives. These were posted on a large chart in the teacher lounge. Teachers had the opportunity to develop tasks, activities, and products that aligned with the various levels, on a K–5 continuum. By using the map, teachers began new cross-grade-level partnerships. For example, 2nd and 5th grade teachers found ways to work together as their students learned about the solar system. This process also enabled special subject area teachers to develop products that aligned with grade-level concepts.

• **The Changing Role of the Coach.** As Conway began professional development in differentiation, the school provided a coach to teach staff about differentiation and to coach teachers through the lessons and help them move forward. After several years, the coach served as an advisor to grade-level teams as they planned lessons and units. The coach also worked with special area teachers in showing them how to support grade-level learning objectives through their lessons. By collaborating with teachers in lesson planning and adding new perspectives when appropriate, the coach's role changed to match the changing needs of the faculty.

The following reflection of a Conway teacher captures many of these concepts key to the evolution of second-order change toward defensible differentiation at the school:

> When differentiation was first introduced, I saw it as a way to deliver curriculum, but when I did it, it was lessons in isolation. As we became more involved I realized that it drives everything you do in the classroom . . . from the way you deliver curriculum to the way you interact with your students to the way students interact with each other. I also realized the importance of the KUD in beginning your lesson planning. I began to feel more comfortable with what I was doing and excited about sharing my work and getting feedback from my peers—still very vulnerable, but willing to take the risk to improve my abilities. At this point in my career, I want to become stronger in differentiation, and I want to share, coach, and plan with a peer. It has been a wonderful journey, and I look forward to more differentiation.

Appendix C
Example of Feedback Provided by the Colchester Teacher Liaison to Colleagues

In his role as a supporter and facilitator for teachers as they implemented differentiation, two very young teachers came to Bill Rich, Colchester High School's teacher liaison, for help. The two teachers taught two sections of a combined English-history class called the American Experience to 10th graders, with approximately 36 students per class. By October of this particular year, they began to really struggle with the classes, feeling that they were moving too slowly for some of their students and still losing some who did not understand the content. Off-task behavior was causing disruptions.

Rich's first advice to the teachers was not to be too hard on themselves. He reminded them that some ambiguity is inevitable in teaching. In examining some of the class issues, Rich told them he had discovered in his own teaching that it was important to challenge the high-ability students first in order to set a good tone and pace for the class. He also advised them to share their thinking about their teaching with the class and to take time to be sure they had the same goals and expectations for the students before they moved forward as a team. He talked with them about developing a survey to elicit insights from the students that could guide an open conversation with the classes. Further, he suggested waiting until a natural break occurred in course content before using the survey.

In addition to conversations with his two young colleagues, Rich provided the following written feedback on a draft of the survey that the two teachers shared with him. It serves as an example of one kind of personalized staff development that is closely linked to the needs of individual teachers. The teachers crafted the survey as a "first quarter huddle," using a football analogy that seemed to fit the fact that the class was completing the first grading period—or first quarter—of the school year and the teachers wanted to have a huddle with the students to make their team stronger:

Hi,

I think your 1st Quarter Huddle looks good. I have a few recommendations, but keep in mind that you should do what feels right to you. You are close to these classes so you will have a better idea of the best way to approach them. That said, here are my ideas.

1. I like your huddle metaphor. In a way, teaching is like running a two-minute offense in football—there is no huddle, it's a little desperate, and often includes a Hail Mary pass or two. I think you are right to emphasize that this is a time to take a pause for the cause in order to calibrate your teaching and their learning now that you've gotten to know each other.

2. I like how you incorporated the "best self" notion, but I would recommend not saying that you want them to always try to be their best selves, only because that will be unattainable for most. What I would recommend is asking that they rise to this occasion and be their best selves while filling out this survey. (I also tend to call on the best self thing on occasions when I really need them to pull through. By only requiring them to do this every so often, it makes it more special and they actually tend then to do it. Asking them to go for it always makes it lose some of its power.)

3. Your first three questions seem to be asking the same thing. Perhaps they can be wed into one question regarding challenge. Do they know about the idea that "People learn best when they do work that is just a little harder than what they are used to"? This might be a way to frame this question. I'm sure you're going to do this, but I'd give them more space to write, and I'd be sure to let them know how important that writing will be to you. I like your last two questions. Sometimes what I do for those two questions is ask students to give three pieces of advice to me, three pieces of advice for the class, and three pieces of advice to themselves that, if followed, would make the class work better for all. I separate these into three different questions, and I actually put in a number 1, 2, and 3 under each one so they are more likely to actually put in three pieces of advice. These distilled responses are usually instructive and easily quotable.

4. If you do what I just mentioned, you might not need the last question. Sometimes I like to end with an open-ended question, something like, "Before we collect this, is there anything else you think we should consider before we come back to you with our plan for making adjustments before we dive into our next marking period?" Most kids don't answer this, but sometimes it elicits a significant response from a few kids.

I think the most important part of this survey will be the tone when you set it up in class. If the kids sense that you are sincere and even being a little vulnerable with them, they tend to respond best. Whatever you can do to talk to them "from the heart" so that they will be their "best selves" in their responses, the better. They should know how seriously you take this and how eager you are to act on their insights. They should know that you will do whatever it takes to make progress. If they know you are sincere in your plan to use their feedback, it can be very powerful, especially when it is in concert with other adjustments (calls home, private conversations, routing for starting class, notes in mailboxes, etc.).

Look forward to having another conversation soon about how I might be able to support your efforts. Keep in mind that teaching can feel like a sprint, but it is a long-distance run. As a baseball fan, I also like to think of it as a long season, filled with streaks and slumps. Rarely as a teacher have I had amazing and dramatic turn-around moments. Often, though, after much turmoil and many adjustments I can see how the aggregate of many small decisions has made things better. Remember the goal: progress, not perfection. Steady progress—not without setbacks—leads to great things over time.

Have a great weekend.

Bill

Following is the form of the survey the two teachers used with their classes as the first quarter of the year ended:

1st Quarter Huddle!

Greetings American Experiencers!

We have just passed the quarter mark for our year and we believe it is important to stop and take stock of where we have been and what we have done well and look ahead to where we are going and what we can improve. We have enjoyed getting to know each of you and look forward to deepening those relationships throughout the year.

We will spend some time talking about this as we transition into the second quarter, but we are moving from the period of the year where we get to know you as learners and get to know the class as a community to the meat of our year, where we expect you to challenge yourself so that you will walk out of here in June feeling good about the effort you made, the skills and knowledge you gained, the experiences you had, and the impression you left on us, your classmates, and yourself. We will focus on "being our best selves" as teachers and will continue to work to challenge you and meet your needs. In this survey, we want you to really think about how you can improve your learning experience and our classroom community, so please try to "be your best self" when answering our questions below.

Please answer all questions honestly and respectfully.

People learn best when they do work that is just a little harder than what they are used to. Please <u>respond</u> to this thought and think about how challenged you feel in this class—are we challenging you enough? Are you challenging yourself? Are you doing the required work? Are you doing your best work?

Think about your participation in this class. Are you participating regularly? If not, why not? Is your participation dominating our air space in a way that makes it difficult for others to participate? If so, how can you improve your participation?

Do you feel that our classroom is a safe learning environment? Please describe why or why not.

What was your favorite(s) subject/topic/activity so far this semester and why?

In order to make this class better and improve your learning experience, please give us some advice. . .

What three pieces of advice would you give us, your teachers?

1.

2.

3.

What three pieces of advice would you give your classmates?

1.

2.

3.

What three pieces of advice would you give yourself?

1.

2.

3.

"He who does the work does the learning."—Anonymous

Please think about this quotation for a moment and then respond by writing a complete paragraph.

- What does this quote mean to you?
- Do you agree or disagree? Why?
- How does it apply to you and your performance, work ethic, and behavior in this class?

_____

_____

_____

_____

_____

_____

_____

_____

_____

Other suggestions/ideas/feedback. . .

As a result of data gleaned from the survey and Rich's advice to the teachers to find two or three things they could change and put into action all at once, the teachers took the following steps:

1. They made a more deliberate effort to differentiate assignments and materials in ways that provided a challenge to high-ability students. At times, this included restricting assignment options they could select.

2. They changed the physical setup of the room and created new seating assignments, which they still do from time to time.

3. They set stricter limits on student behaviors and removed students from the classroom when they could not behave appropriately.

4. They gave students additional choices in assignments and projects.

The advice and support offered to the young teachers by the school's teacher liaison were significant in their growth in using ongoing assessment information to modify their teaching, establishing classroom community, managing a differentiated classroom, and providing more appropriately challenging assignments for high-end learners.

Appendix D
Example of a KUD Lesson Planning Format at Colchester High School

A precursor to sustained, effective differentiation is determining what is essential for students to know, understand, and do (KUD) as the result of a unit. Differentiation then occurs to support all students in developing and, if possible, extending the identified knowledge, understanding, and skills. Many teachers have not thought about their curriculum in that way, and therefore developing KUDs can be frustrating at the outset. Without a KUD format (or some other format that specifies essential knowledge, understanding, and skills), teachers tend to give advanced students more work, to give strugglers less work, and to provide related but ill-focused choices for student work. High-quality differentiation hinges on stating and focusing on what students should understand. Developing those understandings will enable students to recall, retrieve, and transfer what they learn. An example of a KUD planning guide from Colchester follows. The concept-based approach to curriculum helps teachers focus their curriculum planning, and subsequently their plans for differentiation, on essential knowledge, understanding, and skills for all students to master while adhering to the requirements of state standards.

The Human Experience: English

Reading and Writing the Self

Trimester 1

KNOW:

- Literary, poetic, and cinematic terms
- Background material necessary to understand text
- How to read poetry aloud
- How to approach poetry using the "poetry breakdown" method
- Etymological and found vocabulary
- There is a controversy that surrounds Chris McCandless's death
- Jon Krakauer learns about himself by telling Chris's story

UNDERSTAND:

Literacy (reading, writing, and viewing with a critical "eye") is a means for us

—to discover and construct ourselves,

—to examine how *writers* have discovered and constructed themselves, and

—to explore how *characters in literature* have discovered and constructed themselves.

and. . .

–Myths were used to explain the unexplainable.

–People have often tried to "find themselves" by escaping to nature.

Reading	Writing	Literary Community
<u>Myth:</u> *Narcissus* <u>Texts:</u> *Into the Wild* (Krakauer) *Walden* selections (Thoreau) "To Build a Fire" (London) "The Ethicist" (*NY Times*) "This I Believe" (NPR) <u>Poetry:</u> *Poems of the Self* collection <u>Film:</u> *Elephant Man* <u>Honors Texts</u> (Tiered): *Bad Boy* (Myers) *The Wizard of Earthsea* (LeGuin) *Catcher in the Rye* (Salinger)	Regular Journal Writing Write Your Own Myth Dear Chris Letters Ethicist Responses Poetry Nonfiction Writing <u>Culminating Assessment:</u> Statement of Personal Philosophy, whereby students explore how literacy, including literary experiences in this class, influenced their self-knowledge and self-construction (essential writing that all students complete to a high standard)	"Read-alouds" Writing Groups: Personal Philosophy Vocabulary Program

DO (content activities and assessments):

When students successfully complete the culminating assessment (Statement of Personal Philosophy), they demonstrate the following Vermont Grade Expectations for high school.

READING

Students . . .

- RHS: 13 . . . analyze and interpret elements of literary texts, citing evidence where appropriate.
- RHS: 15 . . . generate well-developed and grounded personal responses to what is read through a variety of means.
- RHS: 18 . . . demonstrate the habit of reading widely and in depth.

WRITING

Students. . .

- WHS: 2 . . . demonstrate command of appropriate English conventions.
- WHS: 5 . . . show an understanding of plot/ideas/concepts in literary and informational texts and make thematic connections among texts, prior knowledge, and the broader world of ideas.

Appendix E
Sample Faculty Survey About
Progress on Differentiation at
Conway Elementary School

1. How do you think Conway's students have grown as a result of your
professional development in differentiation?

2. When you differentiate lessons, are students grasping concepts better
than when you do not differentiate?

3. Please list the pros and cons of your work with differentiation from a
professional and personal perspective.

    <u>Pros</u>

    <u>Cons</u>

4. Describe as specifically as possible how your understanding of differentiation has changed over time.

5. Do you believe parent and student opinions about differentiation have evolved over time? If so, what do you think might have influenced that evolution?

6. Outline a wish list for the next steps in staff development or other support for our continued growth in differentiation.

Appendix F
Example of an Exit Card Used to Monitor Professional Development at Colchester High School

Name: _____

1. What did you accomplish today?

2. How does this work advance differentiated instruction?

3. As a result of today's work, do you have any questions related to differentiating instruction?

4. On a 1 to 5 scale (1 = poor, 5 = excellent), how would you rate the overall quality of today's inservice?

| 1 | 2 | 3 | 4 | 5 |

5. Please complete the grid below.

Three things that I enjoyed about today.	Three suggestions for the next inservice.
1.	1.
2.	2.
3.	3.

6. Do you have any other comments or suggestions you'd like to pass along to the Professional Development Committee?

Appendix G
Sample Colchester Student Surveys to Monitor Understanding of Differentiation and Its Effects on Students

I. The American Experience: Ongoing Course Evaluation
After reading each statement, please circle the ONE response (Strongly Agree to Strongly Disagree) that best matches how you feel.

Please comment on *each of your ratings* in the space provided. Help us understand your ratings with a sentence or two.

1. I think that the amount of homework generally has been too little for my challenge level. In other words, I believe that a greater homework load would be better for me academically.

    Strongly Agree   Agree   Disagree   Strongly Disagree

2. I think that the difficulty of homework has generally been too easy for my challenge level. In other words, I believe that more difficult homework would be better for me academically. I'm asking you to "amp it up" for me.

    Strongly Agree   Agree   Disagree   Strongly Disagree

3. What goes on <u>during</u> class generally challenges me. In other words, I find myself doing and thinking about things during class, and this helps me to further my intellect.

Strongly Agree   Agree   Disagree   Strongly Disagree

4. Ms. Mullin and Mr. Blanchette generally try to vary the activities during class and for homework so that a variety of learners and learning styles are taken into account.

Strongly Agree   Agree   Disagree   Strongly Disagree

5. In *The American Experience* my teachers try to know me well enough to tailor my learning to fit my needs.

Strongly Agree   Agree   Disagree   Strongly Disagree

6. *The American Experience* does not stress writing enough. In other words, I would like more writing for homework and during class.

Strongly Agree   Agree   Disagree   Strongly Disagree

7. *The American Experience* does not stress reading enough. In other words, I would like a greater emphasis on reading.

Strongly Agree   Agree   Disagree   Strongly Disagree

8. *The American Experience* does not stress vocabulary enough. In other words, I would like a greater emphasis on vocabulary.

Strongly Agree   Agree   Disagree   Strongly Disagree

9. Ms. Mullin or Mr. Blanchette has graded me appropriate to my readiness (ability) level. In other words, I feel my teacher is generally a fair grader.

Strongly Agree   Agree   Disagree   Strongly Disagree

10. Ms. Mullin and Mr. Blanchette have contributed to a friendly community spirit in our class.

Strongly Agree   Agree   Disagree   Strongly Disagree

Below, add any comments you wish. Thank you for your constructive comments. We promise you that we will take your comments to heart as we plan for the rest of the year.

II. Thinking About Our Class

We need your help. We're going to Chicago to make a presentation to a large group of teachers who want to know what we've learned from teaching this two-year pilot at Colchester High. Specifically, they want to know how to differentiate instruction so that all students can learn well in a heterogeneous class. We have lots of ideas about this, but we want to include your ideas in our presentation.

Below are several questions that will help you consider different elements of learning in this class. Please take this seriously because we will be excerpting parts of your responses to share with teachers from around the country.

1. Why is it especially important to have to have a strong and respectful sense of community in D.I. classes?

2. What are some of the useful ways teachers can build strong communities in diverse classes?

3. What are the advantages of using concepts to organize learning?

4. What learning activities seem particularly appropriate to use with students who have a wide range of interests, learning styles, and readiness levels?

5. Imagine that you had not become part of this two-year, D.I. pilot. How would your life have been different?

6. If you had a neighbor or a sibling who was entering a heterogeneous D.I. class, what advice would you give her?

7. Compose a short memo to a teacher who is considering teaching a diverse group of students. In it, let the teacher know what you think she must keep in mind. Also let her know what mistakes to avoid.

Appendix H
Example Letter Showing Colchester Principal's Communication

January 2003

Colchester Parents and Students:

Two years ago, we embarked on the ambitious mission of ensuring equity and excellence for ALL students in this high school. In spite of budget setbacks, we have remained steadfast in that mission. Let me begin by making it clear that I strongly support Advanced Placement courses. In the last four years we have added, not eliminated, AP offerings. I am committed to continue developing our AP programs. I will continue to advocate strongly for the funding to support them, even with lower-than-average enrollment. I also support a college preparatory curriculum for all students with the option to accelerate within the differentiated classroom.

By many indicators, Colchester High School has improved markedly over the last four years. Our dropout rate is the lowest in Chittenden County. Postsecondary attendance has risen. Student performance on the statewide tests, the New Standards Reference Exams (NSRE), in math and English/language arts has doubled. In many subtests our students perform significantly above the state average. In the science PASS test our students scored well above the state average as well. The school community and I are intent on continuing to be better at what we do.

Differentiated instruction is not a budget issue. It is not in conflict with AP and accelerated courses. To the contrary, differentiation should happen in all classrooms, including the AP and accelerated classes. Why? Because these are the characteristics of differentiated instruction:

- Students are seen as unique individuals who have a variety of interests and learning styles.
- Teachers know it is important to know each student well in order to meet his/her needs.
- Teachers are trained in teaching practices that ensure that each student is highly challenged.
- Classrooms are safe, exciting places where all individuals share in a challenging learning community.

Differentiated instruction is the term used when schools insist that teachers do these things in a thoughtful and intentional way. Differentiated instruction identifies good practices that are already in place—and have been for years. What I just described is good teaching for all. These are our beliefs about the philosophy of differentiation:

- that we are committed to equity and excellence for all students;
- that we will come to know your students very well and that we will take each one of them as far as possible;
- that we have conducted a successful (action research–based) two-year pilot in differentiated instruction: East/West Studies and American Experience;
- that, when done well, student achievement (for all students— advanced through those who struggle) improves in a heterogeneous class that differentiates instruction;
- that this type of instruction requires rigorous professional development for teachers and a commitment of resources (we have begun and will continue);
- and finally that we will use action research to assess and adjust what we are doing and that we will share this information with you at every step along the way (we have begun and will continue).

In humanities this means that every student will be part of East/West Studies, a team-taught course with a challenging curriculum in its third year of implementation. Every team will have students of varying levels of readiness, interests, and learning profiles.

In science, all students will be enrolled in Science 9. Two teachers will assume responsibility for Science 9 and will be given the time and resources to work together and with other 9th grade teachers in delivering a curriculum that meets all students where they are and challenges them to higher levels of achievement. We know from our pilot that, with thoughtful instruction, the achievement of the advanced students is not compromised, in fact it is enhanced, in a differentiated setting.

In math, 9th grade students will be enrolled in one of two settings: Algebra or Geometry, depending on their choices in the middle school. The math teachers anticipate varied levels of readiness and different student needs in each of these courses. They, too, are prepared to support the students who struggle and to challenge the advanced-level students in ways that prepare them for the rigors of upper-level math courses in the future.

In education we cannot shut down the factory to retool the line. We must retool as the line moves along and then examine closely, adjust, change, and reinvent when necessary. In the future, you may hear us mention habits of mind. Ten years ago, when we developed the Common Core and eventually the *VT Framework of Standards*, we were asked to identify the knowledge, skills, and dispositions necessary to succeed in the 21st century. High schools are working hard on the skills and knowledge, but we have not done enough with the dispositions. What are the intelligent and effective qualities a learner must possess when confronted with a problem? Persistence, listening to others with empathy and understanding, thinking flexibly, communicating, creating, and innovating: these are the habits of mind that will enable the struggling learner to experience competence and the student functioning at a high level to perform above the high standard set for him or her. You will hear more about the habits of mind as time goes on.

One final thought: college admission is the most frequently cited obstacle to the changes we are undertaking. I have been assured by college admissions counselors that, with a comprehensive school profile and notations on the transcript, this will not be a problem. On March 20th at 6:30 p.m. we will sponsor an evening to discuss and explain differentiated instruction to our incoming 9th grade parents and students. I cordially invite anyone in the community to attend.

Regards,

Joyce Stone, Principal

References

Bransford, J., Brown, A., & Cocking, R. (2000). *How people learn: Brain, mind, experience, and school.* Washington, DC: National Academy Press.

Burke, P., Christensen, J., & Fessler, P. (1984). *Teacher career stages: Implications for staff development.* Bloomington, IN: Phi Delta Kappa.

Cohen, E., & Goodlad, J. (1994). *Designing groupwork: Strategies for the heterogeneous classroom.* New York: Teachers College Press.

Conroy, P. (2002). *My losing season.* New York: Doubleday.

Danielson, C. (2006). *Teacher leadership.* Alexandria, VA: Association for Supervision and Curriculum Development.

Darling-Hammond, L., & McLaughlin, M. (1999). Investing in teaching as a learning profession: Policy problems and prospects. In L. Darling-Hammond & G. Sykes (Eds.), *Teaching as the learning profession: Handbook of policy and practice* (pp. 376–411). San Francisco: Jossey-Bass.

Darling-Hammond, L., & Sykes, G. (Eds.). (1999). *Teaching as the learning profession: Handbook of policy and practice.* San Francisco: Jossey-Bass.

Downey, C., Steffy, B., English, F., Frase, L., & Poston, W. (2004). *The three-minute classroom walk-through: Changing supervisory practice one teacher at a time.* Thousand Oaks, CA: Corwin.

Duke, D. (2004). *The challenges of educational change.* Boston: Pearson.

Dweck, C. (2006). *Mindset: The new psychology of success.* New York: Random House.

Earl, L. (2003). *Assessment as learning: Using classroom assessment to maximize student learning.* Thousand Oaks, CA: Corwin.

Educational Research Service. (1992). *Academic challenge for the children of poverty.* Arlington, VA: Author.

Evans, R. (1996). *The human side of school change: Reform, resistance, and the real-life problems of innovation.* San Francisco: Jossey-Bass.

Fuchs, L., & Fuchs, D. (2002). *What is scientifically-based research on progress monitoring* (Technical report). Nashville, TN: Vanderbilt University.

Fullan, M. (1991). *The new meaning of educational change.* (2nd ed.). New York: Teachers College Press.

Fullan, M. (1993). *Change forces: Probing the depths of educational reform.* London: Falmer.

Fullan, M. (1995). The limits and potential of professional development. In T. Guskey & M. Huberman (Eds.), *Professional development in education: New paradigms and practices* (pp. 253–267). New York: Teachers College Press.

Fullan, M. (2001a). *Leading in a culture of change.* San Francisco: Jossey-Bass.

Fullan, M. (2001b). *The new meaning of educational change.* (3rd ed.). New York: Teachers College Press.

Fullan, M., Hill, P., & Crevola, C. (2006). *Breakthrough.* Thousand Oaks, CA: Corwin.

Glickman, C. (2002). *Leadership for learning: How to help teachers succeed.* Alexandria, VA: Association for Supervision and Curriculum Development.

Goodlad, J. (1990). *Teachers for our nation's schools.* San Francisco: Jossey-Bass.

Guskey, T. (1995). Professional development in education: In search of the optimal mix. In T. Guskey & M. Huberman (Eds.), *Professional development in education: New paradigms and practices* (pp. 144–131). New York: Teachers College Press.

Hawley, W., & Valli, L. (1999). The essentials of effective professional development. In L. Darling-Hammond & G. Sykes (Eds.), *Teaching as the learning profession: Handbook of policy and practice* (pp. 127–150). San Francisco: Jossey-Bass.

Hoerr, T. (2005). *The art of school leadership.* Alexandria, VA: Association for Supervision and Curriculum Development.

Huberman, M. (1983). Recipes for busy kitchens. *Knowledge: Creation, diffusion, and utilization, 4,* 478–510.

Joyce, B., & Showers, B. (1995). *Student achievement through staff development: Fundamentals of school renewal.* White Plains, NY: Longman.

Joyce, B., & Showers, B. (2002). *Student achievement through staff development.* (3rd ed.). Alexandria, VA: Association for Supervision and Curriculum Development.

Kanold, T. (2006). The flywheel effect. *Journal of Staff Development, 27*(2), 16–21.

Kaufman, H. (1971). *The limits of organizational change.* Tuscaloosa, AL: University of Alabama Press.

Kennedy, M. (2005). *Inside teaching: How classroom life undermines reform.* Cambridge, MA: Harvard University Press.

Kruse, S., Louis, K. S., & Bryk, A. (1994, spring). *Building professional community in schools.* Madison, WI: Center on Organization and Restructuring of Schools, University of Wisconsin.

Kulik, J., & Kulik, C. (1992). Meta-analytic findings on grouping programs. *Gifted Child Quarterly, 36*(2), 73–77.

Lambert, L. (2005, February). Leadership for lasting reform. *Educational Leadership, 62*(5), 62–65.

Marx, G. (2000). *Ten trends: Educating children for a profoundly different future.* Arlington, VA: Educational Research Service.

Marzano, R., Waters, T., & McNulty, B. (2005). *School leadership that works: From research to results.* Alexandria, VA: Association for Supervision and Curriculum Development.

McNamara, B. (2007). *Learning disabilities: Bridging the gap between research and classroom practice.* Upper Saddle River, NJ: Pearson.

Powell, W., & Napoliello, S. (2005, February). Using observation to improve instruction. *Educational Leadership, 62*(5), 52–55.

Reeves, D. (2006). *The learning leader: How to focus school improvement for better results.* Alexandria, VA: Association for Supervision and Curriculum Development.

Rogers, E. (1995). *Diffusion of innovations.* (4th ed.). New York: Free Press.

Safer, N., & Fleischman, S. (2005, February). How student progress monitoring improves instruction. *Educational Leadership, 62*(5), 81–82.

Saphier, J., King, M., & D'Auria, J. (2006). Three strands form strong school leadership. *Journal of Staff Development, 27*(2), 51–57.

Sarason, S. (1996). *Revisiting the culture of the school and the problem of change.* New York: Teachers College Press.

Schlechty, P. (1997). *Inventing better schools: An action plan for educational reform.* San Francisco: Jossey-Bass.

Schmoker, M. (2006). *Results now: How we can achieve unprecedented improvements in teaching and learning.* Alexandria, VA: Association for Supervision and Curriculum Development.

Sergiovanni, T. (1999). *Rethinking leadership.* Glenview, IL: Skylight.

Sparks, D., & Hirsh, S. (1997). *A new vision for staff development.* Alexandria, VA: Association for Supervision and Curriculum Development.

Spillane, J. (2006). *Distributed leadership.* San Francisco: Jossey-Bass.

Spillane, J., Halverson, R., & Diamond, J. (2001). Investigating school leadership practice: A distributed perspective. *Educational Researcher, 30*(1), 23–28.

Sykes, G. (1999). Teacher and student learning: Strengthening their connection. In L. Darling-Hammond & G. Sykes (Eds.), *Teaching as the learning profession: Handbook of policy and practice* (pp. 151–179). San Francisco: Jossey-Bass.

Taylor, R., Baskerville, S., Bruder, S., Bennett, E., & Schulte, F. (2006). Six challenges are key for high-performing schools that aim to achieve more. *Journal for Staff Development, 27*(2), 22–27.

Tomlinson, C. A. (1999). *The differentiated classroom: Responding to the needs of all learners.* Alexandria, VA: Association for Supervision and Curriculum Development.

Tomlinson, C. A. (2003). *Fulfilling the promise of the differentiated classroom: Strategies and tools for responsive teaching.* Alexandria, VA: Association for Supervision and Curriculum Development.

Tomlinson, C. A., & McTighe, J. (2006). *Integrating differentiated instruction and understanding by design: Connecting content and kids.* Alexandria, VA: Association for Supervision and Curriculum Development.

Urbanski, A. (1993). Real change is real hard: Lessons learned in Rochester. *Stanford Law & Policy Review,* Winter 1992–1993, 123–133.

U.S. Department of Education, National Center for Education Statistics. (2006). *The condition of education 2006* (NCES 2006-071). Washington, DC: U.S. Government Printing Office.

Wiggins, G., & McTighe, J. (1998). *Understanding by design.* Alexandria, VA: Association for Supervision and Curriculum Development.

Wiggins, G., & McTighe, J. (2007). *Schooling by design.* Alexandria, VA: Association for Supervision and Curriculum Development.

Index

Note: Page numbers followed by *f* indicate illustrations.

About the Authors

Carol Ann Tomlinson

 Carol Ann Tomlinson's career as an educator includes 21 years as a public school teacher of a differentiated classroom. Her work included 12 years as a program administrator of special services for struggling and advanced learners. She was Virginia's Teacher of the Year in 1974. More recently, she has been a faculty member at the University of Virginia's Curry School of Education, where she is currently professor of educational leadership, foundations, and policy, and codirector of the university's Summer Institute on Academic Diversity and Best Practices Institutes, and where she was named Outstanding Professor in 2004. Tomlinson is the author of more than 200 articles, book chapters, books, and other professional development materials. For ASCD, she has written seven books, including *How to Differentiate Instruction in Mixed-Ability Classrooms*, *The Differentiated Classroom: Responding to the Needs of All Learners*, and *Fulfilling the Promise of the Differentiated Classroom: Strategies and Tools for Responsive Teaching*, and with Jay McTighe she wrote *Integrating Differentiated Instruction and Understanding by Design: Connecting Content and Kids*. Tomlinson's ASCD books have been translated into 12 languages. For Corwin Press, she coauthored *The Parallel Curriculum*

Model: A Design to Develop High Potential and Challenge High-Ability Learners. For the National Middle School Association, with Kristi Doubet she wrote *Smart in the Middle Grades: Classrooms That Work for Bright Middle Schoolers*. She works nationally and internationally with teachers and administrators who want to develop classrooms and schools that are actively responsive to academically diverse student populations. Tomlinson can be reached at the University of Virginia, P.O. Box 400277, Charlottesville, VA 22904, or via e-mail at cat3y@virginia.edu.

Kay Brimijoin

Kay Brimijoin is currently associate professor of education and chair of the Education Department at Sweet Briar College in central Virginia, where since 2000 she has taught in the teacher education program and helped to launch a master's program in differentiated curriculum and instruction. More than 20 years of classroom teaching and school administration, doctoral research on differentiation, and more than 10 years of work with schools and school districts convinced Brimijoin that teacher education programs must equip new teachers with the knowledge, understanding, and skills to differentiate curriculum and instruction. She completed her PhD in educational psychology with a concentration in curriculum and instruction and gifted education at the University of Virginia. She won a High School Curriculum Award (1999), a Research and Evaluation Award (2000), and a Doctoral Student Award (2002) from the National Association for Gifted Children. She also won a Doctoral Dissertation Research Award from the Virginia Association for Supervision and Curriculum Development in 2001. She coauthored a unit in Carol Ann Tomlinson and Cindy Strickland's *Differentiation in Practice: Grades 9–12*, published by ASCD in 2005. Brimijoin is the author of numerous articles, including a 2003 review of the literature supporting differentiation. She has written curriculum with elementary, middle, and high school teachers and presented at numerous local, state, and national conferences. She consults with schools and districts across the country on differentiation, curriculum design, gifted education, mentoring, and teacher education. Brimijoin can be reached at Sweet Briar College, Sweet Briar, VA 24595, or via e-mail at brimijoin@sbc.edu.

Lane Narvaez

Lane Narvaez has been the principal at Conway Elementary in the Ladue School District, St. Louis, Missouri, for the past 12 years. She has served as an administrator at the elementary, middle, high school, and district levels. Narvaez has worked in the public school systems of New York, Arizona, and Missouri, and has 28 years of teaching and administrative experience. She has worked in at-risk as well as affluent school communities. Her degrees include a bachelor of arts from Hunter College in New York, a master's in reading from Manhattan College in New York, and a doctorate in reading from Arizona State University. Her research interests include mentoring the beginning teacher, curriculum and instruction, and schoolwide differentiation. She has presented at the national conferences of the Association of Teacher Educators, American Educational Research Association, and the Association for Supervision and Curriculum Development. She has also presented at the Summer Institute of Academic Diversity at the University of Virginia and the Oxford Round Table in Oxford, England, on her work involving schoolwide differentiation. For the past three years she has worked with Henry County Schools in Virginia to help implement differentiation throughout the district's schools. She has served as a coach in differentiation for schools in Virginia and California, working with teachers and administrators as they implement differentiation. Narvaez can be reached at Conway Elementary School, 9900 Conway Road, School District of the City of Ladue, St. Louis, MO 63124, or via e-mail at lnarvaez@ladue.k12.mo.us.

Related ASCD Resources: Differentiated Instruction

At the time of publication, the following ASCD resources were available; for the most up-to-date information about ASCD resources, go to www.ascd.org. ASCD stock numbers are noted in parentheses.

Mixed Media

Differentiated Instruction in Action (two-disc CD-ROM) (#504031)

Differentiating Instruction for Mixed-Ability Classrooms Professional Inquiry Kit by Carol Ann Tomlinson (#196213)

Differentiated Instruction Professional Development Planner and Resource Package (Stage 1) (#701225)

Differentiated Instruction Professional Development Planner and Resource Package (Stage 2) (#703402)

Print Products

The Differentiated Classroom: Responding to the Needs of All Learners by Carol Ann Tomlinson (#199040)

Fulfilling the Promise of the Differentiated Classroom: Strategies and Tools for Responsive Teaching by Carol Ann Tomlinson (#103107)

How to Differentiate Instruction in Mixed-Ability Classrooms, 2nd edition, by Carol Ann Tomlinson (#101043)

Integrating Differentiated Instruction and Understanding by Design: Connecting Content and Kids by Carol Ann Tomlinson and Jay McTighe (#105004)

Videos and DVDs

At Work in the Differentiated Classroom (three 28- to 48-minute programs on DVD and a 195-page facilitator's guide) (#601071)

Leadership for Differentiating Instruction (one 100-minute DVD with a comprehensive user guide and bonus DVD features)(#607038)

A Visit to a School Moving Toward Differentiation (one 30-minute DVD with a comprehensive viewer's guide) (#607133)

For additional resources, visit us on the World Wide Web (http://www.ascd.org), send an e-mail message to member@ascd.org, call the ASCD Service Center (1-800-933-ASCD or 703-578-9600, then press 2), send a fax to 703-575-5400, or write to Information Services, ASCD, 1703 N. Beauregard St., Alexandria, VA 22311-1714 USA.